Prehistoric, Roman, and post-Roman landscapes of the Great Ouse Valley

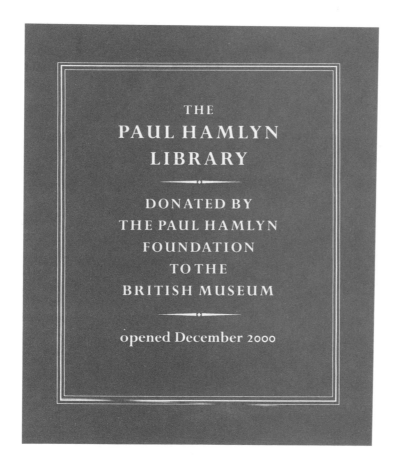

Prehistoric, Roman, and post-Roman landscapes of the Great Ouse Valley

edited by Mike Dawson

CBA Research Report 119
Council for British Archaeology

2000

Published 2000 by the Council for British Archaeology
Bowes Morrell House, 111 Walmgate, York YO1 9WA

British Library Cataloguing in Publication Data
A catalogue for this book is available from the British Library

ISSN 0589-9036

ISBN 1 872414 98 2

This volume is published with the aid of a generous grant from

Anglian Water

Front: The River Great Ouse near Oakley, Bedfordshire
Back: Reconstruction of the Barleycroft Farm Longhouse, see Chapter 9, Figures 9.5 and 9.8

Typeset from authors' disks by Calderdale Typesetting Limited, Ripponden, West Yorkshire
Printed by Pennine Printing Services Limited, Ripponden, West Yorkshire

Contents

List of figures

List of tables

Contributors

Michael Dawson
(formerly of Bedfordshire County Archaeology
Service)
Samuel Rose
Cottage Farm
Sywell
Northamptonshire NN6 OBJ

Christopher Evans
Cambridge Archaeological Unit
Department of Archaeology
University of Cambridge
Downing Street
Cambridge CB2 3DZ

Chris Green
Department of Geography
Royal Holloway University of London
Egham
Surrey TW20 0EX

Alex Jones
Birmingham University Field Archaeology Unit
The University of Birmingham
Edgbaston
Birmingham B15 2TT

Mark Knight
Cambridge Archaeological Unit
Department of Archaeology,
University of Cambridge
Downing Street
Cambridge CB2 3DZ

Fachtna McAvoy
Centre for Archaeology
English Heritage
Fort Cumberland
Fort Cumberland Road
Eastney
Portsmouth PO4 9LD

Tim Malim
Cambridgeshire County Council
Archaeological Field Unit
Haggis Gap
Fulbourn
Cambridge CB1 5HD

Tim Reynolds
Cambridgeshire Archaeology
Libraries and Heritage
Babbage House
Shire Hall
Cambridge CB3 0AP

Rebecca Roseff
Herefordshire Archaeology
PO Box 3
Leominster
HR6 8LU

Rob Scaife
Department of Geography
University of Southampton
Highfield
Southampton SO17 1BJ

Paul Spoerry
Cambridgeshire County Council
Archaeological Field Unit
Haggis Gap
Fulbourn
Cambridge CB1 5HD

Preface

We at Anglian Water are in the business of environmental protection. Our sewage treatment works clean and recycle water originally taken from the environment for public supply and return it to the environment. Our environmental policy commits us to a positive approach to conservation encompassing both the natural and man-made heritage of the region we serve.

One of the ways in which our responsibility and care for the environment is translated into action is through our capital investment programme. We are the largest investor in environmental improvements in the region and over the last ten years we have spent £3 billion, a further £1.4 billion is to be spent in the next five years. This will improve the quality of our environment through investment in river water quality (our River Care Programme), bathing water quality (our Blue Flag Waters Programme) and the wider environment through our Biodiversity Action Plan and sustainability policies.

Through this programme new sewage and water treatment facilities and new pipelines and sewers are being constructed. Whilst these provide improved services to our customers we recognise that our work must be planned carefully to minimise any potential impacts on areas of conservation value. Indeed, in an archaeological context, well planned projects provide an opportunity to extend archaeological knowledge.

Archaeological conservation has become of particular significance to us and through our capital investment programme we have become an important sponsor of archaeological investigations. We would not want less than a rigorous approach to the protection of the archaeological record. To this end we work in partnership with the archaeological community. It is for this reason that we were delighted to attend and sponsor the conference 'Archaeology of the Ouse Valley' and to see the proceedings of that conference through to publication.

Amongst many other projects undertaken in the Ouse Valley the conference discussed our work on the Bedford Southern Orbital Sewer. Construction of this large scheme proceeded along the Ouse Valley in a series of phases for several years. During its progress the scheme revealed a Roman settlement, an extensive Roman cemetery, and a previously unknown Saxon cemetery.

Conferences and publications such as this represent an extremely good way of communicating the partnership message and provide a forum for debating issues. Congratulations to the south Midlands Group of the Institute of Field Archaeologists and particularly to Mike Dawson for his organisational efforts.

We look forward to continuing our close association with the archaeological community.

Paul Woodcock, Head of Water Quality and
Environmental Regulation
Anglian Water
September 2000

Summary

This volume is based on a conference held at Hinchinbrooke House, Cambridgeshire in February 1994 with some additional papers commissioned after the day. The conference was sponsored by Anglian Water Services and organised by members of the South Midlands Group of the Institute of Field Archaeologists and by members of Bedfordshire County Archaeology Service. The volume attempts to draw together the archaeology of the Great Ouse Valley from the post-glacial to the post-Roman period. This is the first occasion on which such a survey of current work has been attempted in this area and the conference was intended to provide the basis for further work as well a forum for discussion on the day. The breadth of the survey was ambitious from the first and to this end several papers were commissioned, after the conference itself, to fill gaps in areas such as the topographic history of the valley. The volume which follows comprises two principle elements: synthetic surveys of specific landscape areas and short case study papers based on current work. The former provide an overview of approaches to landscape study in the area whilst the latter are intended to characterise the range and scale of projects in the Great Ouse Valley in the 1990s. At a time when the formulation of research frameworks is increasingly seen as an important element in shaping the direction of future archaeological work this volume will provide a framework for defining future research well into the next millennium.

Zusammenfassung

Dieser Band enstand im Anschluss an eine Tagung, die im Februrar 1994 in Hinchinbrooke House, Cambridgeshire, stattfand. Er basiert auf die Vorträge der Tagung und enhält zudem einige zusätzliche Beiträge, die später für diesen Band entstanden sind. Die Tagung wurde von Anglian Water Services finanziert und von Mitgliedern der South Midlands Group of the Institute of Field Archaeologists und des Bedfordshire County Archaeology Service organisiert. Dieser Band versucht eine Übersicht über die Archäologie des Great Ouse Flusstals von der Post-Glatialzeit bis zum frühen Mittelalter zu geben. Es ist der erste Versuch einer Synthese der Forschungsergebnisse des Great Ouse Flusstals und die Tagung sollte deshalb als Diskussionsforum dienen und darüber hinweg eine Grundlage fur weitere Untersuchungen legen. Da der Umfang und die Ziele dieses Surveys von Anfang an sehr hoch angesetzt waren, wurden zusäztliche Beiträge in Auftrag gegeben, um während der Tagung unbehandelte Themen, wie die topographische Geschichte und Entwicklung des Flusstals, zu ergänzen. Der hier vorliegende Band enthält zwei verschiedene Elemente: zum einen werden surveys von spezifischen Landschaftsbereichen besprochen, um einen Überblick über die gegenwärtigen Ansätze der Landschaftsarchäologie zu bereiten. Zum anderen werden einzelne Projekte und Fallbeispiele gegenwärtiger Untersuchungen vorgestellt, die die Bandbreite und den Unfang der Projekte im Great Ouse Flusstal in den 90er Jahren charakterisieren sollen. Da die Formulierung von Forschungsfragen und -Ansätzen innerhalb eines fest formulierten Rahmens gegenwärtig immer wichtiger wird, hofft der vorliegende Band diesen Rahmen für zukünftige archäologische Forschung bis weit ins nächste Jahrtausend zu geben.

Sommaire

Ce livre est basé sur un colloque qui s'est tenu à Hinchinbrooke House, Cambridge, en février 1994, ainsi que sur d'autres articles qui ont été réclamés après coup. Le colloque était parrainé par Anglian Water Services et avait été organisé par des membres du Institute of Field Archaeologists, groupe des South Midlands, et par des membres du Bedfordshire County Archaeology Service. Ce livre tente de rassembler l'archéologie de la vallée de la Great Ouse, depuis la période post-glaciaire jusqu'à la période post-romaine. C'est la première fois qu'une telle étude de travail actuel a été tentée dans ce domaine et ce colloque avait pour but de fournir une base de travail ultérieur aussi bien qu'un forum de discussion pour le jour même. Dès le début, le projet était d'ampleur ambitieuse et, à cette fin, plusieurs articles avaient été réclamés, après le colloque, afin de combler des lacunes dans des domaines comme l'histoire topographique de la vallée. Le livre qui suit comprend deux éléments principaux: des études de synthèse concernant des paysages précis et de courts articles portant sur des études de cas basées sur du travail actuel. Les premières fournissent une vue d'ensemble des manières d'aborder l'étude de paysages dans la région alors que les seconds ont pour objet de caractériser la portée et l'échelle des projets dans la vallée de la Great Ouse pendant les années 1990. A une époque où la formulation des structures de la recherche est de plus en plus considérée un élément important dans la détermination de la direction du travail archéologique futur, ce livre fournira une structure de définition de la recherche future pendant les premières années du prochain millénaire.

1 Introduction

by Mike Dawson

The River Ouse has one of the largest catchment areas of any river valley in the British Isles, yet, sandwiched between the Chilterns to the south and the Nene and Welland Valleys to the north, it has not generated a significant archaeological identity (Figures 1.1 and 1.2). This is something of an anomaly and in 1992 it was clear to those working in the Ouse valley and its hinterland that a considerable amount of important work was taking place in the region. However, just as the need to bring this to wider attention was recognised, the pace of development seemed to be eroding the very resource which was about to yield new insights into the past. It is an inherent contradiction of the archaeological enterprise that destruction should lead to the recovery of fresh evidence. The Ouse Valley Conference, which took place in February 1994, therefore was intended not only to draw attention to the diminishing resource but to summarise some of the advances made by current projects.

The conference was also seen as an opportunity in the earliest stages of the application of PPG 16 to set the scene for further research, to provide the basis on which to judge the gaps and omissions in present research and survey. It was organised at a time when the Anglian region, Cambridgeshire, Suffolk, Norfolk, Hertfordshire, and Essex, were preparing a research frameworks document and although this grouping did not include Bedfordshire or Buckinghamshire discussions were taking place with this in mind. A year later, almost to the day after the Hinchinbrooke Conference, the South Midlands group of the IFA organised a research frameworks seminar at Wendlebury, and shortly afterwards Bedfordshire began the preparation of its own frameworks document.

A third and significant element was the involvement of Anglian Water Services. In 1990 PPG 16, through the development control function of local authorities, imposed a duty of care for the archaeological resource on would be developers and Anglian Water adopted such an attitude in their conditions of association. The sponsorship of both the conference and the CBA's publication of the volume by a newly privatised utility characterised much of the cooperative work carried out in the Ouse Valley in the early 1990s.

The Ouse Valley

Probably the first archaeological activity in the Ouse Valley took place in the 17th century when John Aubrey described samian ware from Sandy in *Monumenta Britannica* (1666) as 'an urn, red like coral, with an inscription'. Since then, of course, considerable attention has focused not only on areas such as the Fenland, but on the evidence of all periods, from the lithic scatters of the Palaeolithic to the Roman and historic towns of the Ouse Valley itself. Despite the level of interest, and more recently the increased funding for archaeology, the archaeological resource is diminishing. Speakers at the conference identified three main factors: quarrying; infrastructure and commercial development; and agricultural activity. To this list may be added a myriad of other causes, many deriving from alternatives uses of agricultural land such as golf driving ranges and singular structures such as an elephant amphitheatre at Woburn.

The Great Ouse Valley of the 1990s was extensively served by archaeological organisations and this is to some extent reflected in the range of contributors to this volume. At the time of the conference each of the counties through which the Ouse flows – Cambridgeshire, Bedfordshire, and Buckinghamshire – had their own archaeology service comprising both development control officers and contracting organisations, and each county held the county Sites and Monuments Record (in Bedfordshire the Historic Environment Record). Since 1994 Buckinghamshire County Council has disbanded its field service and no longer has a County Archaeologist. In Bedfordshire the county council no longer has a County Archaeologist. In addition to the local government organisations Cambridge University has a field unit and organisations, for instance, from as far afield as Birmingham, Oxford, and Salisbury have all worked in the Great Ouse Valley. This situation has given rise to an extraordinary range of archaeological publication varying from the county journals – Proceedings of the Cambridge Antiquarian Society, Bedfordshire Archaeology, Records of Buckinghamshire – to client reports prepared by the contracting units for development led projects. Ideally all of these should be available either through the SMRs or in the local studies sections of the county libraries.

In addition to commercial archaeology, often development led, there are several research initiatives, such as the Southern, now English, Rivers Survey and Fenland Survey, which continue to yield results and there are ongoing management strategies, such as MPP and the Fenland Management Programme, all of which contribute to the vibrant atmosphere of change and development in the Great Ouse Valley.

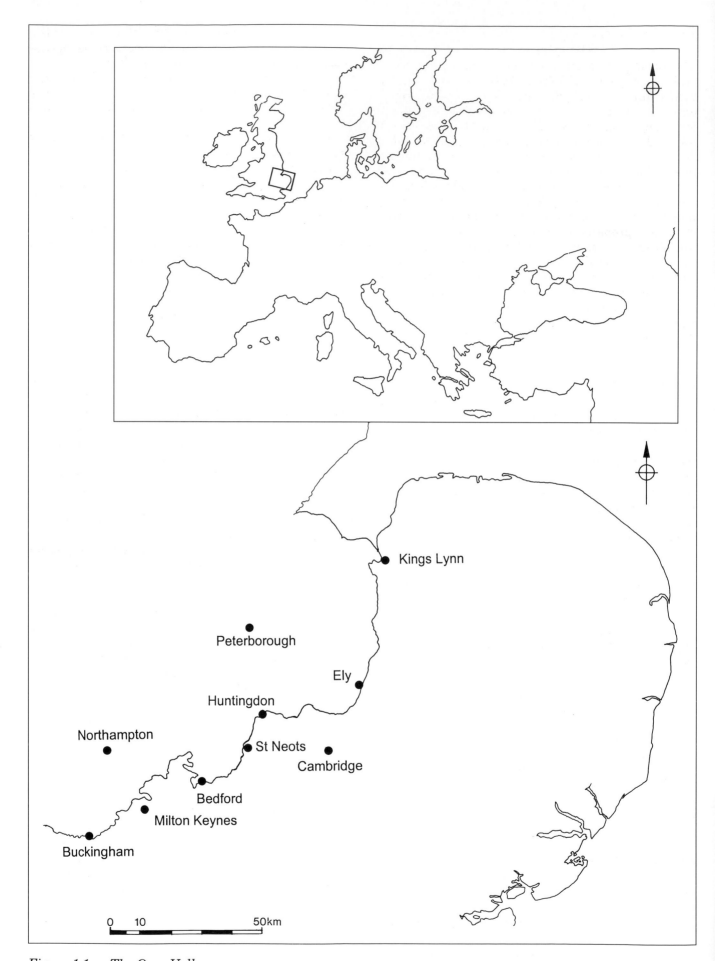

Figure 1.1 The Ouse Valley

Presentation

The report which follows is based largely, but not entirely, on papers presented at the conference held at Hinchinbrooke House, Huntingdon on 19 February 1994, entitled 'The Archaeology of the Ouse Valley'. Almost inevitably because of the limitations imposed by space, timing, and availability of individual speakers the conference programme has been adapted during the transformation into this publication. Some speakers were not able to find the opportunity to convert delivered text into written papers, whilst several individuals who were not present have prepared papers which have contributed significantly to improving the balance of the volume. The framework of this report is straightforward. The opening papers focus attention upon the relief, topography, and environmental history of the valley to provide the basis for a series of chronologically arranged essays which move from the Palaeolithic to the early-medieval period. Where current work permitted there are a series of chronologically arranged chapters focusing on landscapes in the Great Ouse Valley. In addition to these there are several case studies based on individual sites; thus allowing the results of current projects to be seen in the context of wider research.

There are inevitably gaps in this approach. In particular no synthetic work has been undertaken on the Mesolithic of the Ouse Valley and my short paper on this period is intended only to draw attention to the extent to which largely unpublished evidence for this period has grown in the last decade. A second area similarly afflicted is the post-Roman and early-Saxon periods. To some extent this lacuna has been addressed by a recent paper gathering together the largely artefactual evidence for the period from the middle Ouse (Wingfield 1995, but written in 1992). Presently it is clear that several excavations in the middle Ouse as well as the work of the Leverhulme Trust (Lewis *et al* 1993) will greatly enhance our knowledge of early-medieval settlement.

The volume opens with a detailed summary of the geological history of the Great Ouse Valley by Dr Chris Green of Royal Holloway, University of London, whose research and involvement with the Ouse Valley has spanned over twenty years. The second paper by Dr Rob Scaife similarly provides a detailed overview but of the floral environment of the valley. The first paper was not presented at the conference but was written especially for this volume to provide, together with Dr Scaife's essay, the background essential to understanding the human impact and development in the valley. A single case study of the micro-environment is provided by Rebecca Roseff, based on excavations at Little Barford, on the middle Ouse. Her study uses water volumes to argue for episodic flooding which may have had a considerable effect on human habitation patterns.

The early impact of man is addressed by Dr Tim Reynolds, who surveys our current understanding of Palaeolithic archaeology and outlines some of the areas of potential research. Of considerable significance for this period are the difficulties of addressing often deeply buried or redeposited Palaeolithic evidence within the context of PPG 16. It is clear today that much can be learnt from the experience at Boxgrove.

Current work on the Mesolithic period is briefly summarised by myself prior to Tim Malim's review of the considerable evidence for ritual activity in the valley from the Neolithic onwards. He makes the phenomenological argument for the sanctity of place continuing at certain locations from the Neolithic through to the Roman period. Fachtna McAvoy provides the case study from the Neolithic site at Godmanchester to show how the complexity of belief systems were played out in the practicalities of design at a monument complex.

Dr Chris Evans' paper on the landscape of the lower Ouse uses the results of large scale excavation, sampling, and sustained watching briefs to develop a model of the late-Bronze Age landscape in the fenland delta.

My own paper largely reflects Bedfordshire County Archaeology Service's work over a six year period from 1988 to 1994. In it I survey the increasing evidence of sedentary settlement from the beginning of the Iron Age through to end of the Roman period, arguing for significant conflict between pastoralist and arable farmers in the early to middle Iron Age, whilst suggesting that the impact of Rome from the 1st century AD onwards was the first occasion in which settlement agglomeration took place. Alex Jones provides the case study for this period based on his work at Little Paxton, suggesting that the area was occupied by small-scale farms from the Iron Age and throughout the Roman period.

In the final paper Dr Paul Spoerry focuses on the decline of Roman agglomerated settlement and the growth of medieval towns. Although restricted in area this paper provides a metaphor for the transition of the Ouse valley landscape from the Roman period to the medieval.

Bibliography

Lewis, C, Fox, P M, & Dyer, C, 1993 Medieval settlements in Bedfordshire and Northamptonshire: an interim report, *Medieval Settl Res Grp Annu Rep*, **7**, 1992, 15–20

Wingfield, C, 1995 The Anglo-Saxon settlement of Bedfordshire and Hertfordshire: the archaeological view, in R Holgate (ed) *Chiltern archaeology. Recent work. A handbook for the next decade*. Dunstable: The Book Castle, 31–43

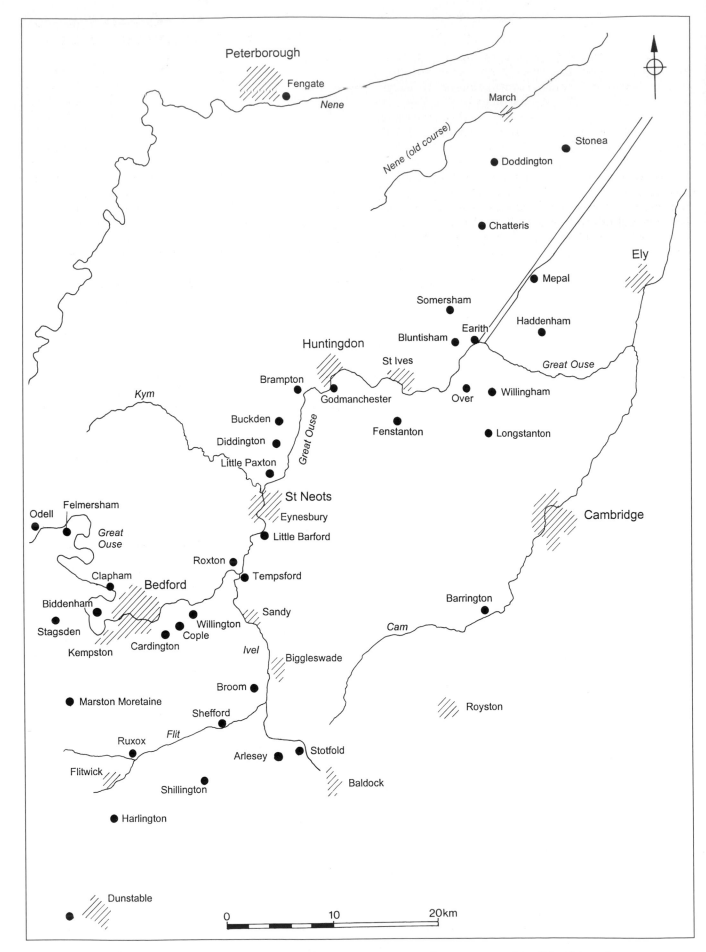

Figure 1.2   The landscapes of the Ouse Valley: contemporary settlements mentioned in this volume

2 Geology, relief, and Quaternary palaeoenvironments in the basin of the Great Ouse *by Chris Green*

Introduction

Considered in terms of either catchment area or stream length, the Great Ouse is one of Britain's larger rivers. The headwaters of the Great Ouse rise in the heart of the English Midlands near the western border of Northamptonshire and the river enters the sea on the southern margin of the Wash at King's Lynn in Norfolk. The present account deals largely with the basin of the Great Ouse upstream from the point where the river enters the Fens, between St Ives and Ely. This part of the river is sometimes called the Bedfordshire Ouse (Fig 2.1). Strictly speaking, the catchment of the Great Ouse includes the basins of the right bank tributaries of its Fenland reach, the Cam, the Lark, the Little Ouse, the Wissey, and the Nar, but these basins, occupying much of the western marches of East

Anglia, lie outside the scope of this account. In fact, the history of the Fenland reaches of the rivers draining to the Wash is somewhat confusing. The waters of the Great Ouse now flow in part into the Old and New Bedford Rivers which are 17th-century drainage cuts, and in part into the Old West River which may itself be an artificial watercourse. Seventeenth-century maps show the Great Ouse flowing northward from the vicinity of Earith to join the River Nene south of March. However, low-lying river terraces flank both this northward course and the Old West River, so the Great Ouse may have followed both courses at different times, or even at the same time, in the past.

The course of the Great Ouse lies entirely within lowland Britain and most of the catchment lies below 200m OD. The relief of the catchment is therefore generally low-lying and subdued, and in

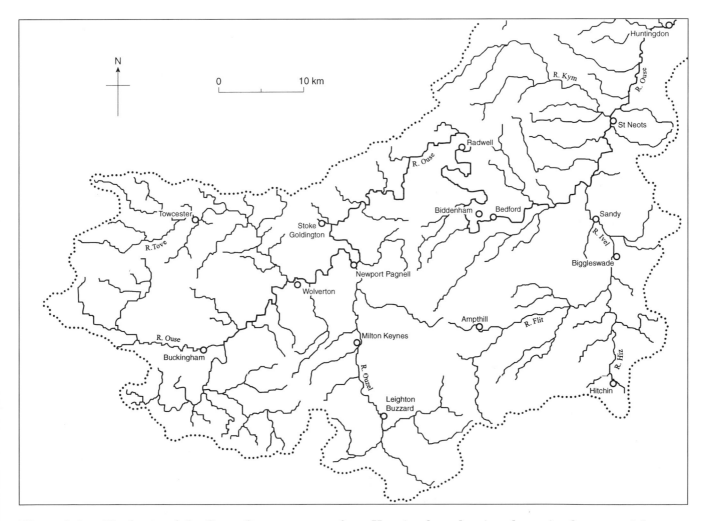

Figure 2.1   The basin of the Great Ouse upstream from Huntingdon, showing the main elements of the stream network

broad terms these characteristics can be attributed to two factors. Firstly, the bedrock underlying large parts of the catchment is clay that offers little resistance to erosion; and secondly, the whole of the catchment was over-run by glacial ice on at least one occasion during the Quaternary.

Solid geology

The bedrock that outcrops in the basin of the Great Ouse is all of Mesozoic age and sedimentary origin (Taylor 1963; Edmonds and Dinham 1965; Shephard-Thorn *et al* 1994). The structural arrangement of the rocks is relatively simple. The strata dip at a very low angle towards the southeast. The dip is often less than 0.5° and rarely more than 5°. The outcrop pattern is correspondingly simple, with the oldest rocks occurring in the northwest of the area and the youngest in the south-east (Fig 2.2).

The oldest beds exposed in the basin of the Great Ouse are of Jurassic age and form part of the Upper Lias. They include dark-grey clays and rubbly limestones. The latter are often shelly and contain phosphatic nodules. The Upper Lias is overlain by the highly variable but generally soft and calcareous

rocks of the Inferior Oolite. In its lower part the Inferior Oolite includes the Northampton Sands and Ironstone. These are oolitic and sandy and, where redistribution of ferric oxides has occurred, may locally form a rock which is resistant to weathering and erosion. In its upper part, the Inferior Oolite comprises the Lower Estuarine Series mainly represented by fine sands, silts, and clays. Similar lithologies form the Upper Estuarine Series in the lower part of the overlying Great Oolite.

An important relief-forming unit in the Great Oolite is the Blisworth Limestone, which outcrops in north-west Bedfordshire and north Buckinghamshire, forming interfluve plateaux and valley side benches. This is a pale buff or creamy limestone usually shelly and sometimes oolitic. The Blisworth Limestone is separated from the overlying Cornbrash Limestone by the narrow and inconspicuous outcrop of the Blisworth Clay. The Cornbrash is a hard limestone composed in its lower part of finely divided shell debris, with shell fragments becoming coarser in the Upper Cornbrash. The Cornbrash Limestone is another relief-forming stratum, giving rise to conspicuously level hill tops and well-defined valley-side benches. All these limestones have been quarried sporadically and are found as building stones over a wide area

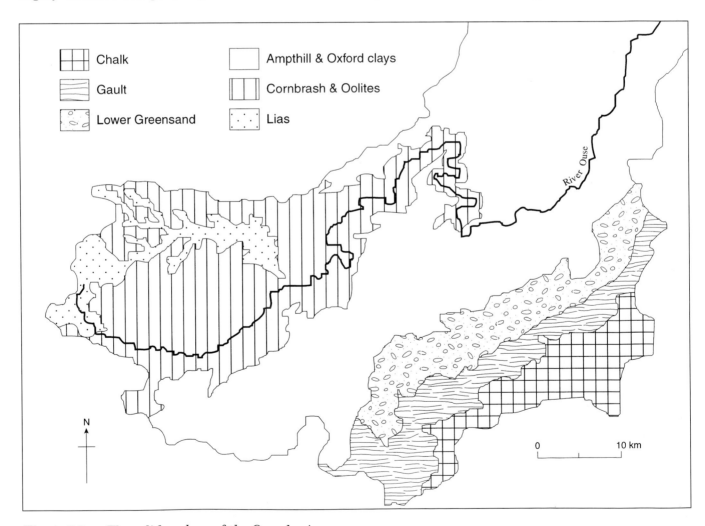

Figure 2.2   The solid geology of the Ouse basin

which, in a southerly direction, extends as far as the Chiltern Hills.

Immediately above the Cornbrash Limestone are the Kellaways Beds – dark-grey mudstones in their lower part, becoming more sandy in their upper part. Topographically the Kellaways Beds are rarely distinguishable from the overlying Oxford Clay which is the most extensive bedrock outcrop in the basin of the Great Ouse. The Oxford Clay is a black, grey, or bluish-grey clay which is generally rather uniform, especially in terms of its relief-forming characteristics. Together with the overlying Ampthill and Kimmeridge Clays it underlies the great lowland vale that extends from the headwaters of the Great Ouse in Northamptonshire north-eastward to and beneath the Fen Basin. The Oxford Clay has an outcrop some 10km in width near Milton Keynes, widening to nearly 30km in width at the Fen edge. The Ampthill and Kimmeridge Clays occupy only small areas to the south and west of Sandy but both outcrops broaden from there in a north-easterly direction. They underlie the low ground between St Ives and Ely where the combined outcrops have a width of some 25km.

The Jurassic rocks described in the previous paragraphs are overlain unconformably by Cretaceous strata. Between Linslade and Sandy the Lower Greensand is an important relief-forming rock, creating an impressive escarpment that overlooks the Oxford Clay vale. Despite its name, the Lower Greensand is usually brown or yellow in colour. The main unit, forming the bulk of the formation, is the Woburn Sands. These are largely unconsolidated but include beds of harder, gritty, iron-cemented sandstone which are responsible for the upstanding character of the relief, and which have been used locally as a building material. The Lower Greensand is an important aquifer, giving rise to numerous springs, especially at its junction with the underlying Jurassic clays, and also having many wells sunk.

The Lower Greensand is succeeded upward by the Gault, a tenacious, dark-grey clay. The Gault has an outcrop some 8–15km in width that forms the low ground separating the Lower Greensand from the Chalk. To the north and east of Sandy, where the Lower Greensand ceases to be a significant relief-forming stratum, the low ground underlain by the Gault is continuous with the broad lowland underlain by the Jurassic clays.

From the vicinity of Whipsnade, to the west of Dunstable, in a north-easterly direction to Ashwell between Baldock and Royston, the watershed of the Great Ouse basin is formed by the escarpment of the Chalk. Near Dunstable the Chalk escarpment rises steeply from the Gault vale, gaining over 90m in less than half a kilometre to reach a height of over 240m OD. Further east, the escarpment is less dramatic but remains an important relief feature. The Chalk is a soft white limestone. Its resistance to weathering and erosion, and hence its importance as a relief forming rock, is the result of its great permeability. This also accounts for its importance as an aquifer. There is a well-marked spring-line at the junction between the Chalk and the underlying Gault Clay.

Relief and drainage

Relief

In very general terms, the Great Ouse and its tributaries drain a lowland basin extending from south-west to north-east across the south-eastern part of the English Midlands. As described above, the extent of this lowland is defined by a broad outcrop of Jurassic and Cretaceous clays. Where the Great Ouse enters the Fens, the ground surface is almost everywhere at a level below 5m OD. Ninety kilometres to the south-west, at the upstream extremity of the basin where the Great Ouse/Thame watershed is located on the Oxford Clay, the lowest point on the interfluve is at approximately 90m OD. These figures help to emphasise the low-lying nature of the Great Ouse basin and the lack of physical barriers within and around it.

Within the basin of the Great Ouse, four main terrain types can be recognised.

1 The Jurassic and Gault Clay lowlands

Wide valley floors pass almost imperceptibly into gentle valley side slopes. Interfluve summits are broad and very gently undulating. In the lowest part of the basin being considered here, the valley of the Great Ouse forms part of the Fen lowland. In the upstream direction there is a gradual increase in the amount of relief and in the steepness of the valley side slopes while the extent of the gently undulating interfluve areas is reduced. However, throughout this large region slopes are very gentle and local relative relief, even in the upper parts of the basin, rarely approaches 60m. In the area downstream from Bedford, around St Neots, interfluve summits mainly rise to between 50m and 60m OD. To the west of Bedford and upstream around Newport Pagnell the interfluves are mainly at a level between 100m and 120m.

2 The limestone country

The headwaters of the Great Ouse itself and its left-bank tributary the River Tove, which is confluent with the Great Ouse near Wolverton, drain a tract of country in which the dominant relief-forming rocks are limestones. The limestone units are, however, discontinuous, separated from one another by less resistant rock types. In this region, both the Great Ouse and the Tove occupy relatively narrow valleys with local benching of the valley sides where resistant limestone beds are present. Interfluve summits are often remarkably flat, reflecting structural surfaces in the limestone sequence. As the uppermost headwaters are approached, steeper valley-side slopes become more common but road gradients, even on minor roads, nowhere reach as much as 1 in 7. Interfluve summits around the Tove headwaters rise to a high point of 189m OD, but for most of its length the watershed between the Great Ouse and Nene catchments is a subdued feature, generally less that 80m above the floodplain of the master stream in either basin.

3 The Lower Greensand ridge

This is a well-defined and distinctive relief feature. Locally, at Lidlington and Bow Brickhill for example, the escarpment rises more than 60m in less than half a kilometre. Between Leighton Buzzard and Ampthill the crest of the ridge rises above 120m OD in many places, with a high point of 171m OD. Both scarp and dip slopes have been vigorously dissected, resulting in many minor valleys, re-entrants, and narrow spurs, creating a landscape that contrasts strongly with the subdued relief developed on either side of the ridge on the Jurassic and Cretaceous clays. Landslip scars and some active landslips are present on the steeper slopes in this region, especially where, for any reason, drainage is poor.

4 The Chalk escarpment

The outcrop of the Chalk within the basin of the Great Ouse is relatively small, but the Chalk escarpment represents the highest ground within the basin. At the south-west extremity of the part of the Chalk escarpment that lies within the Great Ouse basin, the drainage of the Tring Gap is shared between the headwaters of the Great Ouse and the Thame. Passing north-westward, the escarpment is steep and the apron of Lower Chalk in front of the main escarpment is narrow. There is another gap in the escarpment at Dagnall and it then rises to a high point at 243m OD on Dunstable Downs. To the west of Dunstable is Totternhoe, the source of Totternhoe Stone, used as a building material over a wide area both within and beyond the Chilterns. East of Dunstable, the crest of the escarpment is at a lower level, generally between 160m and 170m OD. To the east of Hexton, the line of the escarpment is interrupted by the broad re-entrant marking the Hitchin Gap which passes through the Chalk escarpment at a level of 90m OD. To the east of the Hitchin Gap, the watershed of the area being considered in this account turns northward, away from the Chalk escarpment.

Drainage

The drainage pattern in the basin of the Great Ouse reflects to some extent the influence of geological structure but also displays some interesting departures from a simple structural pattern. From its headwaters downstream to Buckingham the course of the Great Ouse accords quite closely with the regional dip of the Jurassic rocks. Downstream from Buckingham the course is approximately parallel with the strike of these rocks as far as Newport

Pagnall. Here the river turns back to the north-west, against the dip, to Gayhurst where it resumes a course parallel with the strike of the Jurassic rocks, taking it north-east to Sharnbrook. From this point, southward to Bedford the course, though meandering widely, again follows the regional dip. At Bedford the river once again turns to the north-east and, following the strike of the Oxford Clay, makes its way to Huntingdon where it turns eastward, through St Ives, into the Fens.

The Great Ouse has only one substantial left bank tributary, the River Tove. In its upper reaches this flows through Towcester from west to east, somewhat obliquely to the regional dip. East of Towcester, the Tove turns to the south-east, directly down dip to join the Great Ouse at Cosgrove, near Wolverton. The Great Ouse has two substantial right-bank tributaries, the Ouzel and the Ivel, both of which rise in springs at the base of the Lower Chalk. The Ouzel has its headwaters close to the Tring and Dagnall Gaps and flows rather directly northward from there against the regional dip to join the Great Ouse at Newport Pagnall. The Ivel has its headwaters close to the Hitchin Gap and, like the Ouzel, flows directly northward to pass through Sandy and join the Great Ouse at Tempsford.

Pre-Quaternary and Quaternary landform evolution

Pre-Quaternary

Very little has been written about pre-Quaternary landform development in the basin of the Great Ouse. For the wider area of the south and east Midlands accounts are few in number and general and speculative in character. The most common assumption is that throughout eastern England, at some time during the Tertiary, drainage towards the east was established, consequent on the regional dip, and that development of the drainage pattern led to the growth of major subsequent streams following the strike of the less resistant strata (Straw 1979). With major portions of its course running approximately parallel with the strike of the Jurassic rocks, such an origin seems likely for the Great Ouse.

By the end of the Tertiary, it is assumed that a surface of low relief had been created, truncating the Mesozoic rocks and falling in elevation towards the east. In the area immediately to the north-west of the Ouse basin, Kellaway and Taylor (1952) delineated an 'East Midland Surface' that declines eastward from about 230m OD, to the west of Uppingham, to about 70m OD between Oundle and Thrapston. As the topography of the western part of the Ouse basin is closely similar to that of the area examined by Kellaway and Taylor (1952), it seems reasonable to suggest that the same surface may be present there. There has been some speculation about the exact form and origin of this summit relief, in particular whether it represents a single erosional surface which has been tilted towards the east, as Kellaway and Taylor (1952) believed, or a series of less extensive erosional benches at successively lower levels from west to east (Clayton 1979). Whether the surface is of subaerial or marine origin has also been a subject of debate. However these arguments are resolved, it is only the highest ground on the limestone outcrops in the west of the Great Ouse basin that might form remnants of the lower part of this pre-Quaternary feature. In the extreme south of the basin, the summits of the Chalk are also thought to be remnants of a pre-Quaternary erosional surface (Wooldridge and Linton 1955).

Pre-Anglian Quaternary

The Anglian glaciation is perhaps the event that has been most influential in shaping the present-day relief in the basin of the Great Ouse. Superficial geological deposits to which an Anglian age has been assigned are very widely present in the basin of the Great Ouse and it seems likely that the whole basin was over-run by Anglian ice. There is, however, some evidence relating to the form of the immediately pre-Anglian relief, although little has been published to establish its significance. Little is known, for example, about the origin and detailed morphology of the often extensive low-relief surfaces at levels below the summit plateau which, like the summit plateau itself, are generally mantled by Anglian glacial deposits. It seems clear, however, from the distribution of the glacial deposits that pre-Anglian erosion had already reduced the basin to a general level which in most places is no more than 30m above present-day valley floors, and which in some of the river valleys may have been close to, or even below, the level of the modern alluvium.

Depositional remnants of a pre-Anglian drainage pattern have also been recognised in the form of the Milton Sands. These are deposits of sand and gravel which underlie the Anglian glacial deposits in several places in the basin of the River Nene around Northampton. Similar deposits underlying Anglian till have been identified further north in the Rockingham Forest area. No occurrences of the Milton Sands have been recorded within the basin of the Great Ouse, but they are present near Yardley Hastings, close to the Nene–Ouse watershed, where they appear to mark the position of a channel system trending towards the Great Ouse basin (Castleden 1980). The pre-Anglian age of all of these deposits is indicated by a complete absence in them of any of the far-travelled components brought into eastern England by the Anglian ice. Where it has been possible to reconstruct the drainage lines with which these deposits are associated, they all appear to indicate flow towards the east or south-east, broadly in accord with the regional dip. Where it has been possible to reconstruct the gradients associated with the deposits, projection downstream into the western margins of East Anglia suggests links to the drainage system in that area that was over-run by Anglian glacial ice.

The Anglian glaciation

Regional studies of the chalky till in eastern England (Perrin *et al* 1979; Wilmot 1985) indicate that the Anglian glacial ice entered the basin of the Great Ouse from the north-east, across the Fen Basin. The maximum extent of the glacial deposits towards the south-west lies almost everywhere within the basin of the Great Ouse and the glacial limit appears to run closely parallel with the watershed throughout its length from Hitchin, where the Anglian ice passed across the Chalk escarpment into the basin of the proto-Thames, to Blisworth, just south of Northampton. This distribution gives the impression of a marginal lobe of the Anglian ice sheet which was effectively contained within a pre-existing basin of the Great Ouse and unable to surmount the relatively low ground that forms the interfluves.

The most widespread product of the Anglian glaciation is a more or less chalky till which masks the solid geology almost everywhere within the basin of the Great Ouse, except where the present rivers have cut down through it. The till also conceals details of the pre-existing relief and hence varies in thickness, usually from a few metres up to as much as 50m. Thicknesses up to *c* 15m are not unusual; thicknesses greater than this seem to be associated with well-defined linear sub-drift depressions. The till is usually a bluish-grey to dark-grey clay with an admixture of chalk in the form of clasts up to 30mm long and variable amounts of finely divided material. The clay is probably mainly derived locally from the Jurassic clay bedrock. The upper 1–2m of the till is often brown or yellowish-brown in colour as a result of weathering, and may be decalcified. The stone content commonly includes, in addition to chalk, Jurassic limestones and mudstones, flint, quartz, quartzites derived from Triassic conglomerates, occasional igneous and metamorphic clasts, Carboniferous limestone, cherts and sandstones, and the highly distinctive Rhaxella chert from the Corallian of the Howardian Hills in Yorkshire. This latter rock type, which was transported southward in substantial quantities by Anglian ice has become an important marker lithology in the study of Middle Pleistocene sequences in eastern England. Fluvioglacial gravel deposits are not uncommon in close association with the Anglian till, either as lenses or more extensive beds within the till, or beneath or above it.

An interesting feature of the glaciated landscape within the basin of the Great Ouse is the existence of a system of deep linear sub-drift depressions or buried valleys (Hill 1908; Woodland 1970; Horton

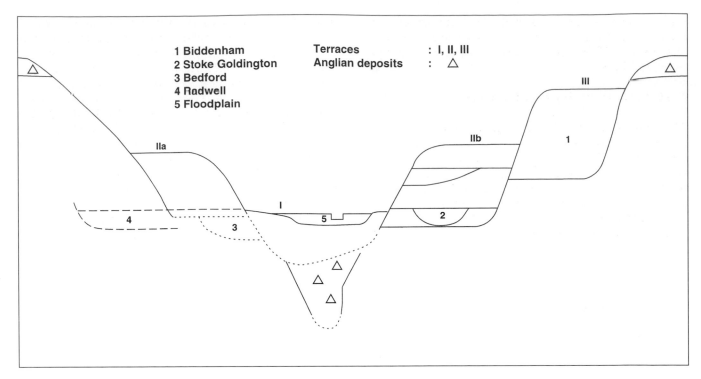

Figure 2.3   Schematic section across the valley of the Great Ouse, illustrating the occurrence of three terraces (I-III) flanking the modern valley, and a tunnel valley underlying the valley floor. Anglian glacial deposits occupy the interfluves and infill the tunnel valley. Temperate Pleistocene fossil assemblages are known from four different stratigraphic contexts in the Ouse valley. The stratigraphic position of key sites (1-4) is indicated. Holocene fossil assemblages are present in the floodplain deposits (5)

1970). Such depressions have been identified from borehole records in several separate localities within in the basin and although continuity between such localities has not been proven, it seems likely that an integrated drainage system and a common origin are indicated. In most cases the buried feature and the modern drainage follow closely similar alignments. A sub-drift depression has been traced beneath the valley of the Great Ouse from Huntingdon upstream to the confluence with the Ivel. At Offord, just south of Huntingdon, where the valley floor is at a level of about 10m OD, the floor of the buried valley is at a level of -20m OD. The buried feature can be traced upstream from the confluence, beneath both the Great Ouse and Ivel Valleys. In the Great Ouse Valley a sub-drift depression has been recorded as far upstream as Cardington. In the Ivel Valley the buried feature is known to extend upstream to Biggleswade and a possible continuation is known to exist beneath the Hitchin Gap. This latter feature has a total length of some 19km and for much of its length comprises two roughly parallel depressions. Several boreholes in the Hitchin Gap passed through more than 100m of infill to bottom at levels of more than 60m below OD. A similar depression has been identified beneath the Ouzel Valley between Stoke Hammond and Newport Pagnall. This feature is about 500m wide and has a maximum depth beneath the valley floor of over 40m. In the upper reaches of the Great

Ouse Valley, near Stony Stratford, and beneath parts of the Tove Valley, the presence of sub-alluvial depressions is inferred from borehole records and from the fact that till mantling the valley sides can be seen to pass below the valley floor alluvium. Deep sub-drift depressions are not confined to alignments that coincide with modern valleys. Borehole records indicate a linear depression, possibly several kilometres in length and up to 50m deep, extending from south-west to north-east through the Hatleys, where no major drainage line is present today.

The favoured explanation for all these depressions is as pre-glacial valleys. Some, particularly those with a deep and relatively narrow cross-section, have undoubtedly served as sub-glacial meltwater conduits in which large hydrostatic pressures encouraged deep erosional excavation into the weak Jurassic clays. This explanation is supported by the fact that the down-valley gradients of the depressions are undulating and irregular, and also by the nature of the sediments infilling the depressions. These comprise deposits of glacial till and outwash which in several cases are accompanied by thick lacustrine deposits, indicating the transformation of the depressions into ice-marginal lakes, either as the ice advanced into the area, or as it withdrew, or both. The advance of the Anglian ice into the basin of the Great Ouse from its lower end, and the likely eventual wasting of the ice from the headwater regions progressively towards the mouth of the basin suggests obvious opportunities for the impounding of drainage and the development of ice-marginal lakes.

Post-Anglian valley development

The main outcome of post-Anglian geomorphological activity has been the excavation of the present-day river valleys (Fig 2.3). From the location of these valleys, coinciding as they do in many cases with major sub-drift depressions, it would appear that following the wasting of the Anglian ice, large parts of the drainage system were re-established in their pre-Anglian positions. There are important exceptions to this situation, most notably in the case of the Great Ouse itself which has a seemingly anomalous course between Newport Pagnall and Bedford. This reach has the appearance of a great northward loop that carries the river away from a course which is otherwise rather closely aligned with the strike of the Jurassic rocks. The widely meandering and deeply entrenched reach of the river between Sharnbrook and Cardington is particularly distinctive and impressive.

The stratigraphic record of post-Anglian valley development is preserved in the form of river terraces and terrace sediments which flank the valleys of the Great Ouse and its larger tributaries. The terraces are usually underlain by deposits of sand and gravel. These sediments are largely the product of braided rivers which were characterised by the presence of active, interconnecting channels occupying much, if not all, of the valley floor. A periglacial origin is usually inferred for such rivers in southern Britain. During high stage events, coarse gravel (up to 64mm) was moving in these channels, creating longitudinal bars in which horizontal bedding prevails. At lower stages, or away from the principal active channels, sand deposition has occurred, resulting in beds and lens-like bodies of sand within the gravel. Cross-bedding is often visible in the sands.

The main local components in the gravel deposits are Jurassic limestones, and ironstones from the Northampton Sands or the Lower Greensand. Chalk pebbles are usually present and, in the type of river indicated by these gravel deposits, are unlikely to have survived transport over a distance of more than a few tens of metres. Thus, away from the Chalk outcrop in the south of the basin they must be derived locally from the ubiquitous chalky till. Durable components include flint, which may come in part from the Chiltern Hills, but is probably also mainly derived from the chalky till and will therefore have originated to the north of the Ouse basin in Lincolnshire or Yorkshire. Minor components include quartz, igneous rocks, and Rhaxella chert, all derived largely, if not entirely, from the till.

In these braided river deposits, organic remains and archaeological material rarely survive, or if they do occur, usually only the more robust materi-al is present and this is usually in a heavily rolled condition. Deposits laid down by the rivers in hydrological conditions similar to those of the present and yielding fossils indicative of temperate climatic conditions are known from only a small number of sites in the basin of the Great Ouse. They have been noticed from an early date (De La Condamine 1853) and several have now been the subject of modern palaeoenvironmental investigation.

For the earlier part of the post-Anglian period in the basin of the Great Ouse, the stratigraphic record is poorly known. Three terrace stages are recognised in the whole of the post-Anglian/pre-Flandrian interval, in contrast to the situation in the adjoining Middle Thames basin, where at least five post-Anglian terraces are usually recognised. Field investigation of the Great Ouse terraces shows, however, that a three-terrace model is rather arbitrary, and that fragments of terrace are locally present at intermediate levels. Assigning individual terrace fragments to particular terraces is sometimes difficult, especially where the topographic feature separating the first and second terraces is weakly developed.

Third terrace

A third terrace has been recognised at levels between 10.0m and 18.0m above the modern alluvium at a number of localities from Over, on the southern edge of the Fen Basin (Bell 1970), as far upstream as Olney (Dury 1952). This feature appears to be the earliest post-Anglian evidence of river development in the Ouse valley. Different views have been expressed at various times (Dury 1952; Horton 1970) about the height range of the third terrace above the alluvium, about where it is preserved, and about the reconstructed gradient of the terrace. In a survey of the terraces of the Great Ouse between Buckingham and Wyboston, Rogerson (1986) recognised only three remnants of the third terrace – at Biddenham, Blunham, and Wyboston. Only at Biddenham, where the terrace is c 11.5m above the modern alluvium, have the deposits underlying this terrace been the subject of systematic investigation. The earliest records of the terrace deposits at Biddenham are given by Prestwich (1861). He records 4.1m of sand and gravel in which several horizons containing Mollusca were present. At the time that Prestwich was writing, the site was already known to have yielded Palaeolithic artefacts and 'a considerable quantity of the teeth and bones of the *Elephas primigenius*, *Rhinoceros tichorhinus*, and of the Horse, Ox and Deer' (Prestwich 1861).

The Biddenham locality attracted considerable attention, particularly as a source of Palaeolithic material (Wyatt 1861, 1862, 1864; Evans 1862, 1872; Lyell 1863; Prestwich 1864), and the fossil material there was found to include the remains of straight tusked elephant (*Palaeoloxodon antiquus*) and the thermophile mollusc *Belgrandia marginata*. Reinvestigation of the Biddenham locality by

*Figure 2.4
Hartigan's Pit at
Stoke Goldington in
October 1981. The
working faces show
the braided river grav-
els which overlie the
organic sediments of
OI Stage 7 age. The
figure on the right
stands on the top of
the OI Stage 7
deposits*

Young (1984), Rogerson (1986), and Harding *et al* (1992) has confirmed the stratigraphy described by Prestwich (1861) and yielded a temperate mollus-can fauna, including *Belgrandia marginata,* and a quantity of Palaeolithic flint work. These modern investigations were in the Spinney Pit (now an SSSI) on the south side of the A428. Woodward (1906) reports that the site visited by Wyatt, Preswich, Evans, and Lyell in the 1860s lay on the opposite side of the road.

Attempts to date the deposits at the Spinney Pit, using uranium series and amino acid racemisation methods, have so far failed to give consistent results. The recognition of an Oxygen Isotope (OI) Stage 7 age for material beneath the lower-lying second terrace at Stoke Goldington, suggests that the Biddenham deposits represent an earlier temperate episode, possibly OI Stage 9.

Second terrace
Terrace remnants at levels between 5m and 10m above the modern alluvium occur in several places in the valley of the Great Ouse, at least as far upstream as Little Linford and downstream to Brampton, near Huntingdon. They have generally been assigned to the second terrace. A second terrace is also reported in the valley of the Ouzel at levels of 2–4m above the modern alluvium (Shephard-Thorn *et al* 1994) and in the valley of the Tove (Horton *et al* 1974). The gravels and sands beneath the second terrace are accompanied in some places by organic deposits of Ipswichian age, but in at least one place, Stoke Goldington, by organic deposits that relate to OI Stage 7 (Green *et al* 1996). Complex stratigraphic relationships of this sort are common in the post-Anglian terrace record of the Great Ouse.

The terrace sediments at Stoke Goldington rep-resent several stages of valley development (Fig 2.4). The terrace surface is about 8m above the mod-ern alluvium and a thickness of some 7–8m of ter-race sediment is present (Green *et al* 1996). The oldest deposit is a typical periglacial river deposit of sand and gravel that predates the OI Stage 7 mate-rial. The mainly fine-grained OI Stage 7 sediments, which are between 1.0m and 2.0m thick, occupy a depression in the pre-existing sands and gravels and represent the progressive infilling of a flood-plain pond which originated as an active river chan-nel. The associated fossil assemblages suggest a largely treeless environment but climatic conditions not unlike those of Midland England today. Both uranium series analysis and amino acid racemisa-tion data indicate an OI Stage 7 age for this mater-ial. Particularly significant for an understanding of valley development is the fact that the level of the modern alluvium lies within the height range of the OI Stage 7 deposits. This shows that already, during a cold interval preceding OI Stage 7, the valley had been cut down to its present level. Overlying the OI Stage 7 sediments at Stoke Goldington are braided river deposits which can be referred to OI Stage 6. These have in turn been locally affected by a cut-and-fill episode with the fill material containing Mollusca assigned to OI Stage 5 on the basis of amino acid determinations. Infill during or after OI Stage 5 is indicated.

The second terrace is probably also represented to the north-west of Bedford where the railway occupies a cutting through a low hill with a summit elevation about 8.0m above the nearby alluvium. At the time of its excavation in the 19th century the cutting is reported by Prestwich (1861) and Evans (1862) to have yielded large quantities of bones. The species represented were said to include both *Hippopotamus* and horse. *Hippopotamus* is now generally regarded as indicative in Britain of a last interglacial (Ipswichian) age for the deposits in which it occurs. Thus it seems likely that organic beds of Ipswichian age were preserved beneath the second terrace at this locality. However horse has never been found in modern investigations in association with *Hippopotamus* in deposits of Ipswichian age, so the fauna reported from this site may have included material from more than one horizon. Horse is common in deposits of OI Stage 7 age and also in Devensian deposits.

Attempts to relocate the fossiliferous deposits at the Bedford Railway Cutting were made in 1982 when machine excavations were opened beside the cutting at intervals along its eastern side. No fossil material was found and the drift consisted of rather uniform, structureless sand to a depth of about 2.0m. A detailed inspection of the whole of the railway cutting was also made but failed to locate any fossiliferous material.

A further locality at which fossiliferous deposits may have been present beneath the second terrace is Summerhouse Hill, to the east of Bedford. The fullest description of this site is given by Wyatt (1864). He records the summit of the hill at a level of 11m above the modern alluvium and states that a gravel deposit was present on the north-eastern flank of the hill. This deposit had 'a depth of 15 feet [4.6m] at the foot of the hill, gradually decreasing in thickness until near the top, where it ceases altogether' (p184). This description suggests that the gravel may have extended up to the level of the second terrace. Wyatt reports that large quantities of bones were recovered from gravel workings at Summerhouse Hill. Among the species he recorded were *Palaeoloxodon antiquus* and *Hippopotamus*, but also reindeer. The juxtaposition of these species indicates that deposits of more than one age were present at Summerhouse Hill. The occurrence of *Hippopotamus* shows, however, that the sequence included beds of Ipswichian age.

Summerhouse Hill is now largely occupied by an Anglian Water Authority water treatment works. Rogerson (1986) examined the records relating to successive stages of the construction of this works, but found that these contained no indication of the gravel deposits described by Wyatt on the higher flank of the hill, although gravel was encountered around its lower margins.

Paterson and Tebbutt (1947) refer to a site at Brampton which they treat as the 'Middle Terrace' of the Ouse and as separate from the 'low terrace gravel' around St Neots. Terrace sediments at the Brampton locality yielded bones of *Hippopotamus* and '*Cervus giganteus*' (?*Megaceros giganteus*). This may therefore be another locality where the second terrace of the Great Ouse is underlain by deposits of Ipwichian age.

First terrace

The first terrace is preserved as an extensive but discontinuous feature throughout the whole length of the Great Ouse, from at least as far upstream as Buckingham and downstream into the Fen Basin. It is also present in the valleys of the larger tributaries of the Ouse. The surface of the terrace in the Great Ouse valley extends up to levels at least as high as 4.5m above the modern alluvium. In the tributary valleys it is generally less than 2m above the alluvium. The lower edge of the terrace often merges imperceptibly with the surface of the alluvium. The terrace deposits underlying the first terrace are commonly between 3m and 4m in thickness and occupy the whole of the valley floor, passing beneath the modern alluvium which lies in a shallow channel cut into them. Gravel pits and foundation works have exposed the first terrace sediments in many places. Records of most of these temporary sections are tantalisingly brief. Banton (1924), Mantle (1926), and Tebbutt (1927) are among the more extended accounts. For only four localities are there accounts of modern environmental investigations.

At Somersham, on the southern edge of the Fen Basin, an aggradational surface is present at a level between 2m and 3m OD. Beneath this surface river sediments are present which are thought to be deposits of the Great Ouse. An investigation of the flora and faunas from this site (West *et al* 1994) reveals a complex situation which has important implications for the terrace record elsewhere in the basin of the Great Ouse. The lowest beds at Somersham from which organic samples were obtained are temperate brackish water sediments, assigned to the Ipswichian on the basis of their pollen content. They contain a molluscan fauna of temperate aspect which includes both *Belgrandia marginata* and *Corbicula fluminalis*. Both these species are now extinct in Britain and *C. fluminalis* has never been found in beds of undisputed Ipswichian age, although it is often present in deposits of OI Stage 7 age, including Stoke Goldington. The Somersham assemblage may therefore include material reworked from earlier deposits. Reworking has certainly occurred at higher levels in the Somersham sequence. The upper beds at Somersham are Devensian cold-stage sediments and occupy a depression cut into the Ipswichian deposits. The cold-stage faunas include taxa of arctic affinity, but are mixed with temperate taxa which are interpreted as having been derived from pre-existing warm-stage sediments. The full complexity of the situation is indicated by the fact that the temperate assemblage in the Devensian cold-stage sediments is not one that could have been derived from the immediately underlying temperate sediments but must have originated elsewhere in the locality.

Ipswichian deposits are found again beneath the first terrace of the Great Ouse at Galley Hill, near St Ives. Here Preece and Ventris (1983) describe a temperate fossil assemblage, including such typical Ipswichian thermophiles as the gastropod *Belgrandia marginata* and the maple *Acer mon-*

spessulanum. The remains of *Hippopotamus* are reported by Wyatt (1864) from a locality at Goldington on the south-eastern outskirts of Bedford, where the ground surface is at the level of the first terrace. However, the great majority of the mammalian bones recovered from beneath the first terrace in the basin of the Great Ouse are of species that belong in a cold-stage fauna. Finds of mammoth are recorded in Bedford Museum from several places within the built up area of the town of Bedford and from sites in Kempston and Clapham. Mammoth has also been recorded from Harrowden and Willington and from first terrace sediments at Little Paxton. *Rhinoceros*, red deer, reindeer, horse, and *Bos* or *Bison* have also been found in many places beneath the first terrace, but most of the records provide little information about the detailed context of the finds. The assumption is usually made that all this material is of last glacial (Devensian) age.

Modern palaeoenvironmental investigations of Devensian cold-stage deposits have been undertaken at Somersham (West *et al* 1994), at Earith on the southern edge of the Fen Basin near Somersham (Bell 1970), and at Radwell, about 9km to the north of Bedford (Rogerson *et al* 1992). The Radwell site gives another clear indication of the complexity of the post-Anglian terrace record in the valley of the Great Ouse. At Radwell, silts and sands form a channel fill within the sands and gravels of the first terrace. The terrace surface here is at a level only 1–2m above the alluvium. Plant macrofossils, Mollusca, Coleoptera, and ostracods mainly indicate cool climatic conditions. Radiocarbon dates of 43,250 +2010/-1610 BP (SRR-2980) and 40,500 +1380/-1180 BP (SRR-2981) suggest an age in the mid-Devensian (Upton Warren) Interstadial. However, these dates were obtained from wood charcoal which proved to be of the species *Abies alba*. Not only is the Upton Warren Interstadial particularly noted for its treeless character, the species *Abies alba* was probably absent in Britain in the Devensian and, although well established in the Cromerian and Hoxnian interglacials, was rare or absent in the Ipswichian. It does occur, though not abundantly, in the temperate OI Stage 7 deposits at Stoke Goldington. It seems likely therefore that the Radwell channel deposit includes material derived from pre-existing temperate deposits elsewhere on the valley floor. This possibility is supported by the presence in the basal horizons at Radwell of plant macrofossils of other thermophile woodland species, including alder, prunus, and elder. If this material, together with the *Abies* charcoal, is indeed derived from earlier sediments, the radiocarbon dates must obviously be regarded as infinite.

The account of the Earith site (Bell 1970) tends to confirm the widespread occurrence in the valley of the Great Ouse of reworking of organic material from older into younger beds. The organic sediments at Earith occur beneath the undivided first and second terrace. The largely cold-adapted flora is referred by Bell (1970) to the Devensian. A finite radiocarbon date of 42,140 +1890/-1530 BP (Birm-86) suggests accumulation during the Upton Warren Interstadial. However, an infinite date was also obtained and the plant beds included macrofossils of hornbeam, hazel, dogwood, and a number of somewhat thermophile herbs. Bell suggests that reworking has occurred from Ipswichian deposits, presumed by her to exist nearby.

Periglacial features

Evidence of periglacial conditions is widely present in the basin of the Great Ouse, both as superficial structures affecting the near surface geology and in the form of superficial deposits which generally have the effect of softening the relief outlines. The upper layers both of terrace deposits and of bedrock are affected in many places by periglacial involutions which contort the original bedding, often very severely. Ice-wedge casts seem to be less common but are reported by Bell (1970) in the sands and gravels underlying the low terrace of the Ouse near Earith. She was also able to trace on aerial photographs the associated polygonal patterns where these are visible on the terrace surface. Many valley side slopes, even where the slope angle is as little as 3°, are mantled by head deposits. These are usually a layer of material not more than a metre in thickness which has moved downslope across a diffuse shear zone. On the floors of some minor tributary valleys thicker accumulations of this material may be present and towards the valley axis may grade into, or interdigitate with, alluvial sediments. Sometimes the downslope movement of material has taken the form of a shallow translational landslide, especially on steeper slopes or where impeded drainage exists. These features may be marked by areas of uneven and poorly drained ground.

Alluvium

The alluvium of the modern rivers generally occupies a channel cut into, or in some places through, the deposits that underlie the first terrace. The alluvium may also spread out beyond its channel to overlap the first terrace sediments and feather out towards the valley side. Up to 6m of alluvium have been recorded in boreholes but thicknesses of 2–3m are more likely to be encountered. The bulk of the alluvium is a calcareous, grey-brown, silty clay, often decalcified in its upper part and tending to become greyer downwards. Its lower part may be quite gravelly, and stringers of gravel and isolated pebbles can occur throughout. Shelly horizons may be present and occasionally beds of peat with plant macro-fossils and bones. Kennard and Woodward (1922) provide a faunal list for Mollusca from the alluvium for a site near Bromham. Radiocarbon assay of material from the bottom and top of a gravelly horizon at the base of the alluvium near Wolverton gave dates, respectively, of 3813 ± 45 and 3552 ± 40 BP (Horton *et al* 1974).

Stratigraphical complexity of the terrace sequence

The distribution of fluvioglacial and fluvial sediments in the valley of the Great Ouse shows that, within a height range of less than 2m above and below the level of the modern alluvium, material representing separate aggradations of Anglian, OI Stage 7, Ipswichian, Devensian, and Flandrian age is present. Even the sediments beneath the third terrace, possibly of OI Stage 9 age, reach down at their base to within only 5–6m of the modern alluvium. All of these aggradations are represented by at least several metres of sediment. The scope for reworking between deposits of different age is obvious and the interpretation of the terrace sequence must therefore be approached bearing this potential complexity in mind.

Physical factors and human occupation

From the foregoing account it will be apparent that, although the basin of the Great Ouse is one of low relief and relatively uncomplicated bedrock geology, there are, nevertheless, many distinctive relief facets and an even greater variety of subsurface materials and superficial structures which may affect the distribution and preservation of archaeological remains. The bedrock geology exerts a major influence on water supply and largely dictates the local availability of building materials. Relief, in terms of slope steepness, can rarely have been the overriding factor affecting the choice of settlement sites. Impeded drainage, especially on valley floors and in the clay lowlands in general, is likely to have been a more discouraging factor, especially when, as in the past, these areas were densely wooded, remaining so until comparatively late in the historic period. Not only are physical factors within the basin of the Great Ouse generally manageable in terms of human occupation, there are virtually no serious physical barriers to movement and communication within and through the region. It is not surprising therefore to find evidence of human occupation from an early date, with continuity of occupation extending back, in some places, into the prehistoric period.

Bibliography

Banton, J T, 1924 Notes on the gravels of the Great Ouse basin, *Geological Magazine*, **41**, 328–30

Bell, F G, 1970 Late Pleistocene flora from Earith, Huntingdonshire, *Phil Trans Royal Soc London*, **B258**, 347–78

Castleden, R, 1980 The morphological implications of the Milton Sand, near Northampton, *East Midland Geographer*, **7**, 195–203

Clayton, K M, 1979 The Midlands and southern Pennines, in A Straw & K M Clayton (eds) *The geomorphology of the British Isles – Eastern and Central England*. London: Methuen, 141–240

De La Condamine, H M, 1853 On a freshwater deposit in the "Drift" of Huntingdonshire, *Quarterly J Geological Soc*, **9**, 271–4

Dury, G H, 1952 Some long-profiles of the Great Ouse system, *J Northamptonshire Nat Hist and Field Club*, **32**, 135–40

Edmonds, E A, & Dinham, C H, 1965 Geology of the Country Around Huntingdon and Biggleswade, *Memoirs of the Geological Survey of Great Britain*, Sheets **187** & **204** (England and Wales). London: HMSO

Evans, J, 1861 Flint implements in the drift, being an account of further discoveries on the continent and in England, *Archaeologia*, **39**, 1–69

Evans, J, 1872 *The ancient stone implements, weapons and ornaments of Great Britain*. London: Longmans

Green, C P, Coope, G R, Jones R L, Keen, D H, Bowen, D Q, Currant, A P, Holyoak, D T, Ivanovich, M, Robinson, J E, Rogerson, R J, & Young, R C, 1996 Pleistocene deposits at Stoke Goldington, in the valley of the Great Ouse, UK, *J Quat Sci*, **11**, 59–87

Harding, P, Bridgland, D R, Keen, D H, & Rogerson, R J, 1992 A Palaeolithic site rediscovered at Biddenham, Bedfordshire, *Bedfordshire Archaeol*, **19**, 87–90

Hill, W, 1908 On a deep channel of drift at Hitchin (Hertfordshire), *Quarterly J Geological Soc London*, **64**, 8–26

Horton, A, 1970 The drift sequence and sub-glacial topography in parts of the Ouse and Nene basins, *Rep Inst Geological Sci*, **70(9)**

Horton, A, Shephard-Thorn, E R, & Thurrell, R G, 1974 The geology of the new town of Milton Keynes, *Rep Inst Geological Sci*, **74(16)**

Kellaway, G A, & Taylor, J H, 1953 (for 1952) Early stages in the physiographic evolution of a portion of the East Midlands, *Quarterly J Geological Soc London*, **108**, 343–75

Kennard, A S, & Woodward, B B, 1922 The post-Pliocene non-marine Mollusca of the East of England, *Proc Geologists' Assoc*, **33**, 104–42

Lyell, C, 1863 *Geological evidences of the antiquity of Man*. London: Murray

Mantle, H G, 1926 The superficial deposits in the valley of the Great Ouse between Willington and Wybaston (*sic*), *Proc Geologists' Assoc*, **37**, 414–19

Paterson, T T, & Tebbutt, C F, 1947 Studies in the Palaeolithic succession in England, No III: Palaeoliths from St Neots, Huntingdonshire, *Proc Prehist Soc*, **13**, 37–46

Perrin, R M S, Rose, J, & Davies, H, 1970 The distribution, variation and origins of pre-Devensian tills in eastern England, *Phil Trans Royal Soc London*, **B287**, 535–70

Preece, R C, & Ventris, P.A. 1983 An interglacial site at Galley Hill, near St Ives, Cambridgeshire, *Bull*

Geological Soc Norfolk, **33**, 63–72

Prestwich, J, 1861 Notes on some further discoveries of flint implements in beds of post-Pliocene gravel and clay; with a few suggestions for search elsewhere, *Quarterly J Geological Soc London*, **17**, 362–8

Prestwich, J, 1864 On the geological position and age of the flint-implement-bearing beds and of the loess of the south-east of England and north-west of France, *Phil Trans Royal Soc London*, **154**, 246–310

Rogerson, R J A, 1986 The terraces of the River Great Ouse. Unpublished PhD thesis, University of London

Rogerson, R J A, Keen, D H, Coope, G R, Robinson, E, Dickson, J H, & Dickson, C A, 1992 The flora, fauna and palaeoenvironmental significance of deposits beneath the low terrace of the River Great Ouse at Radwell, Bedfordshire, England. *Proc Geologists' Assoc*, **103**, 1–13

Shephard-Thorn, E R, Moorlock, B S P, Cox, B M, Allsop, J M, & Wood, C J, 1994 Geology of the country around Leighton Buzzard, *Memoir of the British Geological Survey*, Sheet **220** (England and Wales). London: HMSO

Straw, A 1979 Eastern England, in A Straw & K M Clayton (eds) *The Geomorphology of the British Isles – Eastern and Central England*. London: Methuen, 1–139

Taylor, J H, 1963 Geology of the country around Kettering, Corby and Oundle, *Memoir of the Geological Survey of Great Britain*, Sheet **171** (England and Wales). London: HMSO

Tebbutt, C F, 1927 Palaeolithic industries from the Great Ouse gravels at and near St Neots, *Proc Prehist Soc East Anglia*, **5**, 166–73

West, R G, Knudsen, K L, Penney, D N, Preece, R C, & Robinson, J E, 1994 Palaeontology and taphonomy of Late Quaternary fossil assemblages at Somersham, Cambridgeshire, England, and the problem of reworking, *J Quat Sci*, **9**, 357–66

Wilmot, R D, 1985 Mineralogical evidence for sediment derivation and ice movement within the Wash drainage basin, eastern England, *Clay Minerals*, **20**, 209–20

Woodland, A W, 1970 The buried tunnel-valleys of East Anglia, *Proc Yorkshire Geological Soc*, **37**, 521–78

Woodward, B B, 1906 Excursion to Bedford, *Proc Geologists' Assoc*, **19**, 142–46

Wooldridge, S W, & Linton, D L, 1955 *Structure, surface and drainage in south-east England*. London: Philip

Wyatt, J, 1861 Flint implements in the drift, *Bedfordshire Architect & Archaeol Soc Trans*, 3–17

Wyatt, J, 1862 On some further discoveries of flint implements in the gravel near Bedford, *Quarterly J Geological Soc London*, **18**, 113–14

Wyatt, J, 1864 Further discoveries of flint implements and fossil mammals in the valley of the Ouse, *Quarterly J Geological Soc London*, **20**, 183–8

Young, R C, 1984 Aspects of the Middle and Upper Pleistocene of the Upper Ouse basin. Unpublished PhD thesis, University of London

3 The prehistoric vegetation and environment of the River Ouse valley *by Rob Scaife*

Introduction

Bedfordshire is one of the counties in the southern half of England for which there are few pollen data available for reconstructing the vegetational and environmental history of the Holocene or indeed earlier glacial and interglacial periods. This is unfortunate considering the relatively varied geology, which spans the Jurassic to Cretaceous, and the cover of Pleistocene glacial tills. Given the archaeological diversity outlined in other papers in this volume, the availability of more pollen data would have helped to present a picture of the environment in which human communities lived and the way in which they altered and created the landscape which pertains today. It is a region which has been overshadowed by the Fenlands to the east which have continued to provide detailed information on vegetation history since the early days of pollen analytical techniques. Recognition of environmental archaeology as a discipline within archaeology has resulted in the examination of a range of soils and sediments which have started to yield data on the changing environments of the last 10,000 years. This report provides a summary of some of the information now available from pollen and plant macrofossil analyses undertaken on sites in Bedfordshire (Fig 3.1) largely in collaboration with the work of the Bedfordshire County Archaeology Service.

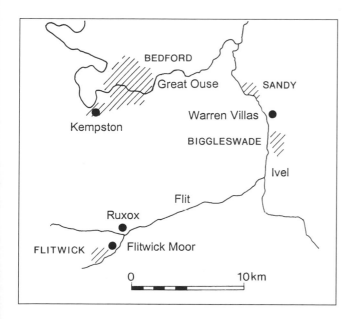

Figure 3.1 Location of sites

Sources of data

Much of our knowledge of past vegetation and ecological change comes from the study of sub-fossil pollen and spores preserved in suitable (usually anaerobic) peat deposits, alluvial and lacustrine sediments, and soils. Sequential sampling at intervals through such material and laboratory extraction, identification, and counting of statistically valid numbers of pollen grains allow the reconstruction of vegetation communities and changes spanning the period in which the deposit was laid down. Such analyses presuppose the availability of such pollen preserving deposits. Peat bogs and lake sediments have long been the principal source of polliniferous sediments by virtue of their waterlogged and anaerobic nature. Knowledge of Bedfordshire suggests a paucity of such sites and where these have existed in the past, they have been largely destroyed through peat cutting, draining for agriculture, or neglect of wetland withy beds. In spite of the varied geology of Bedfordshire, there are few areas where high ground-water levels exist allowing the accumulation of organic/plant material. Areas of existing peat accumulation occur along the floodplains of the principal rivers and are frequently covered by alluvial clay and silt. These valley peat (topogenous) mires contrast markedly with the frequently analysed, and more extensive, upland raised and blanket mires of the north and west of Britain. Examination of the most recent flora (Dony 1978) and earlier surveys by Saunders at the end of the last century have been used to deduce those areas of wetland peat mire by virtue of their typical wetland floras. These consistently show that Flitton Moor/Flitwick Moor and Westoning Moor, on the River Flit, were the most extensive peat bogs in the county, with smaller areas in Westoning Heath. Fortunately, the presence and excavation of the Iron Age/Romano-British site at Ruxox, on the edge of Flitwick Moor, has enabled dating and pollen analysis of the remaining peat. Other pollen-preserving environments, including soils buried under archaeological field monuments such as barrows, field boundaries, and henge banks, may provide evidence from soil pollen analysis of vegetation 'on site' immediately prior to the construction of such features. At present, no data are available since no excavation of such features has taken place in recent times. More specific evidence of human palaeoeconomy has, however, been advanced in the last decade through the recovery and analysis of charred plant remains, usually cereals and associated weeds (ruderals and segetals), from archaeological excavations at Ruxox, Bedford Southern Orbital Sewer, Shillington, Biggleswade West, Biddenham Bunyan Centre, and Norton Road, Shotfold. Although there is the potential for such preservation of food resources by charring from any prehistoric or late site where fire has been used, the greater preponderance of Iron Age and Romano-British sites and the crop varieties cultivated during these periods has led to a correspondingly greater knowledge of agricultural economy from these periods. This contrasts with the earlier Neolithic and Bronze Age periods, where such remains are generally scant although some data has been forthcoming from the Bunyan Centre development (Steadman 1998). Thus, there are substantial gaps in our knowledge of the changing flora, environment and past agricultural economy of Bedfordshire. The reasons for these gaps centre upon the paucity of suitable preservational environments and the chance nature of the sample that results from modern archaeological mitigation.

The Devensian background

It is not practicable here to discuss the characteristics of the vegetation of the Quaternary period as a whole. Suffice it to say that the last two million years have seen major climatic fluctuations in glacial and interglacial periods, each having their own characteristics. The advent of oxygen isotope dating of ice cores and deep sea sediments and amino-acid dating has helped to indicate that the standard Quaternary divisions, still found in many texts, are in reality much more complex. This has, as a result, caused a reappraisal of both the inter-

glacial vegetation models from classic sites such as Hoxne and the relative ages of Palaeolithic sites found typically on the river terrace gravels of, notably, the Ouse (see Chapter 2 this volume).

Before an understanding of the vegetation of the present interglacial period (Holocene) can be attempted, it is necessary to realise that the last glacial/cold stage finished only 10,000 years ago. This stage, the Devensian period, forms the 'background' to the sequence of vegetation changes which have occurred during the subsequent warm stage.

It is now generally recognised that the last (Devensian) cold stage was itself not a period of homogeneous climate but was in fact a complex of warmer and colder phases with corresponding degrees of vegetation and woodland development. Counties surrounding Bedfordshire have yielded organic deposits from the Devensian period (taken from *c* 80,000–10,000 BP) occurring in the fluvioglacial outwash gravels with evidence of the vegetation of the coldest periods (especially 28,000–15,000 BP) and warmer interstadial periods (eg Upton Warren and Chelford). In Middle Ouse, organic muds filling a palaeo-river channel have been found at Radwell on the Great Ouse (NGR TL 00585857). The various levels have been attributed to the last interglacial and (Ipswichian) middle Devensian (Rogerson *et al* 1992). The former shows evidence of scrub woodland of temperate character, whilst upper levels show low-growing herbs but with evidence of *Juniperus* (juniper) and *Abies* (fir). The presence of fir has been the cause of much debate since this tree has not previously been recorded at this late stage of the Pleistocene.

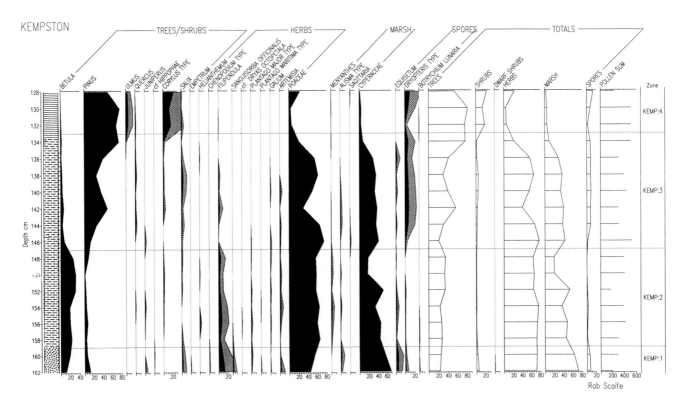

Figure 3.2   Selected pollen and spore taxa from the early-Holocene site at Kempston

Data obtained from Huntingdonshire (Bell 1969,1970) are more typical, showing that the cold stage was represented by open herbaceous tundra types growing in a permafrost environment. Plant communities were of a phytogeographically diverse character with vegetation communities/elements living in close proximity, which are today only found in the Arctic, Alpine, or locally in disjunct refugia in parts of northern Britain. Plant communities which occurred included species-rich, short, turf grass, similar to 'old' chalk downland pasture today; plants of disturbed ground, caused by periglacial freeze–thaw action; marsh and bog communities; dwarf shrub communities (Ericaceae dominated); and tall herb type pasture typical of sub-Alpine meadow or even similar to the old water meadows of Bedfordshire rivers today. More 'extinct' elements of the vegetation undoubtedly included arctic alpine varieties (saxifrages, gentians etc). At Earith, Huntingdonshire, F G Bell (1969,1970) recovered clear evidence for arctic steppe vegetation dominated by Chenopodiaceae, *Artemisia* and, interestingly (but typically), salt-loving/tolerant plants (halophytes) today found only along coasts and in mountains (also motorway verges through salting of roads!). These she attributed to the extreme temperature conditions and mineral soils giving locally saline-rich habitats. Such data on the Devensian vegetation, whilst not seen from Bedfordshire sites, are well documented from other localities. With the exception of the warmer interlude of the Windermere (Allerød) interstadial from *c* 12,000–11,000 BP this diversity of low-growing herb vegetation existed until *c* 10,000 BP, when temperatures rose markedly at the start of the present (Holocene) interglacial period.

The Windermere interstadial period witnessed perhaps the first fluctuations in temperature heralding the onset of the Holocene. This short-lived phase has, in other areas, shown the development of *Betula* (birch) and possibly *Pinus* (pine). However, a short return to the extremely cold conditions of the Loch Lomond stadial (*c* 11,000–10,000 BP) saw a reversion to open herb-rich vegetation. Some evidence of this is seen at Kempston on the River Ouse (NGR TL 015486). Here, a meander cut-off or depression in the bedrock contained inorganic sediments, the base of which are attributed to the period just prior to 10,000 BP. These sediments yielded pollen dominated by grasses, sedges, and other herbs including, for example, *Plantago maritima* (sea plantain), *Filipendula ulmaria* (meadow sweet), and possibly *Dryas octopetala* (mountain avens), in a largely treeless environment. A few birches and junipers may have existed. Selected taxa are represented in the basal levels (160–164cm) of this profile (Fig 3.2) where Cyperaceae (sedges; 70%) and Poaceae (grasses) attain 50–60% of total recorded pollen in pollen zone KEMP:1.

The Holocene

Undoubtedly, it is the past 10,000 years of the present interglacial, the Holocene (Flandrian), which is most relevant to most of the archaeology of Middle Ouse. As noted, there are few sites which have been studied in the region and the data presented here come from a number of assessment studies and sites which are to be published fully at a later date.

The early Holocene – Mesolithic: Flandrian I

Excavations at Biddenham Loop, at Kempston on the River Ouse (NGR TL 015486), and the Southern Orbital Sewer (NGR TL 012509) contain material in their lowest levels which is attributed to the end of the last cold stage. Subsequently, the pollen evidence shows typical early Holocene changes in woodland development and structure. In the lowest levels dating to the cold stage, herbs are dominant, making up some 70–75% of total pollen. This open environment rapidly gave way to woodland due to temperature amelioration and the migration of trees from refugia in which they survived during the cold stages. Thus, here we see the expansion of juniper (*Juniperus*), followed rapidly by birch (*Betula*), as pioneer colonisers of the open landscape shortly after 10,000 BP, subsequently followed by pine (*Pinus*) associated with hazel (*Corylus avellana*). The importance of these taxa is seen at Biddenham Loop/Kempston (Fig 3.2) and at Field 5669 (NGR TL 014485) which have pollen percentages for pine of, respectively, up to 67% and 60% of total pollen present. Whilst pollen analysis is no longer regarded as a 'tool' for dating, being superseded by radiocarbon measurements, it is possible to say that this early dominance of pine took place at *c* 9000 BP in what has been called the Boreal (pine hazel) period (Godwin's 1956, 1975a pollen zone V), Flandrian Chronozone Ib (Mangerud *et al* 1974). However, the migration and expansion of vegetation types during the early part of this interglacial was asynchronous across the country and radiocarbon dating is much needed to establish an absolute chronology of these changes in vegetation and environment. This time of pine and hazel dominance saw the incoming of oak (*Quercus*) and elm (*Ulmus*) and their rise to dominance in the middle and later Boreal from *c* 8500 BP, ousting large areas of the pine woodland. Such rapidly changing vegetation thus represents a major successional change, from pioneer to climax woodland types, due to a rapid temperature rise (at 10,000 BP) and migration of trees, replacing heliophilous herbs and shrubs, and then progressive replacement and dominance of more competitive woodland elements. These changes were also mirrored by the progressive maturation of the soils. By the end of the early Holocene at *c* 7000 BP oak, elm, and hazel woodland was fully established, perhaps with some remaining pine woodland.

It is during this period from 10,000 to 7000 BP

that the early-Mesolithic habitation took place. Traditionally, these communities have been viewed as having a solely hunting and foraging subsistence. There has been much debate in the past on the possibility of these communities affecting the vegetation and environment, directly or indirectly (Smith 1970; Turner 1970). Whilst the effects are certainly visible in peat sites in upland 'fragile' ecosystems such as the North York Moors and Dartmoor (Simmons 1975), such effects in the lowland zone are not generally proven. Dimbleby's work on Iping Common, Sussex, on poor (sandy) soils (in Keefe *et al* 1965) perhaps illustrated the effects of short term occupation causing soil deterioration and expansion of acidophilous heathland communities. At present there is not enough detailed pollen work available from Bedfordshire to address the question of human disturbance during this phase and only the general environment of occupation, as described above, can be outlined. This is unfortunate given the range of Mesolithic artefacts produced in recent fieldwalking surveys (Dawson pers comm).

The middle Holocene – late Mesolithic: Flandrian II

The period from *c* 7000 BP to 5000 BP has frequently been regarded as the middle-Holocene climatic optimum for this interglacial, with higher temperatures and humidity than the preceding Boreal period. However, recent work suggests that the early Holocene may, in fact, have had higher temperatures associated with a continental regime rather than the greater humidity of the middle Holocene. Because of the greater humidity/precipitation, the so-called Atlantic period (Mangerud *et al* 1974) is also notable in that Britain became an island. The post-glacial rise in sea levels bridged the English Channel gap during the early part of this period, effectively preventing further migration of tree taxa into the country.

There is now a substantial amount of data from central, eastern, and southern England which illustrate the vegetation of this, the later Mesolithic period. Unlike the instability and successional changes of the early Holocene endured by Mesolithic communities, the Atlantic period was, in contrast, one of environmental stability. The pine domination of the early Holocene was superseded by dominance of deciduous woodland. Higher temperatures, well-developed soils, and the arrival into the country of thermophilous and slowly migrating tree species resulted in the maximum development of 'natural' woodland in the country. At present, no deposits definitely dated to this period have been found in Bedfordshire, although tentative acclamation has been made for peats along the Bedford Southern Orbital Sewer (Scaife unpublished assessment). However, in spite of this absence of data, a picture of the environment can be made. Rather than the traditional view of a landscape dominated by mixed deciduous woodland, a polyclimax view is

preferable (Godwin 1975b); that is simply that different soil types had differing woodland types. Pollen data from throughout Britain now show marked regional and local variations in the dominant tree types (Birks *et al* 1975; Birks 1989). Here, *Quercus* (oak), *Ulmus* (elm), and *Corylus* (hazel) woodland were undoubtedly of importance, but they were possibly dominant on the heavier clay soils of the county. The better drained soils of the river terraces and the chalklands would have supported *Tilia* (lime/linden), whilst wetter valley bottoms supported tracts of alder carr with willow.

The later prehistoric period – Flandrian III

From *c* 5000 BP in Britain, the Neolithic marks the first clearances for agriculture of the 'natural' woodland of the mid-Holocene, Atlantic. In pollen diagrams this is diagnostically indicated by the first evidence of deforestation on a small scale and the introduction and first occurrence of cereal pollen and associated segetal taxa (weeds of cultivation). Forest clearances have frequently been shown to be of ephemeral character with subsequent abandonment and regeneration of these areas by secondary woodland. Such Neolithic 'Landnam' clearances (Iversen 1941, 1949), originally postulated as lasting some 25–30 years, are now shown to have lasted some hundreds of years, as in the Isle of Wight (Scaife 1980, 1987) and at Hockham Mere, Norfolk (Simms 1973). Frequently associated with, and just prior to, these clearances is the much discussed 'elm decline', a distinctive pollen horizon dated more or less synchronously at *c* 5300–5000 BP. Though many explanations have been given for this significant event, including climatic change, use of elm leaves for fodder, and clearance through ring-barking (see Smith 1970; Turner 1970; Scaife 1987 for discussion), it is now held to be the result of elm bark beetles (*Scolytus*) and fungal disease (*Ceratocystis*) carried by these beetles. Girling (1987), based on pollen data and discovery of elm beetles in pre-elm-decline peats at Hampstead Heath (Girling and Greig 1977, 1985), suggests that the arrival of a Neolithic economy and the opening-up of woodland promoted the geographical expansion of beetles and disease across most of the forests of Britain. Whilst it was once thought that the Neolithic people were responsible for large-scale woodland clearances in such areas of the chalk downland and limestone regions from the early Neolithic, it has now been shown that the overall effect of the period was to create a mosaic landscape of such agricultural clearances set in remaining climax and secondary woodland. In the later Neolithic, there is clear evidence from pollen records for southern Britain of woodland regeneration giving rise to extensive secondary woodland.

Recent analyses of peats and sediments are now beginning to produce data which relate to the later-prehistoric period. These analyses include a palaeo-

Flitwick Moor

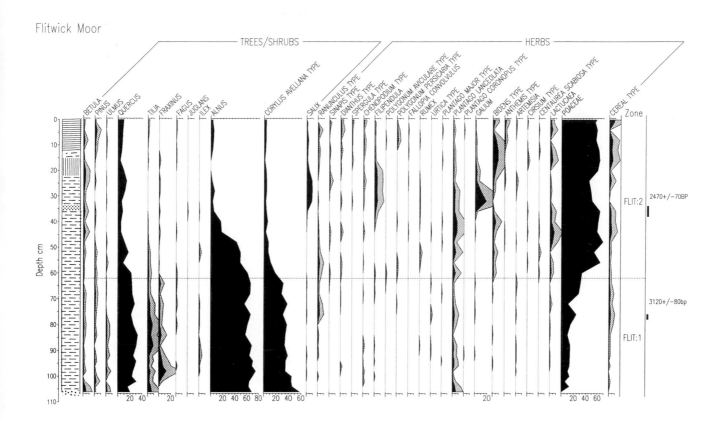

Figure 3.3a   Flitwick Moor, Ruxox. Selected pollen and spore taxa from the late-Holocene peat deposits

Flitwick Moor cont.

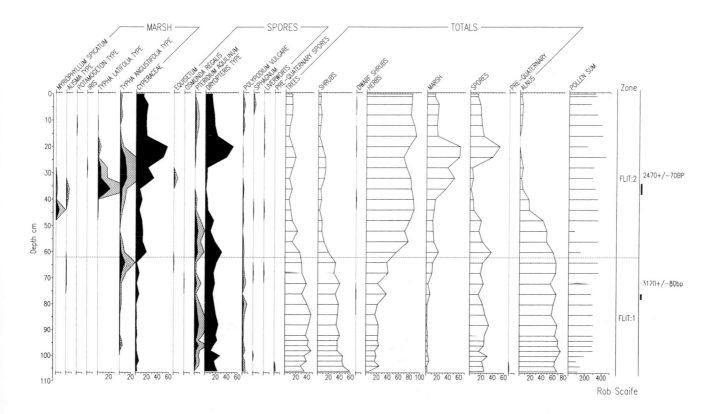

Rob Scaife

Figure 3.3b   Flitwick Moor, Ruxox. Selected pollen and spore taxa from the late-Holocene peat deposits (continued)

river channel at Warren Villa adjacent to the River Ivel (Greig 1993), Salford (Wiltshire 1998), and at Ruxox on the River Flit (see below). These data are now providing more detailed evidence for environment and land-use changes during the later prehistoric and early-historic periods in areas where data were not previously available.

Flitwick Moor, Ruxox – a detailed pollen study in Bedfordshire

At Ruxox, on the River Flit (near Flitwick, NGR TL 046363), pollen analysis has been carried out on the peat deposits of Flitwick Moor and a Romano-British ditch adjacent to the Romano-British settlement (see Chapter 10). This work was carried out in association with excavation of this archaeological site along the route of a (Anglian) water pipeline and has produced a record of vegetation change which spans the late Neolithic (although radiocarbon dates are still awaited) to the Romano-British period.

At the base of this pollen profile (see Figure 3.3) there is strong evidence for secondary woodland of *Fraxinus* (ash), *Ilex* (holly), and *Fagus* (beech). These elements are all grossly under-represented in pollen spectra, through insect pollination in the former and poor dispersal of heavier pollen grains in the case of the latter. Typical, also, is the domination of *Quercus* (oak) and *Corylus avellana* (hazel) and some remaining *Ulmus* (elm). Extremely high values of *Alnus* (alder) through the lower half of the peat profile represent the dominance of alder carr woodland on the moor and adjacent river valleys, including the sample site at Ruxox. Herbs such as *Plantago lanceolata* (ribwort plantain), Chenopodiaceae (goosefoots), Poaceae (grasses), and cereal-type pollen suggest local cereal agriculture and possibly pastoralism.

Of note is the 'curve' for *Tilia* (lime/lindens) since,

as with taxa noted above, it is insect pollinated and greatly under-represented in pollen spectra. Thus, although pollen percentages of up to 10% are found, this shows its substantial importance in the local vegetation of this region. From a depth of 0.70m in the peat there is a significant reduction in *Tilia* values. As with the Neolithic elm decline at *c* 5000 BP, the 'lime decline' is a similarly diagnostic phenomenon in the geographical region of lime growth (southern and eastern England). However, this is not a synchronous phenomenon and dates as early as the late Neolithic have been noted (Scaife 1980,1987) and as late as the Saxon period have been discussed (Baker *et al* 1978; Greig 1982). Whilst the cause of decline was originally attributed to climatic change from continental conditions of the sub-Boreal period to wetter sub-Atlantic at *c* 3000 BP, it has been demonstrated that it had human causes and in the pollen record is often associated with weeds of cultivation (Turner 1962). Although the dating range, as noted above, is broad, the majority of dates fall within the late Bronze Age. This is perhaps associated with increasing land pressure related to the reorganisation of land-use during this period, which certainly appears to be the case in chalkland areas of southern Britain (Ellison and Harris 1972; Fowler 1978). At Ruxox there is a similarly close correspondence with increasing weeds (ruderals/segetals) such as Brassicaceae spp, Polygonaceae spp, Asteraceae spp, *Plantago lanceolata*, and cereal pollen with the decline of lime. A radiocarbon date of 3120 ± 80 BP (Beta-117412, cal BC 1525–1145) at 0.76m similarly places the lime decline here to the late Bronze Age, which is comparable with the majority of dates obtained from southern and eastern England. Greig (1993), as noted above, has produced pollen data from Warren Villa, in the valley of the River Ivel (see Figure 3.4). Here, a 1.2m stratigraphical sequence of peat overlain by gravel and alluvium

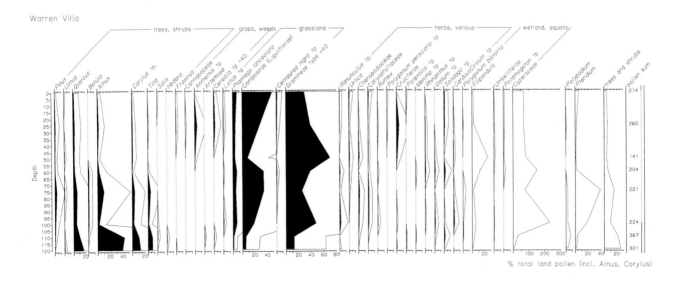

Figure 3.4   Warren Villas. Pollen analysis carried out by James Grieg

Ruxox RB Ditch

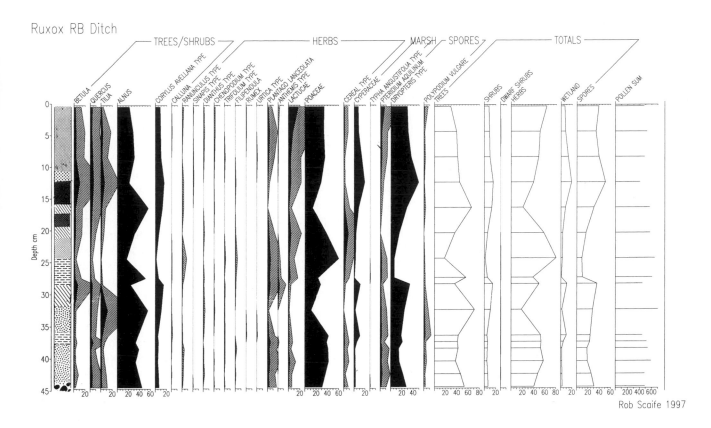

Rob Scaife 1997

Figure 3.5   Selected pollen and spore taxa from the Romano-British ditch profile, Ruxox

shows a similar sequence of events as that of Ruxox. Lower levels are dominated by *Alnus*, which was dominant in the river valley, whilst *Quercus, Corylus avellana*, and *Tilia* are the dominant terrestrial elements (wildwood). A clear *'Tilia* decline' from 1.00m is similarly associated with a very marked expansion of herb types attributed to pastoral rather than arable activity. Although radiocarbon dating is not yet available, a middle/late-Bronze Age date again seems most likely for the sequence.

In the upper half of both the Ruxox and Warren Villas pollen profile there is a marked change in the ecology of the valley mire from alder carr woodland to sedge fen, and an increase in *Salix* (willow) and marginal and aquatic taxa (*Typha latifolia*/lesser reed mace, *Typha angustifolia* type/bur reed and common reed mace, *Iris*, and aquatic taxa). This implies water-logging of the valley bottoms in these locations. The similarity of the two pollen profiles is interesting and whilst such changes are usually viewed as local responses to changing water tables, it is possible that we are here seeing a more regional response to changes in hydrology. This cannot yet be corroborated, but it is tentatively suggested that further and more widespread woodland clearance may have caused rising ground-water tables through reduction in evapotranspiration and increased surface run-off. At both sites there is a reduction in dry-land tree types. This may have taken place during the Iron Age. Alternatively, rising sea levels during the final millennium BC

(Waller 1994) may have caused ponding back of the River Ouse system and its tributaries. Importance of *Salix* (willow) at Ruxox may be attributed to coppicing activity in close proximity to the site.

The Romano-British period

There are now a number of sites which represent this period, particularly the Ruxox farmstead excavations. The work of Greig (1993) at Warren Villas (Fig 3.4) and Wiltshire (1998) at Salford have both provided information which can be compared with the Ruxox site. At Ruxox, excavation produced substantial quantities of charred cereal and seed remains from a variety of sediment filled ditches. One of these ditches contained 0.45m of finely laminated red and brown silt and clay, charcoal, and organic deposit and may have been from outwash products into a still pond from an industrial process. Pollen preservation in this context was excellent and produced a diverse assemblage, providing clear evidence for the local environment of the site (see Figure 3.5). The pollen spectra can be correlated with the upper pollen levels obtained from the nearby, and older, peat deposits of Flitwick Moor. Thus, in addition to the continuation of local alder carr woodland, which was dominant in the extensive moors area, there is also evidence of *Tilia* woodland in the local area. This is an important and interesting record since with some exceptions (Epping Forest: Baker *et al* 1978), such woodland had been largely cleared during the later Bronze Age period (Turner 1962; Greig 1982; Scaife 1980; Waller 1994). However, comparison with Figure 3.3a from Flitwick Moor shows lower values and appears to correlate with the upper part of the lower sequence in Figure 3.3b. This shows that while the main lime decline took place during the Bronze Age, some areas remained into the historic period. The continued importance of lime into the later-prehistoric and early-historic periods may rest with its value for obtaining bast fibres. In comparison to *Tilia*, there appears a significant reduction in the alder, oak, and hazel woodland noted above. This possibly shows increasing pressure on woodland, perhaps as a source of fuel for local pottery kilns or for extension of occupation and/or agriculture. In contrast to this woodland is the clear evidence for arable agriculture with substantial values for pollen of cereals and a diverse range of associated weeds typical of arable and waste ground (ruderals and segetals).

The evidence for cultivated crops

The character and importance of cereal cultivation is clearly seen from analysis of the charred plant remains from suitable 'on-site' preserving contexts such as pits, ditches, and kilns. Interest in Bedfordshire was shown by John Percival and Hans Helbaek as long ago as 1937 with their examination of Iron Age and Romano-British cereal grain from Totternhoe Castle, where two-row barley, bread wheat, and Rye Brome grass (*Bromus secalinus*) were identified from excavations by C F Hawkes (Caruthers 1990). Subsequently, little work has been undertaken until recent years. A number of recently excavated Bedfordshire archaeological sites have produced quantities of charred plant remains using now standard flotation techniques. These include excavations at Stagsden, the Bedford Southern Orbital Sewer excavations (SO90), and Shillington Bury Iron Age and Ruxox Romano-British settlements. Stagsden in particular has produced substantial quantities of charred plant material from early–middle Iron Age, pre-Belgic and post-Belgic Iron Age, and Romano-British domestic contexts (Scaife in Dawson forthcoming).

Whilst the pollen evidence from sites such as Ruxox illustrates the presence of arable cultivation, it is the analysis of charred grain and weed assemblages which provides the more detailed evidence for crop types and preferences. It is known that the Neolithic saw the introduction of domestication with cereal cultivation (and domestic animals) at c 5500–5000 bp. Because of the paucity of Neolithic sites excavated in Bedfordshire, it is assumed that the principal cereals were similar to other British sites (Jones 1981) which included emmer wheat (*Triticum dicoccum* Schubl.), hexaploid bread wheats (*Triticum aestivum* type), and barley (*Hordeum* sp). Neolithic contexts at the Bunyan

Centre (Scaife in Steadman 1998) have provided evidence of the former (emmer wheat) and the early cultivation of peas. Bronze Age agricultural activity continued with these types, especially with barley, until significant changes in preferences occurred during the Iron Age. Jessen and Helbaek (1944) and Helbaek (1952) showed that spelt wheat (*Triticum spelta* L.) became particularly important from the Iron Age and continued to be so into the Roman period. For the Iron Age this importance is seen from sites at Stagsden and the along the Bedford Southern Orbital Sewer excavations (Scaife in Dawson forthcoming) where substantial quantities of grain and chaff were found in domestic contexts (pits, ditches, and kilns) associated with Iron Age roundhouses. The quantities of this grain (and emmer wheat) are in part due to the fact that these glume wheats require parching (heating) in kilns to release the grain from the wheat ears and there is, therefore, a greater likelihood of accidental burning and thus preservation. Substantial numbers of weed seeds and cereal chaff debris found in some contexts attest to 'on-site' crop processing (winnowing, threshing, and sieving). Waste material was burnt and has similarly produced fine assemblages of seeds from weeds associated with the crop cultivation. Whilst the importance of these glume wheats is perhaps over-emphasised because of their greater chance of preservation, there is, nevertheless, evidence for other crop types including *Hordeum* (barley), *Avena* sp (oats), *Triticum aestivum* type (bread wheat), *Pisum sativum* L. (pea), and *Vicia faba* L. (Celtic bean).

Romano-British contexts examined at Stagsden, Bedford Southern Orbital Sewer (SO90), and Ruxox (RU90) typically show few differences from the previous period, crop types showing a continuation of those grown in the preceding Iron Age. Thus, spelt (*Triticum spelta* L.) and emmer wheat (*Triticum dicoccum* Schubl.) remain especially important with barley (*Hordeum*), oats (*Avena*), and pea and Celtic bean also present at a number of sites. Typically there appears to be an increasing importance of free-threshing bread wheat (*T. aestivum* type) during the Romano-British period. Evidence of this change has also been found near Peterborough (Scaife 1994). From evidence elsewhere in eastern England, it seems likely that spelt wheat and emmer had become less popular by the Saxon period, to be replaced by bread wheats. The Saxon to medieval period represents another lacuna for which sites yielding plant remains are required.

Conclusions

From the above discussion it will be apparent that there are very significant gaps in our knowledge relating to certain periods of Middle Ouse vegetation and environment. In particular, there are few prehistoric sites of Neolithic and Bronze Age date which could provide both pollen evidence for the date and the extent of vegetation clearance which occurred (eg the elm decline and possible 'Landnam' clearances) and of charred (or waterlogged) plant remains to characterise fully, the development of prehistoric agriculture in Bedfordshire. Similarly, sites of Saxon to medieval date are required to provide evidence of the changing crop preferences in the post-Roman period. Given the current nature of archaeological excavations responding to developmental threats, the discovery of sites which might 'fill' these gaps in our knowledge must rely on chance.

Bibliography

Baker, C A, Moxey, P A, & Oxford, P A M, 1978 Woodland continuity and change in Epping Forest, *Field Stud*, **4**, 645–69

Bell, F G, 1969 The occurrence of southern, steppe and halophyte elements in Weichselian (Last-Glacial) floras from southern Britain, *New Phytologist*, **68**, 913–22.

Bell, F G, 1970 Late Pleistocene floras from Earith, Huntingdonshire, *Phil Trans Royal Soc London*, **B258**, 347–78

Birks, H J B, Deacon, J, & Peglar, S, 1975 Pollen maps for the British Isles 5000 years ago, *Proc Royal Soc*, **B189**, 87–105

Birks, H J B, 1989 Holocene isochrone maps and patterns of tree-spreading in the British Isles, *J Biogeography*, **16**, 503–40

Caruthers, W J, 1990 Percival and Helbaeks archive of plant remains, *Circaea*, **8**, 65–70

Dawson, M, forthcoming (2000) *Archaeology in the Bedford Region*, BAR Brit Ser

Dony, J G, 1978 *Flora of Bedfordshire*. Ilkley, West Yorkshire: Scolar Press

Ellison, A, & Harris, J, 1972 Settlement and land use in the prehistoric and early history of southern England, in D L Clarke (ed) *Models in Archaeology*. London: Methuen, 911–62

Fowler, P J, 1978 Lowland landscapes, in S Limbrey & J G Evans *The effect of man on the landscape: the lowland zone*, CBA Res Rep **21**. London: Council for British Archaeology, 1–12

Girling, M A, 1987 The bark beetle *Scolytus scolytus* (Fabricius) and the possible role of elm disease in the early Neolithic, in M Jones (ed) *Archaeology and the flora of the British Isles*. Oxford: Oxford University Committee for Archaeology, 34–8

Girling, M A, & Greig, J R A, 1977 Palaeoecological investigations of a site at Hampstead Heath, London, *Nature*, London **268**, 45–7

Girling, M A, & Greig, J R A, 1985 A first fossil record for *Scolytus scolytus* (F.) (Elm Bark Beetle): its occurrence in Elm Decline deposits from London and the implication for the Neolithic Elm Decline, *J Archaeol Sci*, **12**, 347–51

Godwin, H, 1975a *The history of the British flora*, 2nd edition. Cambridge: Cambridge University Press

Godwin, H, 1975b History of the natural forests of Britain: establishment, dominance and destruction, *Phil Trans Royal Soc*, **B271**, 47–67

Greig, J R A, 1982 Past and present lime woods of Europe, in M Bell & S Limbrey (eds) *Archaeological Aspects of Woodland ecology*, Assoc Env Archaeol Symposia Vol 2, BAR Int Ser **146**. Oxford: British Archaeological Reports, 23–55

Greig, J R A, 1993 Assessment of a pollen profile from Warren Villa, Bedfordshire WV90. Unpublished report

Iversen, J, 1941 Landnam i Danmarks Stenalder, *Danm geol Unders*, **R11** (66), 1–67

Iversen, J, 1949 The influence of prehistoric man on vegetation, *Danm geol Unders*, Ser IV, **3** (6), 1–25

Helbaek, H, 1952 Early crops in southern England, *Proc Prehist Soc*, **18**, 194–233

Jessen, K, & Helbaek, H, 1944 *Cereals in Great Britain and Ireland in prehistoric and early historic times*. Det. Kongelige Danske Videnskabernes Selskab Biologistie Skrifler 3(2) Copenhagen

Jones, M, 1981 The development of crop husbandry, in M Jones & G Dimbleby (eds) *The Environment of man: the Iron Age, Roman and Anglo-Saxon Periods*, BAR Brit Ser **87**. Oxford: British Archaeological Reports, 95–127

Keefe, P A M, Wymer, J J, & Dimbleby, G W, 1965 A Mesolithic site on Iping Common, Sussex, England, *Proc Prehist Soc*, **31**, 85–92

Mangerud, J, Andersen, S T, Berglund, B E, & Donner, J J, 1974 Quaternary stratigraphy of Norden, a proposal for terminology and classification, *Boreas*, **3**, 109–28

Rogerson, R J, Keen, D H, Coope, G R, Robinson, E, Dickson, J H, & Dickson, C A, 1992 The flora and palaeoenvironmental significance of deposits beneath the low terrace of the River Great Ouse at Radwell, Bedfordshire, England, *Proc Geologists' Assoc*, **103**, 1–13

Scaife, R G, 1980 Late-Devensian and Flandrian palaeoecological studies in the Isle of Wight. PhD thesis, University of London, King's College

Scaife, R G, 1987 The elm decline in the pollen record of south east England and its relationship to early agriculture, in M Jones (ed) *Archaeology and the flora of the British Isles*. Oxford: Oxford University Committee for Archaeology, 21–33

Scaife, R G, 1994 The plant remains, in C A I French (ed) *The archaeology along the A605 Elton-Haddon Bypass, Cambridgeshire*, Fenland Archaeol Trust Monogr **2**. Peterborough/ Cambridge: Fenland Archaeological Trust/ Cambridgeshire County Council, 154–67

Simmons, I G, 1975 Towards an ecology of Mesolithic man in the uplands of Great Britain, *J Archaeol Sci*, **2**, 1–15

Simms, R E, 1973 The anthropogenic factor in East Anglian vegetational history: an approach using A.P.F. techniques, in H J B Birks & R G West (eds) *Quaternary Plant Ecology*. Oxford:

Blackwell Scientific, 223–36

Smith, A G, 1970 The influence of Mesolithic and Neolithic man on British vegetation: a discussion, in D Walker & R G West (eds) *Studies in the vegetational history of the British Isles*. Cambridge: Cambridge University Press, 81–96

Steadman, S, 1998 A later Neolithic and Bronze Age mortuary complex and Iron Age settlement at the Bunyan Centre, Bedford, *Bedfordshire Archaeol*, **23**, 2–32

Turner, J, 1962 The *Tilia* decline: an anthropogenic interpretation, *New Phytol*, **61**, 328–41

Turner, J, 1970 Post-Neolithic disturbance of British vegetation, in D Walker & R G West (eds) *Studies in the vegetational history of the British Isles*. Cambridge: Cambridge University Press, 97–116

Waller, M, 1994 *The Fenland Project, Number 9: Flandrian Environmental Change in Fenland*, East Anglian Archaeology **70**. Cambridge: University of Cambridge, Cambridgeshire Archaeological Committee

Wiltshire, P E J, 1998 Palynological analysis of Iron Age 'pond' sediments at Salford Quarry, Bedfordshire. Unpublished report

4 Alluviation and landscape change at Little Paxton

by Rebecca Roseff

Background to the site – the Ouse and its catchment

The River Great Ouse, with a drainage basin of approximately 8400km² and 250km in length, is the third largest river in England. In general it is a low lying river, with two thirds of its length below 20m OD. The river rises in the west where it is called the Tove, at the foot of the Cotswolds in the Northampton Uplands, and in the Chilterns to the south, where it is called the Ouzel or Lovat, and flows in a north-easterly direction through the counties of Buckinghamshire and Bedfordshire and the towns of Milton Keynes, Newport Pagnell, and Bedford. Additional tributaries join the Ouse below Bedford, including the Cam, Little Ouse, and Wissey, as the river continues its route to the sea through Cambridgeshire and Norfolk, flowing through the Fens and out into the North Sea at The Wash. The port of King's Lynn lies at its mouth.

The Ouse drains a varied geology, flowing through areas of chalk, clay, and sand (Fig 4.1). In its western headwaters the river crosses Jurassic limestone, clay, and shales. In the middle reach, upstream from Little Paxton, it flows over the Jurassic Oxford Clay, which consists of clay and shales, and the Jurassic Kellaway beds, which are mainly composed of sands. Over much of the catchment the solid geology is overlain by glacial deposits of sand, gravel, and boulder clay. The boulder clay varies in depth and texture but generally consists of stony and chalky clay (Edmonds and Dinham 1965; Horton *et al* 1974; Knight 1984). River terrace deposits and alluvium are mapped along much of the middle reaches of the river. Such a varied geology means that alluvium deposited by the Ouse is

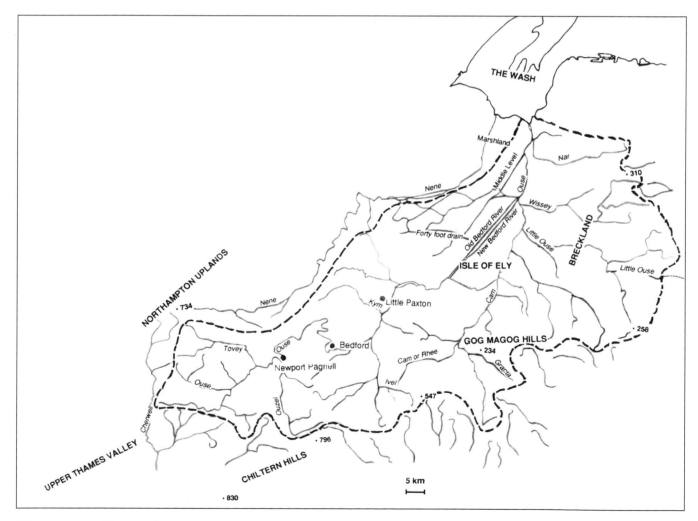

Figure 4.1   The catchment and location of Little Paxton

hard to source, as the chalky deposits, sand, and clays could all potentially derive from a variety of primary or secondary (ie glacial and periglacial) unconsolidated sources.

The low gradient of the catchment and the deep soils, with their high water-retention capacity, mean that, with certain exceptions, the Ouse is a sluggish river with a delayed reaction to rainfall, slow to rise and slow to fall.

The Little Paxton site

Little Paxton lies about 20km downstream from Bedford above the confluences with the Cam, Little Ouse, and Wissey, and approximately half way along the length of the river. The nearest recording station to Little Paxton is at Offord (NGR TL 220664) about 1.5km downstream from the excavation site (Institute of Hydrology 1993). At Offord the upstream catchment is 2570km². At this point in its course the river flows in a south to north-north-easterly direction. The study area (Fields 1 and 2, Fig 4.2) is situated about 700m from the west bank of the river. On this west side the Ouse valley is flat for about 2.5km, rising only slightly from a 12m OD level at the river to 13m in the centre of the site and 14m at the west edge of the site. On the east bank, in contrast, the land rises sharply to 20m OD.

A deserted village, still visible as earthworks, lies adjacent to the site on its western side at 14m OD. When the study site was first stripped of topsoil, marks of ridge and furrow were observed trending west to east across the site at the 13m OD level, indicating that it once formed part of an open field, probably used for arable agriculture and probably dating to the medieval period.

The river terrace gravels

The site lay on river terrace gravels, which varied in depth from less than one metre in the west to six metres in the south-eastern area, with an average thickness of 2.7m. The gravels were composed of predominantly sub-angular and angular flint pebbles (80–90%) with minor amounts of quartzite and chalk. Coarseness increased with depth. The silt fraction was about 5% and the sand content 53%. The average overburden consisted of around 1.0m topsoil and 0.4m hoggin (a mixture of soil and gravel) (MacLean 1990).

The geological survey and memoir place Little Paxton on the lower, first terrace (Edmunds and Dinham 1965). The classification into first, second, and third river terraces given in the geological memoir is, however, not certain and ongoing research seeks to clarify the chronology, development, and sequence of these deposits (Green, this volume).

Modern flooding patterns

Flooding occurs annually to the 12m level and, until very recent times, this flooded land was used as meadow. The study site, at approximately 13m, floods only exceptionally, the last time in living memory was in 1947. Flooding is not known to have occurred at the 14m level in living memory.

The flow of the river is accurately known from the nearby recording station at Offord. For example, the mean daily naturalised flow (the calculated flow after removing the effects of abstraction) in 1972, which was a dry year, was 12.058 cubic metres a second (cumecs). The average for January, which was the highest month, was 31.34 cumecs and for October, the lowest month, 2.832 cumecs. The minimum flow in any one day was 2.2 cumecs and the maximum 59.3 cumecs. Rainfall and flow is generally highest between December and March and at its lowest from July to November, but it fluctuates and it is not unusual for high flows to occur at any time of the year.

These figures show that a large difference between the lowest and highest flows is normal for the Ouse and that the main cause of flooding today, as in the past, is prolonged and heavy rainfall. However, climatic and sea level changes, and land and river management developments will have had some effects.

Deforestation, except in very heavy and prolonged rainfall, leads to more rapid runoff, flooding, and erosion. It is thought that this had occurred by the Iron Age (Reed 1979; Simmonds and Tooley 1981; Simco 1984).

River management schemes, such as the construction of the 100 foot river in the mid-17th century, and the Eau Brink Cut in the 19th century, have, by speeding the flow downstream of Little Paxton, possibly reduced flooding. On the other hand, widespread agricultural drainage, urbanisation, and the creation of water-filled gravel pits, by speeding drainage and taking up the floodplain's water-holding capacity, would all tend to hasten the rate of flow, causing the river to rise and fall more quickly than it would have done in the past.

Before the construction of the Denver Sluice in the 17th century, which largely eliminated tidal influence inland, fluctuating sea levels would also have affected flooding patterns. The sea level in East Anglia has fluctuated throughout the Holocene, with seven episodes of higher tides and marine transgressions, and higher flood risk, and six episodes of lower tides and marine regressions, and lower flood risk, since 6500 BP (Jones and Keen 1993, 260). A transgressive period was apparently experienced in the Iron Age, and a regressive in the Romano-British period. A transgressive period followed in the early Anglo-Saxon period, followed by a short regressive period. From the Norman period until today there has been a period of sea level rise.

In conclusion it seems likely that flash flooding is more likely to occur in recent times, with modern drainage and a largely treeless landscape, than in prehistoric and early-historic times.

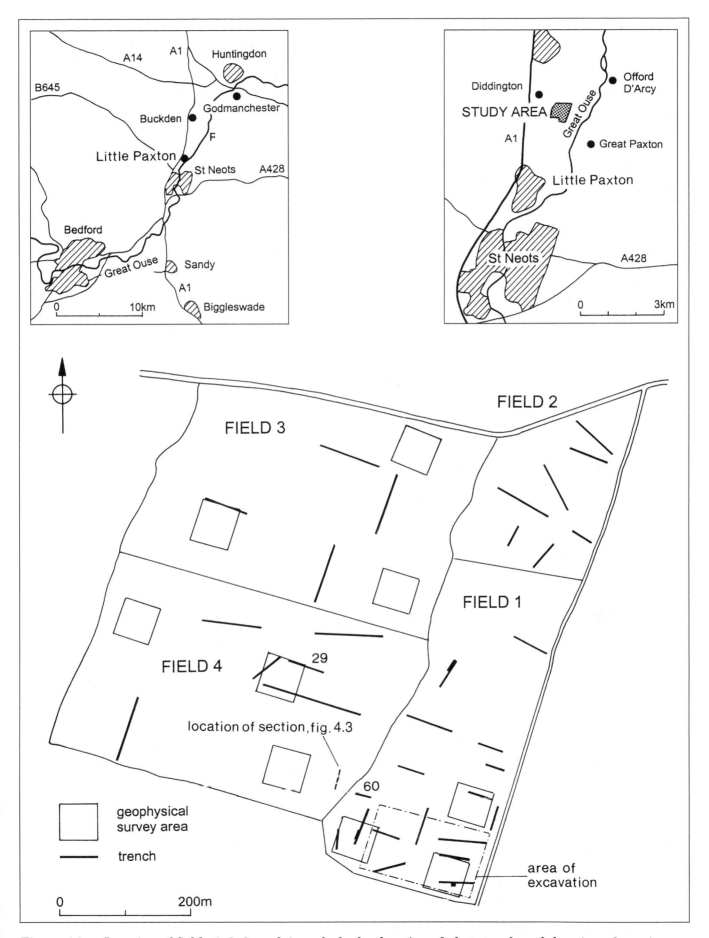

Figure 4.2   Location of fields 1, 2, 3, and 4 marked, plus location of photograph and drawing of stratigraphy on west edge of quarry (Figs 4.3 and 4.5) and Trench 60 (Fig 4.4)

Soils and fertility

The soils at Little Paxton are formed on bands of sand, gravel, and sand with small and medium stones in the 10YR colour range, overlain by bands of darker, redder sand, gravel, and sand with small and medium stones in the 7.5YR range. The topsoil is a plough soil of about 0.5m – a sandy loam with 10% stones. In places this lies directly over the C horizon, while elsewhere there is a B horizon of about 0.2m. The pH is high (A horizon 7.7, B horizon 7.4, C horizon 7.5).

With the low clay content the soil is unlikely to have a high natural fertility and its sandy, easy-draining nature means that crops are subject to drought. Heavy applications of manures and a wet summer are needed for a good yield. The clay soils on the east side of the river give higher and more reliable yields and consequently are preferred for arable crops (P Firbanks pers comm).

Study of soils and sediments

Soils and sediments were studied by field observation by Dr C French during the first assessment at Little Paxton (French 1992) and by the author in Field 1 and on the east edge of Field 4 during the main excavation of 1994. Sections were recorded along the main east–west and north–south quarry stripping faces (both longer than 200m) that marked the edge of the quarry in Field 1 in May 1993. In addition, a 60m trench was purposely dug

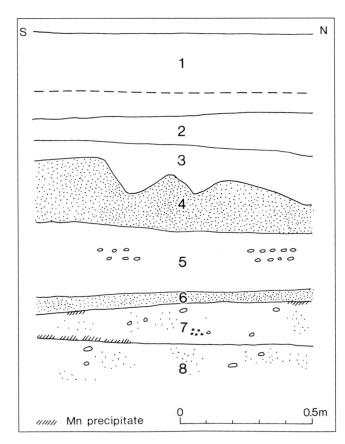

Figure 4.3   Section at west end of quarry

for sediment recording at the western edge of the excavation, and an accelerator date obtained within the upper bands of the gravels from this trench (Trench 60, Figs 4.2 and 4.4). General recording of soils and ditch fills, to observe particle size, water-logging levels, gleying, and iron pans, was also used to interpret alluviation and flooding patterns. Sediments below and predating the river terrace gravels were recorded in one area on the east side of Field 1.

Charred plant remains were recovered by flotation from a range of features. In all, 82 contexts from the Romano-British site and 104 from the Iron Age site were sampled, with more than 410 buckets of soil processed. Mollusca, beetle, pollen, and waterlogged samples were collected as appropriate, though full analyses of these samples have yet to be carried out.

Sediments below the river gravels
The gravels were approximately 3m in depth and overlay a grey deposit consisting of sorted and banded, very dark grey, chalky silt and sand, and chalky clay and fine sand. This probably represented a Pleistocene lacustrine deposit lain down at a pre-Devensian stage of the Pleistocene.

River gravels and subsoil
Figure 4.3 depicts a section through the underlying gravels, exposed during quarrying on the eastern edge of Field 4 in May 1991, some 800m from the River Ouse today. The upper 1.2m of sediment consisted of bands of horizontally laid stones and sand. What is significant and interesting about this section was that the bands clearly were darkened with organic matter to at least 1.2m below the surface. By inference these layers were post-glacial, although they had been laid down by high energy water.

In the main north–south quarry section, the uppermost bands of sand, and sand with stones, similar to those in Figure 4.3 were observed to continue across the site, a distance of more than 200m. In the east–west section they were also apparent, but at one point were cut in the west by a stream at least 20m wide. This was probably a small palaeochannel of a former wide, shallow stream course. This feature exists today in a much restricted form as a sinuous drainage ditch marking the boundary between Field 1 and Field 4 (Fig 4.2).

Trench 60 was dug to further examine the sediments lying below the topsoil (Fig 4.4). In the 60m section of this trench the subsoil began at 12m OD and consisted of a yellow-brown sand (10YR6/8) with mixed small and rounded stones, not horizontally laid, of about 0.3m depth. This layer was cut by several small, shallow features with silty, organic, and gleyed fills. They were interpreted as small streams. Below these features and the subsoil, along the length of the trench, were bands of chalky sand and gravel, yellow sand, and chalky bands of horizontally laid small rounded stones. These layers were clearly water-laid high-energy deposits.

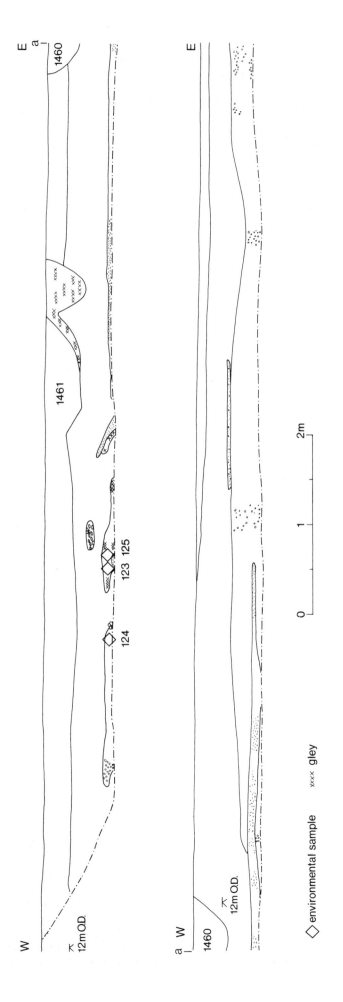

Figure 4.4   Trench 60, showing location of C14 date. Figure in two parts

At the westernmost edge, organic lenses with small pieces of humified wood were found stratified within the sand and gravel bands (Fig 4.4). A sample was taken for accelerator dating, which gave a calibrated date of 3360 to 2940 BC (Beta-69286).

The sand and gravel layers in Trench 60 are probably best interpreted as glacial gravels, reworked by a shallow, meandering stream system that was active in the Neolithic, in the vicinity of the stream shown in Fig 4.2 between Fields 1 and 4.

Further evidence that the upper river gravels and 1.2m of hoggin and soil had been altered and/or laid down in the post-glacial, was found during a watching brief in Field 4, to the south of the east end of Trench 29 (Fig 4.2). Thin bands of charcoal were noted in the quarry face, stratified within the bands of gravels and sand, below the topsoil and hoggin, at levels of about 1.5–2.0m below the top of the gravel (Alex Jones pers comm).

Overlying sediments and water levels

The Iron Age and Romano-British features were cut into the upper bands of sand and through the overlying hoggin layer in Field 1. Overlying them was approximately 0.45–0.5m of plough soil.

The base of many of the Iron Age features in Field 1, on the west, were at 11.9m OD and were not waterlogged; features were gleyed at 11.8m OD. On the east of Field 1, on the Romano-British site, waterlogging occurred below 11.45m to 11.55m OD, at a similar level to today, and several features contained waterlogged material. On this evidence it would seem that the water level in the Romano-British period was similar to today. The gleyed layers above were interpreted as the higher, winter water-table.

Discussion

The sections shown in Figures 4.3, 4.4, and 4.5, and the charcoal revealed within the upper quarry gravels in Field 4 (Fig 4.5), clearly point to a post-glacial deposition of the upper 1.2m of sediment at Little Paxton. This would have been through the agency of turbulent, high-energy water. Today these layers lie 0.7–1.4km west of the modern course of the river. Their presence indicates that the river has moved eastwards since the Neolithic. A braided river, periodically fast flowing and turbulent, probably crossed the Little Paxton site in prehistory. The streams may have been affected by tidal changes and they probably reworked the glacial river-terrace gravels rather than deposited allochthonous material. The radiocarbon date indicates the river was still active, and in this form, in the Neolithic, while the archaeological features cutting the upper bands of sand and gravels show that it had abandoned this form by the Iron Age.

Some alluviation of finer grained sediment, which now forms the topsoil, has occurred since the

Figure 4.5   Photograph of section shown in Fig 4.3, west end of quarry

Neolithic. This took place in part by the filling of abandoned channels, as was observed in Trench 60, but probably also by over-bank flooding. It is unfortunately not possible to say whether the alluviation pre- or postdated the Iron Age and/or Romano-British period, for ploughing has destroyed the integrity of the stratigraphy in the upper layers. After the floodplain built up due to the deposition of alluvium, the majority of the river became confined to one meandering channel. The ridge and furrow that was present over the study area, indicative of medieval communal arable farming, implies that major flooding and alluviation was not occurring in the medieval period or post-medieval period and that flooding patterns were much the same as today.

These interpretations are different to those reached about the two sites on the Ouse downstream of Little Paxton, studied by Robinson (1992, 198), where the water level rose in the Romano-British to medieval period but with no alluviation, while alluviation occurred in the medieval period, and flooding without alluviation in the post-medieval period. This pattern is comparable to that from the Welland Valley (French et al 1992) where some alluviation occurred in the late Neolithic, the water level rose in the late Bronze Age and Iron Age, while alluviation occurred in the late-Romano-British to early-medieval periods.

Bibliography

Edmonds, E A, & Dinham, C H, 1965 Geology of the Country Around Huntingdon and Biggleswade, *Memoirs of the Geological Survey of Great Britain*, Sheets **187** & **204** (England and Wales). London: HMSO

French, C A I, 1992 Soils assessment, in P Leach, Little Paxton Quarry Diddington, Cambridgeshire, Archaeological Assessment Phase 1. Birmingham University Field Archaeology Unit unpublished report

French, C A I, Macklin, M G, & Passmore, D G, 1992 Archaeology and Palaeochannels in the Lower Welland and Nene Valleys: Alluvial Archaeology at the Fen Edge, Eastern England, in S Needham and M G Macklin (eds) *Alluvial Archaeology in Britain*, Oxbow Monogr **27**. Oxford: Oxbow, 169–77

Horton, A, Shephard-Thorn, E R, & Thurrell, E G, 1974 The geology of the New town of Milton Keynes, *Rep Inst Geological Sci*, **74**(16)

Institute of Hydrology, 1993 *Hydrological Data United Kingdom 1993 Yearbook*. Wallingford: Institute of Hydrology

Jones, R L, & Keen, D H, 1993 *Pleistocene environments in the British Isles*. London: Chapman & Hall

Knight, D, 1984 *Late Bronze Age and Iron Age Settlement in the Nene and Great Ouse Basins*, BAR Brit Ser **130**(i & ii). Oxford: British Archaeological Reports

MacLean, D, 1990 ECC Quarries Ltd, Little Paxton Quarry. Unpublished report for English China Clays Quarries Ltd (now CAMAS group)

Reed, M, 1979 *The Buckinghamshire Landscape*. London: Hodder & Stoughton

Robinson, M, 1992 Environment, archaeology and alluvium on the River gravels of the south Midlands, in S Needham & M G Macklin (eds) *Alluvial Archaeology in Britain*, Oxbow Monogr **27**. Oxford: Oxbow, 197–209

Simco, A, 1984 *A survey of Bedfordshire, the Roman Period*. Bedfordshire County Council/RCHM(E)

Simmonds, I, & Tooley, M, (eds) 1981 *The environment in British Prehistory*. London: Duckworth

5 The Palaeolithic of the Ouse Valley

by Tim Reynolds

Introduction

The English Heritage sponsored English Rivers Project, which will include an evaluation of the potential for Palaeolithic research on the deposits of rivers north of the Thames Valley, has now concluded. It is appropriate, therefore, to draw together the present evidence of Palaeolithic settlement in the lower reaches of the River Great Ouse and discuss some of the key research issues upon which it can inform. Whilst the English Heritage projects pull together existing data and produce a useful synthesis of the extant materials (Wessex Archaeology 1992), there is an urgency for such study to go further and assist development control archaeologists because of the extent of mineral extraction and plans for future destruction of this irreplaceable resource for understanding England's earliest inhabitants. This paper concentrates on the River Great Ouse between Bedford and Ely (including the modern major tributary in this stretch, the Cam) where substantial gravel extraction has produced a significant amount of material and existing permissions for extraction span the next ten years. After this time, the archaeological resource will be substantially reduced.

The archaeological record for later prehistoric periods is also threatened by development and so evaluation and mitigation strategies are applied to preserve, in some form, the surviving materials. Regular synthesis, landscape modelling, and interpretation are vital for this process to be effective and this applies to Pleistocene landscapes as much as any other. However, the Palaeolithic suffers in that planning archaeologists are not adequately informed by existing records to permit effective evaluation, mitigation, or preservation. Palaeolithic archaeology can only be poorly served through the application of PPG16. It is hoped that this summary of the Great Ouse resources, together with the preliminary, but pioneering, recommendations in development control archaeological briefs in Cambridgeshire, may lead to an effective and productive future for Pleistocene archaeology and planning in the Ouse valley.

This paper, then, presents a brief account of the Pleistocene archaeology of the River Great Ouse between Bedford and Ely, including an introduction to the main research area for which the Ouse has significant data, and the geology of the river valley, before presenting the Palaeolitic materials and discussing the problems and potential for their future study.

Terminology

The British Isles have been occupied for at least 500,000 years (Roberts 1986), during which time substantial environmental changes have taken place. These environmental changes have been sequenced and plotted, and both compared and correlated with continental evidence. As a result of the development of research into these environmental changes, several different terminologies have been applied to the Pleistocene sequence. In this paper, stages will follow the sequence put forward by Mitchell *et al* (1973) and Sparks and West (1972), which runs as follows:

Name	Climate	Date (Years BP)
Flandrian	Warm	12,000–Present
Devensian	Cold	105,000– 12,000
Ipswichian	Warm	130,000–105,000
Wolstonian Complex	Cold/Warm	360,000–130,000
Hoxnian	Warm	425,000–360,000
Anglian	Cold	440,000–425,000
Cromerian Complex	Warm/Cold	525,000–440,000

Dating for the sequence remains tentative, as problems with obtaining dates and correlations are many. The above named sequence is based upon type sites from terrestrial locations, whilst the fullest record is provided by oxygen isotope studies of deep sea core materials (Shackleton and Opdyke 1973). Many difficulties exist in attempting correlations and this issue will be returned to later.

The origins of modern humans

A combination of DNA studies and fossil evidence has demonstrated that the human lineage diverged from that of the African apes *c* 4 million years ago. The 'missing link' is, therefore, something less of a problem than it was in the past and research now centres upon identifying the reasons for the divergence – the behavioural and the intellectual capabilities of pre-modern human species. Since the mid 1980s more attention has also focussed on another key area, that of the origins of our own sub-species, *Homo sapiens sapiens*. There has been considerable debate as to the status of Neanderthals and whether they were direct ancestors to modern humans or an offshoot with no significant input to ourselves (Mellars 1990; Stringer and Mellars 1989).

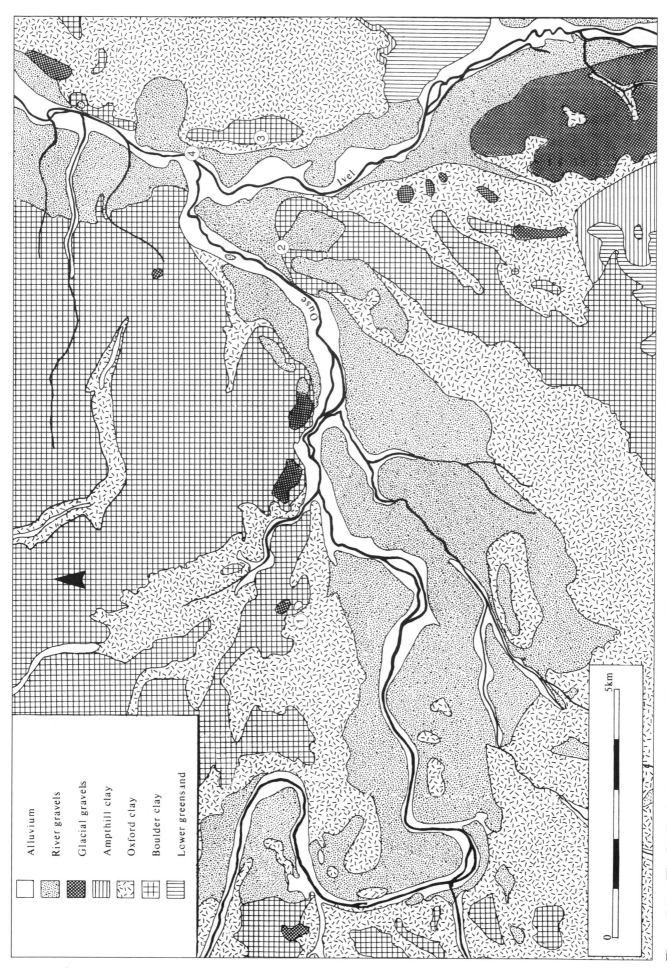

Figure 5.1   The Bedfordshire Ouse. 1 Biddenham, 2 Willington, 3 Tempsford, 4 Tempsford

Alluvium

River gravels

Glacial gravels

Ampthill clay

Oxford clay

Boulder clay

Lower greensand

5km

0

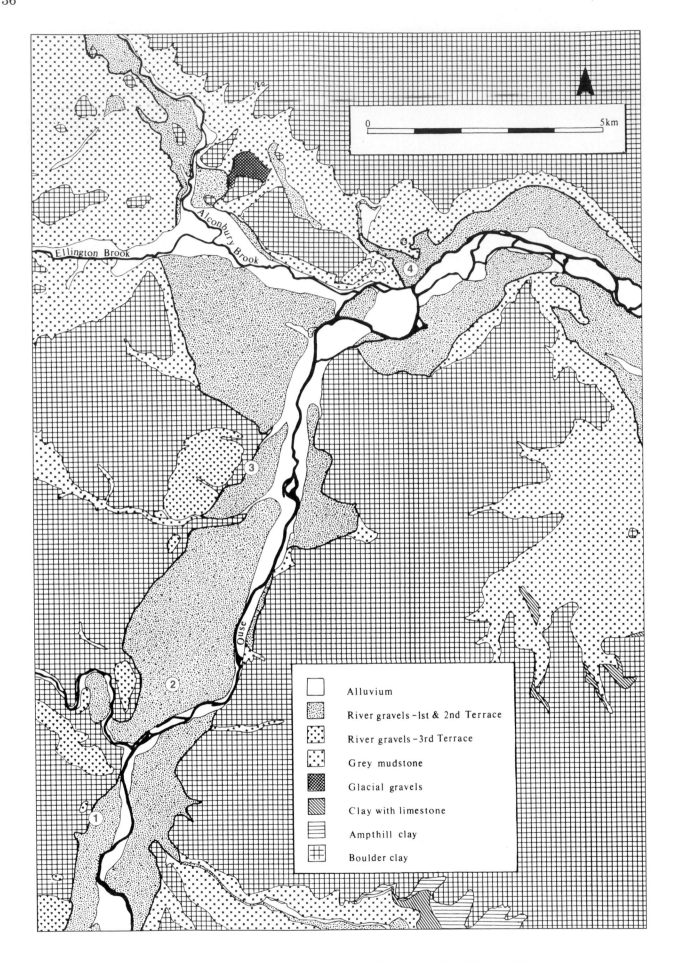

Figure 5.2   The Huntingdon Ouse. 1 St Neots, 2 Little Paxton, 3 Buckden, 4 Huntingdon

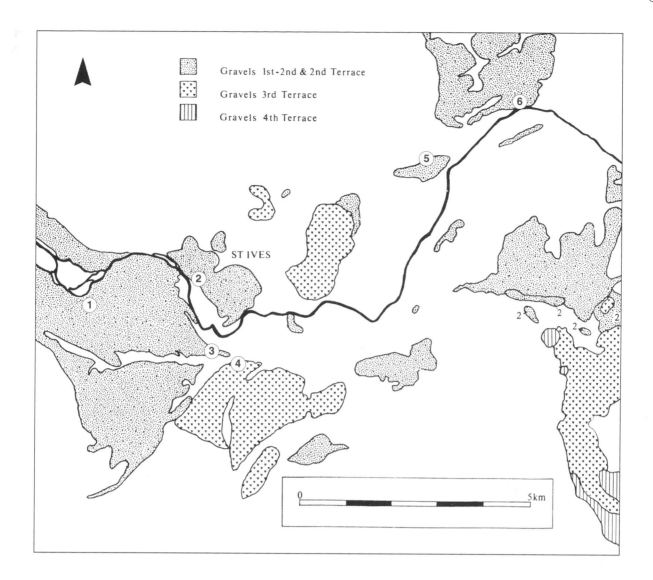

Gravels 1st-2nd & 2nd Terrace

Gravels 3rd Terrace

Gravels 4th Terrace

ST IVES

0   5 km

Figure 5.3   The Cambridgeshire Ouse. 1 Godmanchester, 2 Hartford, 3 Fenstanton, 4 Fen Drayton, 5 Bluntisham, 6 Earith

The associated archaeological evidence for this debate in Europe lies in the Mousterian and the Middle to Upper Palaeolithic transition (Reynolds 1991). Did the major changes in behaviour evident in this cultural transition spring from the arrival of a new hominid type?

The date for the change, in Europe, was placed between 40,000–30,000 BP. Recent work in Africa and Asia, however, has demonstrated that modern humans appeared prior to, or at the time of, the Ipswichian (ie 130,000–105,000 BP). This is substantially before the European Middle to Upper Palaeolithic transition. Additionally, both types of hominid, Neanderthals and modern humans, have now been found in association with the Mousterian and indeed, in Israel, Neanderthals replace modern humans as climatic conditions deteriorate, only to be superseded by modern humans later. The simple correlation between the Mousterian and Neanderthals and the Upper Palaeolithic and modern humans is no longer acceptable and it is increasing-

ly apparent that no single or simple explanation will suffice for the history of hominids in Europe and the Near East between 130,000–30,000 BP. The cultural, behavioural, and genetic relationships are by no means clear and this is made more problematic by the lack of evidence from key areas and dates.

The main research questions may be summarised thus:

(1) Did modern humans appear in, and spread through Europe, at any time prior to the Middle to Upper Palaeolithic transition?

(2) Is the brief increase in blade use in north-western Europe within the Acheulean techno-complex during the Ipswichian a product of modern humans, either in the form of resident populations or as a 'bow-wave effect'?

(3) What is the evolutionary relationship between Neanderthals and modern humans?

(4) What do the archaeological materials for this time monitor – can they make any contribution to understanding the evolutionary questions?

It is clear that any site dating to between 130,000–30,000 BP is of international importance as it may inform upon issues relating to the origins of ourselves. In the context of the River Great Ouse an additional factor to consider is that such evidence will be derived from the then limits of the occupied world and local adaptations may be particularly informative about behavioural flexibility and intellect. Thus, the importance of the Ouse gravels should be seen in this light and included in any policies relating to the extraction of minerals of this date.

Geology

The geology of the Cambridge area has been studied for a long time (Marr 1919, 1926; Seeley 1866; Worssam and Taylor 1969) and the gravels found along the river valleys are well known (Figs 5.1–5.4 through section). The long history of interest in the Cam gravels means that much of the following account is based on the Cam rather than the Ouse, but terrace deposits from one system map into the other (Edmonds and Dinham 1965). The Pleistocene landscape was very different from that of the present day in the form of its drainage systems, valley formations, and topography. Areas now drained by the Thames system once ran out around the Chilterns and through the Cam-Ouse area to combine with a greater Rhine river system running across what is now occupied by the North Sea. The Thames system separated from that of the Ouse as a result of the Anglian ice sheet blocking the Vale of St Albans (Gibbard 1985; Wymer 1991) and through river capture. The basis for the present river system was laid down after two ice sheets, the Anglian and the Wolstonian, had passed across the region. All the existing Pleistocene terrace deposits of the Ouse between Bedford and Ely are believed to postdate the Wolstonian, but the patchy distribution of boulder clay on uplands derives from both the Lowestoft Till of Anglian age and the Gipping Till of Wolstonian date. The earliest deposit of interest to this paper is that of the Observatory gravels which lie on a ridge between the Observatory and Girton village near Cambridge. These gravels are not, in fact, river gravels of the present Cam-Ouse system but result from glacial outwash dating to the end of the Wolstonian. These gravels have produced Acheulean tools (handaxes and flake scrapers) at the Traveller's Rest Pit, west of Huntingdon Road, Cambridge (Burkitt 1931a and b; Marr 1919). These materials set the scene for the river terrace finds in demonstrating a pre-Ipswichian Acheulean presence in the area.

A total of four terraces have been identified within the Cam-Ouse system (Edmonds and Dinham 1965; Gallois 1988; Worssam and Taylor 1969) between Bedford and Ely, dating successively younger as terrace height decreases. The fourth terrace, mapped at Longstanton, is tentatively dated to the Ipswichian but has not produced any floral or faunal remains to support such a date. The third terrace, by way of contrast, has produced a considerable amount of evidence and is much more widely distributed. The terrace is particularly well-studied at Histon Road in Cambridge where pollen shows a sequence from interglacial zone f, which is mixed oak forest, through g (forest dominated by hornbeam) to h and i (forests with pine and then birch in significant numbers). This sequence shows a move from optimum interglacial conditions such as the mixed oak forest, to a cooler climate dominated by conifers. Freshwater marls at the same site yielded mollusc assemblages which confirmed this pattern of environmental change (Sparks and West 1959).

A gravel deposit at Barrington, in Cambridgeshire, is recorded as third terrace and produced *Hippopotamus* remains along with other species which indicate a warm climate, whilst at Barnwell, in Cambridge, third terrace gravels produced *Corbicula fluminalis* which today lives in Syria and the Nile (this species also occurred at Histon Road). The third terrace lies between 64–40ft (19.5–12.2m) OD in the Huntingdonshire Ouse valley.

The second terrace has been studied at a site in Sidgwick Avenue, Cambridge, where well-drained calcareous soils were present in a variety of marsh and shallow water conditions. The terrace surface was built up as a series of constantly shifting braided channels crossed it. The terrace is attributed to early-glacial (Devensian) times although the presence of *Corbicula fluminalis* at Milton Road pit, Cambridge might suggest a late-Ipswichian date. The second terrace lies 33–16ft (10.1–4.9m) OD, but it grades into the first terrace at c 16ft (4.9m). In terms of mapping, the Geological Survey often group the first and second terraces together.

Where the first terrace can be separated from the second, it lies between 10–16ft (3.0–4.9m) OD. The terrace has yielded Arctic flora and cold climate mollusc, insect, and mammal faunas at a pit near Barnwell, Cambridge.

Patterns of earlier drainage channels within the existing Cam-Ouse system can occasionally be plotted and a good example of this may be seen in Worssam and Taylor (1969, 90) for the area north of Cambridge.

In summary of the geology, four terraces are known, intermittently present, with the highest (fourth) present and mapped only near Longstanton whilst the remaining three are more widespread. Dating evidence for the fourth terrace is lacking but the third terrace is well-placed within the central and later part of an interglacial. The second terrace is sometimes difficult to separate from the first terrace and dates to either the end of an interglacial or the start of an early glacial. The first terrace is the last in the sequence and has biological indicators of glacial conditions

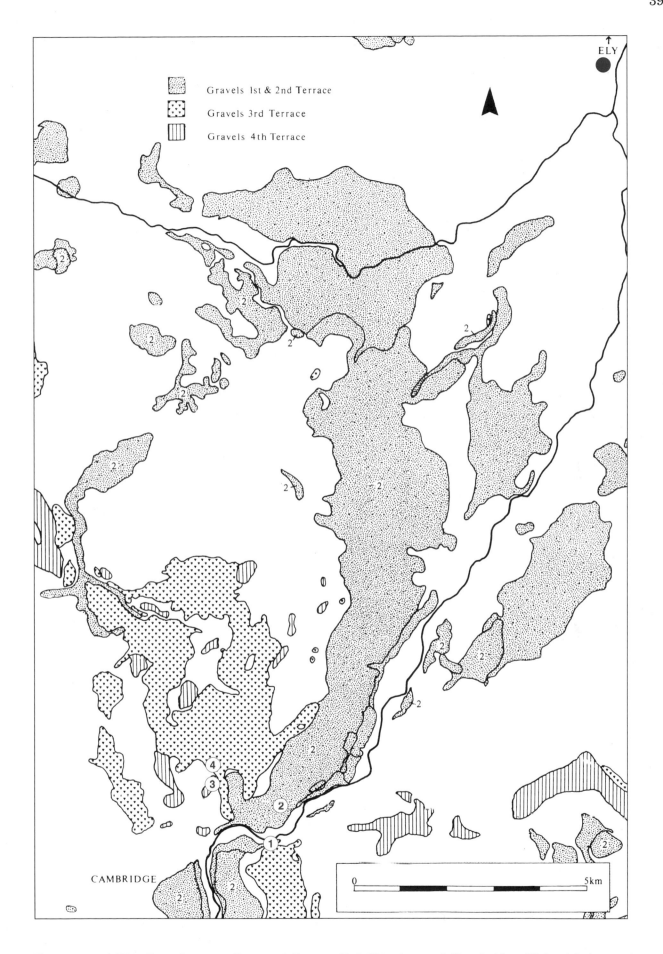

Figure 5.4   The Cam-Ouse confluence. 1 Barnwell, 2 Chesterton, 3 Cambridge (Sidgwick Avenue), 4 Cambridge (Histon Road)

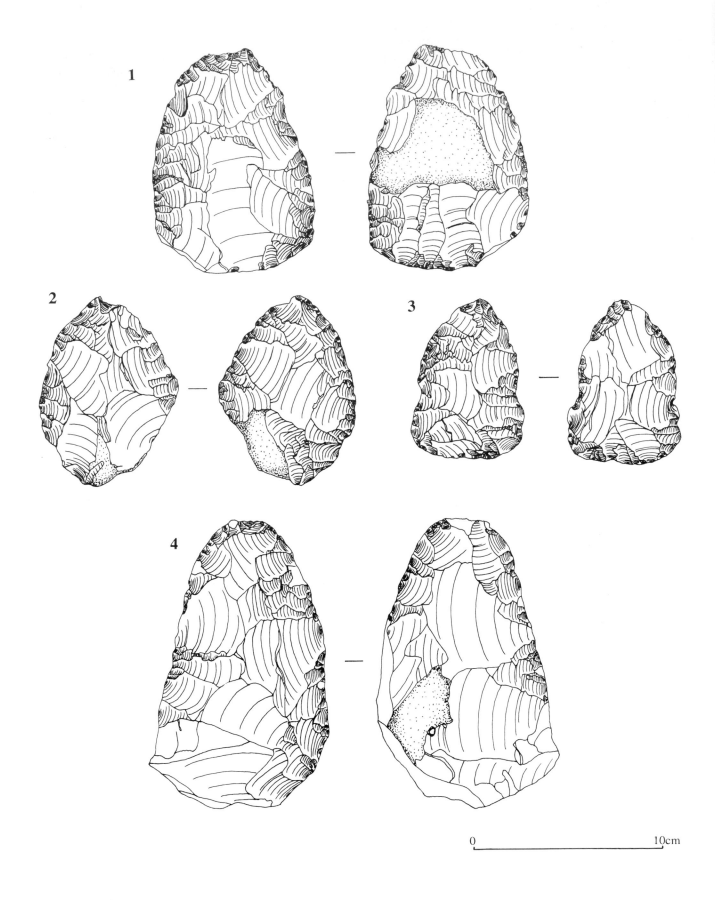

Figure 5.5   Series of bifaces from Fen Drayton

0 _____ 10cm

Archaeology

The earliest finds of Palaeolithic materials from the Cam-Ouse system were made in the 1860s (Evans 1879), immediately following the publication of Darwin's *The Origin of Species by Means of Natural Selection...* in 1859 and the acceptance of the antiquity of handaxes found in the Somme gravels in northern France. The first find from the Ouse was at Biddenham, near Bedford, in April 1861, whilst the first find from the Cam came from Barnwell in 1862. The Barnwell find was particularly interesting in introducing a new component, a worked elephant rib-bone, to the cultural assemblage. After these finds, antiquarians were drawn to the Cam-Ouse terraces and a series of isolated finds reported (AGCC 1977; Bedfordshire SMR; Burkitt 1931a and b, 1945; Cambridgeshire SMR; Coote 1948; Garood 1929, 1933; Griffith 1879; Hughes 1884; Marr 1909; Reid Moir 1923; Smith 1915; Wright 1886). All these finds had more or less the same pattern, handaxes (and, more rarely, the occasional scraper) from gravel pits which were mostly found on spoilheaps. Finds *in situ* were then, and are now, very rare. The handaxes recovered were a variety of shapes; pointed and ovates being the most common forms, whilst edge conditions also varied from sharp to very abraded and what would today be termed rolled. This pattern of occasional and isolated finds remains to the present day but there are occasionally larger numbers of pieces found, of particular note are the collections of materials from Little Paxton, St Neots, and St Ives, all in Cambridgeshire (Broad 1989; Paterson and Tebbutt 1947; Roe 1968a; Tebbutt 1927) and Biddenham and Kempston in Bedfordshire (Roe 1968, 1981). Once again these collections are not huge and do not all derive from a single site (for each parish) but there is a clear pattern to the material recovered. The materials so far collected comprise a Levallois-using late-Acheulean complex which is dominated by the production of *bout coupe* and ovate handaxes (Figs 5.5 and 5.6). The frequency of handaxes has certainly been exaggerated by the selective action of collectors but hundreds of such tools have been recovered, with the majority being either ovate or *bout coupe* in form. Other handaxe forms present include triangular, amygdaloid, and ficron types. Most of the axes seen by the author have been made on large flakes rather than cobbles, and exploitation of the terrace gravels themselves is likely to have provided most of the used raw materials. Occasionally handaxes occur which retain some cortex, usually on the butt or platform end. Where this occurs the cortex is worn and hard, no soft fresh chalky cortex remains. The patterning of handaxe industries in England has been studied by Roe (1968b) and the Ouse materials fall within a late-Acheulean grouping.

Coupled to this biface production is use of Levallois technique – typical tortoise cores occur at Fenstanton, St Ives, and Little Paxton (Reynolds forthcoming; Roe 1981). The Levallois flakes produced include both oval and elongate (blade-like) forms with platform preparation. A typical 'Baker's Hole'

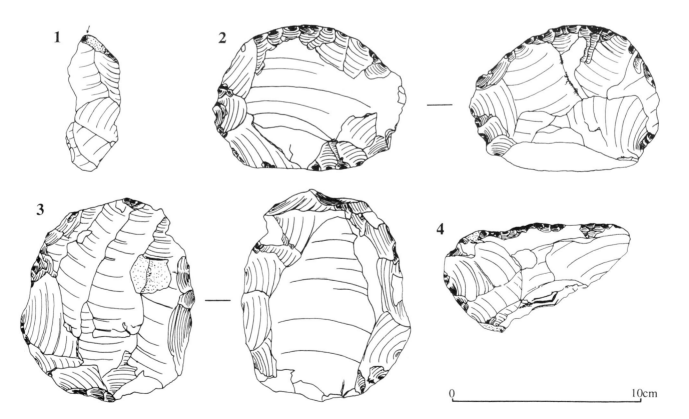

Figure 5.6   Palaeolithic artefacts. 1 burin (Bluntisham), 2 scraper (Fen Drayton), 3 Levallois core (Fen Drayton), 4 flake (Bluntisham)

Levallois flake, of a non-local flint and retouched on one edge, was recovered from Somersham in 1998. Flakes and flake tools are relatively rare, probably as a result of collector bias, but the usual Acheulean tool forms occur: a variety of scrapers on flakes (including transverse forms), notches, and denticulates. There are few pointed forms in the flake component but the occasional blade occurs.

Edge conditions of the material are very variable with some very fresh material and even possible refits present in some Paxton collections, whilst from the same pit came rolled and abraded pieces. Patination states vary from the orange-browns of ferruginous gravels to cream and white.

A second bone tool was discovered in Somersham in 1933 (Garood 1946), but the organic element of assemblages is generally lacking.

At the time of Roe's Gazetteer of Lower and Middle Palaeolithic sites (Roe 1968a), a total of over 100 handaxe yielding sites were known in Cambridgeshire alone. This number has been increased through chance finds during gravel extraction and very occasionally during archaeological investigations (Macaulay 1994; Roberts 1995), although major excavations are still lacking. At the time of writing (originally 1995) there are 115 provenanced Palaeolithic finds and 65 unprovenanced finds in Cambridgeshire and at least 60 entries on the Bedfordshire SMR. An important collection of material, handaxes, cores, and flakes was discovered during 1993–4 at Fen Drayton and Bluntisham, which has been placed in the Museum of Archaeology and Anthropology, University of Cambridge, whilst an assemblage of faunal remains, including mammoth, bovids, cervids, and lion, was also recovered during this time from a gravel quarry at St Ives. Recent quarrying at St Ives briefly uncovered a Pleistocene lake deposit with preservation of molluscs, leaves, and wood. All these recent finds derive from first to second terrace gravels. Evidence for some six mammoths has been observed since this paper was first written.

All the Cam-Ouse terraces, except the fourth terrace, have produced archaeological materials and well-preserved faunal remains also occur. It is clear that archaeologists are currently missing a significant amount of potential information whilst gravel extraction continues unmonitored. It is unfortunate that this material has not been synthesised earlier, as a substantial amount of gravel extraction has taken place unmonitored while sharp and fresh conditioned artefacts have been occasionally collected. The study of associations between artefacts and between artefacts, fauna, and environment is potentially one of the most valuable contributions the River Great Ouse can make to archaeology. It is clear that the materials collected so far span the Ipswichian–Devensian periods, on the basis of floral and faunal correlations which would put the material in the date range of 130,000–10,000 BP. Given the typology and technology of the artefacts, dates of between 130,000–40,000 are acceptable. The first

and second terrace handaxes are dominated by *bout coupe* forms, whilst the third terrace has greater variety of handaxe forms. The variety of forms in the third terrace is matched by the earliest evidence in the region so far, from the Traveller's Rest Pit. This pattern is presently obscure because of collection bias and the difficulty in associating any isolated finds with specific terrace deposits, but if it can be demonstrated more effectively a significant pattern in the typological sequence would be established. Presently, comparable material occurs on the continent spanning the same period, but there the *bout coupe* handaxe has been taken as a type fossil of the Mousterian of Acheulean tradition, which is a late form of Mousterian generally dated to between 60,000–40,000 BP. If the tentative pattern suggested above can be established for Ouse valley handaxe forms these comparisons may become more effective.

There are, however, problems in correlating artefacts with the deposits in which they are found, this is particularly the case for the collected material which has no clear association with individual deposits within terrace formations. These problems are compounded by the reworking of terrace gravels during their deposition and subsequently by periglacial action. These problems were discussed in a Cam-Ouse context by Hughes (1897, 1912) and are well described in Wymer (1992). It should be noted, however, that fine-grained deposits do occur within the Ouse terrace formations, that fresh edged materials and well preserved fauna also derive from these sediments, and so the research potential of these deposits for Palaeolithic archaeology is high. The important issue is to recognise such deposits when they are exposed during the extraction process and to be in a position to mobilise appropriate resources quickly to gain the most information possible.

Discussion

It is clear that the Cam-Ouse system between Bedford and Ely has yielded substantial numbers of artefacts dating between 130,000 and 40,000 BP. At present no whole, *in situ* assemblages have been recovered, and associating cultural material with environmental data remains to be effectively accomplished. There is sufficient evidence, however, to suggest that, subject to monitoring, it is only a matter of time until mineral extraction impacts upon an *in situ* Palaeolithic campsite. What would such a site look like and what could it tell us?

The site would be relatively small, c 10m^2, and comprise a series of scatters of material, both lithic and faunal. Hearths may, or may not, be present. This may appear somewhat uninspiring, however, the information such a site might yield is great.

● Firstly, it would be the first assemblage to date from this period to be investigated in modern times in Britain and would provide a pivotal study around which re-examination of previous finds could be based.

- It would enable the associations of lithics and fauna to be examined and thereby inform upon the economy of the hominids.

- It could provide a means of obtaining firmer dates for the deposits and so enhance our current understanding of the sequence.

- It would provide materials which could be compared with the Continental evidence and so identify local, from more general, adaptations.

- It should inform the current discussion of modern human origins and provide material to contribute to answering the questions listed above (p37).

Additionally, it is important to re-examine the dating of the terraces and the materials themselves, for the *bout coupe* is a late (60,000–40,000 BP) type fossil on the continent but appears to be earlier in the Cam-Ouse system. Is this correct?

The question arises here as to how material is dated to the Ipswichian. At the time of the cited studies at Histon Road, Cambridge, and the dating of the Great Ouse/Cam terraces, dates were calculated using terrestrial correlations. This is problematic because the terrestrial sequence is often truncated by erosional events. Since the terraces were dated, deep sea core research has produced a continuous sequence of $^{16}O:^{18}O$ ratios, which are a direct reflection of the amount of ice present at any time and thence climatic conditions. This continuous sequence has shown that there is another warm period (Oxygen Isotope Stage 3) between the Flandrian and the Ipswichian (which is Stage 5). Could it be that the Cam-Ouse terrace system dates, not to Stage 5, but to Stage 3?

If the latter view is correct then the typological pattern of the Cam-Ouse artefacts would be a better fit to those of the continent. This issue requires further work.

Finally, it is worth reiterating the need for urgent inclusion of Palaeolithic archaeology with the mineral plans of local authorities and their planning teams. A preliminary step has been taken in Cambridgeshire, where a housing development using deep services was planned adjacent to the Histon Road site and a monitoring of geological test pits was requested in the brief. This important step needs to be developed further with regular requirement for such monitoring and certainly for monitoring of gravel extraction. Once again, the Cambridgeshire County Council archaeologists are exploring this potential with limited monitoring of gravel extraction at Brampton. It should be noted that Palaeolithic materials can occur well within one metre of the surface and so a variety of developments can pose a threat to Pleistocene remains. Until regular monitoring of developments affecting Pleistocene deposits is undertaken, the internationally important potential of the Cam-Ouse system will not be met.

Acknowledgements

The author wishes to thank Caroline Gait-Utime for the illustrations and Stephen Coleman for asistance with the records held on Bedfordshire County Sites and Monuments Record and Nesta Rooke for help with the Cambridgeshire County Sites and Monuments Record.

Bibliography

AGCC, 1977 Archaeological Gazetteer of the City of Cambridge, *Proc Cambridge Antiq Soc*, **65** (Part I)

Bowen, D Q, *et al*, 1989 Land-sea correlations in the Pleistocene based on isoleucine epimerization in non-marine molluscs, *Nature*, **340**, 49–51

Broad, D A, 1989 *The History of Little Paxton*. Little Paxton: D Broad

Burkitt, M, 1931a Six Interesting Flint Implements now in Cambridge, *Antiq J*, **11**, 55–7

Burkitt, M, 1931b Cambridge Notes, *Proc Prehist Soc*, **6**, 382–3

Burkitt, M, 1945 A Levallois Flake in Babraham Park, Cambridgeshire, *Antiq J*, **25**, 147

CBA, 1962 *Council for British Archaeology Bulletin for Group 7*, **9**(1)

CBA, 1963 *Council for British Archaeology Bulletin for Group 7*, **10**(1)

Coote, C M, 1948 Notes, Fenstanton and St Ives, *Trans Cambridgeshire and Huntingdon Archaeol Soc*, **7**, 41

Edmonds, E A, & Dinham, C H, 1965 Geology of the Country Around Huntingdon and Biggleswade, *Memoirs of the Geological Survey of Great Britain*, Sheets **187** & **204** (England and Wales). London: HMSO

Evans, J, 1897 *The Ancient Stone Implements, Weapons and Ornaments of Great Britain* (2nd Edition). London: Longmans, Green & Co

Gallois, R W, 1988 Geology of the Country Around Ely, *Memoirs of the British Geological Survey*, Sheet 173 (England and Wales). London: HMSO

Garood, J R, 1929 Recent Discoveries in Huntingdonshire, *Antiq J*, **9**, 9

Garood, J R, 1933 Palaeoliths from the Lower Ouse, *Antiq J*, **13**, 313–15

Garood, J R, 1946 A Bone Implement from the Gravel at Somersham, Huntingdonshire, *Antiq J*, **26**, 186

Gibbard, P, 1985 *The Pleistocene History of the Middle Thames*. Cambridge: Cambridge University Press

Griffith, A F, 1879 On a Flint Implement found at

Barnwell, Cambridge, *Proc Cambridge Antiq Soc*, **4**, 177–80

Hughes, M C, 1884 Palaeolithic Implements from Cambridge, *Nature*, **30**, 632

Hughes, T McKenny, 1897 On the Evidence Bearing upon the Early History of Man which is derived from the Form, Condition of Surface, and Mode of Occurrence of Dressed Flints, *Archaeol J*, **54**, 363–76

Hughes, T McKenny, 1912 On Sources of Error in Assigning Objects found in Sands and Gravels to the Age of those Deposits, with special reference to the so-called Eoliths, *Archaeol J*, **69**, 205–14

Macaulay, S P, 1994 *Post-Medieval Gravel Quarrying at Sweetings Road, Godmanchester*, Cambridgeshire Archaeology 'A' Report **31**

Marr, J E, 1909 On a Palaeolithic Implement found in situ in the Cambridgeshire Gravels, *The Geological Magazine*, **6**, 534–7

Marr, J E, 1919 The Pleistocene Deposits around Cambridge, *Quarterly J Geological Soc London*, **75**, 204–44

Marr, J E, 1926 The Pleistocene Deposits of the Lower Part of the Great Ouse Basin, *Quarterly J Geological Soc London*, **82**, 101–43

Mellars, P A, 1990 *The Emergence of Modern Humans. An Archaeological Perspective.* Edinburgh: Edinburgh University Press

Mitchell, G F, *et al*, 1973 A Correlation of Quaternary Deposits in the British Isles, *Geological Soc London Special Report*, **4**, 1–99

Paterson, T T, & Tebbutt, C F, 1947 Studies in the Palaeolithic Succession in England, No III Palaeoliths from St Neots, Huntingdonshire, *Proc Prehist Soc*, 13, 37–46

Reid Moir, J, 1923 A Series of Solutre Blades from Suffolk and Cambridgeshire, *Proc Prehist Soc*, **4**, 71–81

Reynolds, T, 1991 Revolution or Resolution? The Archaeology of Modern Human Origins, *World Archaeol*, **23**, 155–66

Reynolds, T, forthcoming, Recent Palaeolithic Discoveries in Cambridgeshire, *Proc Cambridge Antiq Soc*

Roberts, J, 1995 *Bluntisham Water Tower to Earith Road, Colne – An Archaeological Watching Brief*, Cambridgeshire Archaeology 'A' Report **49**

Roberts, M B, 1986 Excavation of the Lower Palaeolithic Site at Amey's Eartham Pit, Boxgrove, West Sussex: A Preliminary Report, *Proc Prehist Soc*, **52**, 215–45

Roe, D A, 1968a *A Gazetteer of British Lower and Middle Palaeolithic Sites*, CBA Res Rep **8**. London: Council for British Archaeology

Roe, D A, 1968b British Lower and Middle Palaeolithic handaxe groups, *Proc Prehist Soc*, **34**, 1–82

Roe, D A, 1981 *The Lower and Middle Palaeolithic Periods in Britain*. London: Routledge & Kegan Paul

Seeley, H, 1866 A sketch of the Gravels and Drift of Fenland, *Quarterly J Geological Soc London*, **20**, 470–80

Shackleton, N, & Opdyke, N, 1973 Oxygen Isotope and Palaeomagnetic Stratigraphy of Equatorial Pacific Core V28-238, *Quat Res,* **3**, 39–55

Smith, R A, 1915 Prehistoric Problems in Geology, *Proc Geologists' Assoc*, **26**, 1–20

Sparks, B, & West, R G, 1959 The Palaeoecology of the Interglacial Deposits at Histon Road, Cambridge, *Eiszeitalter und Gegenwart*, **10**, 123–43

Sparks, B, & West, R G, 1972 *The Ice Age in Britain*. London: Methuen

Stringer, C B, & Mellars, P A, (eds) 1989 *The Human Revolution: Behavioural and Biological Perspectives on the origins of Modern Humans.* Edinburgh: Edinburgh University Press

Tebbutt, C F 1927 Palaeolithic Industries from the Great Ouse Gravels at and near St Neots, *Proc Prehist Soc East Anglia*, **5**, 166–73

Wessex Archaeology 1992 *The Southern Rivers Palaeolithic Project Report No.1– The Upper Thames, the Kennet Valley and the Solent Drainage System*. Old Sarum: Wessex Archaeology

Worssam, B C, & Taylor, J H, 1969 Geology of the Country Around Cambridge, *Memoirs of the Geological Survey of Great Britain, England & Wales*, Sheet **188**, 1 Inch. London: HMSO

Wright, A G, 1886 Palaeolithic Implements in Cambridgeshire, *Nature*, **34**, 521–2

Wymer, J J, 1991 The Lower Palaeolithic Period in the London Region, *Trans London and Middlesex Archaeol Soc*, **42**, 1–15

Wymer, J J, 1992 Palaeoliths in alluvium, in S Needham & M Macklin (eds) *Alluvial Archaeology in Britain*, Oxbow Monograph **27**. Oxford: Oxbow, 229–34

6 The Mesolithic interlude

by Mike Dawson

Introduction

In 1979, when Megaw and Simpson wrote what became *the* undergraduate text book on British prehistory, the Mesolithic period was divisible into two broad phases based on technological changes to flint implements and the increased appearance of bone and antler artefacts. If, in the earlier phase the flint artefacts were becoming smaller, the later half of the Mesolithic was 'characterised by an extended range of narrower geometric shapes of individual blades'. Cultural labels Maglemosian and Sauveterrain for the artefact assemblages tended to emphasise the continental extent of Mesolithic culture in the period prior to the formation of the English channel. Yet, even within this broad model, regional characteristics were beginning to be recognised (Megaw and Simpson 1979, 63). The development of such characteristics had been emphasised by Mellars (1976a) who stressed the impact that local resources and localised climates must have had upon early communities increasingly restricted by the rising sea level and reduction in hunting areas. Throughout the Mesolithic period climatic conditions are acknowledged to have been a major determinant in adaptive strategies, but the impact of hunter-gatherer societies on the landscape was also beginning to be recognised. Thus by the mid 1970s many of the major themes in the regional archaeology of the Mesolithic were developing. However, one

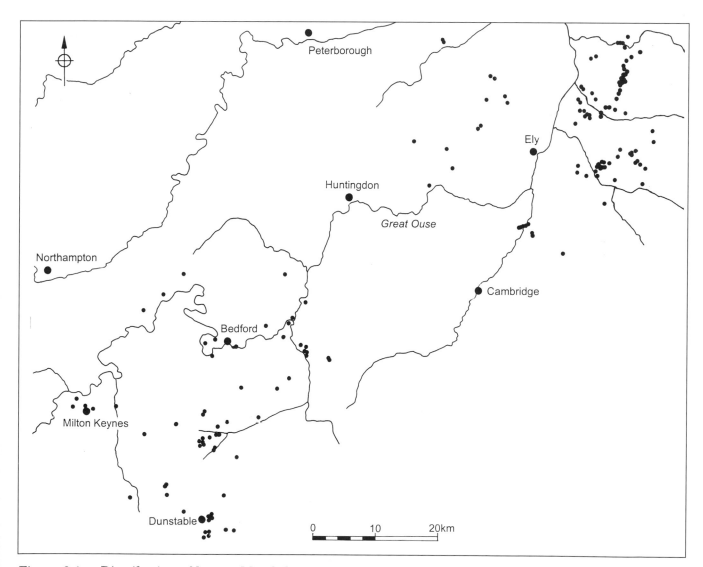

Figure 6.1   Distribution of known Mesolithic sites in the Great Ouse Valley (based on the Fenland Survey, Bedfordshire HER, and Buckinghamshire SMR)

of the main constraints to the development of a detailed regional archaeology was the need to rely upon evidence from either type sites such as Hengistbury Head, Hampshire, or Starr Carr, Yorkshire, or from a relatively restricted number of structured field artefact collection surveys. In a few instances such as High Furlong, Lancashire, C14 dates were beginning to provide a framework beyond that of typology. Nevertheless, a large body of evidence still comprised artefact assemblages, collected with little spatial information, which were assigned to the period on typological grounds.

Dating assemblages on typological grounds is still a problem in prehistoric archaeology generally, and this was recognised in the formulation of the MPP surface lithic scatters and stray finds project which sought to quantify lithic assemblages as the basis for, amongst other things, future research potential (Schofield 1994, 1995). Preliminary results from the Buckinghamshire component of this survey suggest the extent to which Mesolithic assemblages remain unpublished, and therefore without analysis, in the county sites and monuments record. To a degree, Buckinghamshire can be taken as typical of the remainder of the Great Ouse Valley, which, with the exception of the Fenland Survey area and the well known site at Shippea, remains largely a blank. Nevertheless some advances have been made in perceptions of the Mesolithic of the area and in particular in the Middle Ouse (Fig 6.1).

Until recently, interpretation of Mesolithic activity in the Ouse Valley remained largely dependent upon the framework discussed by Megaw and Simpson nearly twenty years ago. In 1987 the Mesolithic material from the Bedfordshire area south of the Ouse Valley was catalogued (Ward 1987); nineteen sites were located on the chalk of the Chilterns and their hinterland, with the remaining ten found north towards the Ouse, including sites on the greensand ridge. Ward listed a further fourteen sites in north Bedfordshire of which, all bar one, were in the Ouse Valley. Ward's conclusions were heavily dependent upon typology, drawing on Clark's 1934 definition of early-Mesolithic assemblages – 'the axe, burin and non-geometric microlith' – to identify early sites. Equally orthodox was his approach to changes in the use of flint and the type of tools produced, concluding that many were environmentally determined. This is perhaps surprising in that, in the absence of any C14 sequence, environmental conditions were deduced from analogies with other regions. However, Ward's catalogue was useful, not only in quantifying the spatial extent of Mesolithic activity in the region, but in pointing to the differences which existed between the middle Ouse Valley and the Chilterns to the south.

The regional difference between the Ouse, the Chilterns, and the Upper Thames was made explicit by Holgate in 1990 (Holgate 1995). He noted that there were few early sites and many of the later sites on the Chilterns were represented by short-stay task-specific assemblages. In contrast to evidence from the Chilterns, the Upper Thames sites in riverine locations produced comparatively high quantities of flint: Tolpits Lane (site B), Moor Park, Hertfordshire, 2100 flints; Stratford Yard, Chesham over 4000, suggesting these may have been either 'base or short stay camps' (Holgate 1995, 8). Holgate was able to argue, from the correlation of C14 dates, that there was a movement away from lower valley locations commensurate with the rise in sea level in the 6th to 4th millennium BC.

In 1990, the publication of PPG 16 suddenly provided the opportunity to include field artefact collection within the scope of development led archaeology, and a succession of field artefact collection projects was instituted (Fig 6.2). In the Ouse Valley area this meant two significantly extensive projects: at the Biddenham Loop, west of Bedford; and along 26km of the M1 as it crossed the Middle Ouse catchment from the headwaters of the River Lea, in the Chilterns; to Salcey forest, east of the headwaters of the Tove. In Biddenham an area of over 100 ha was subject to evaluation. A field artefact collection strategy was determined which assumed the ar-

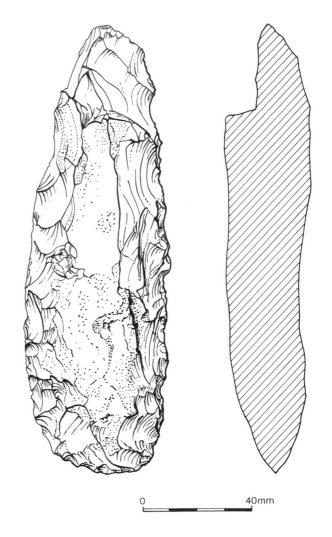

Figure 6.2   Tranchet axe from field 69 near Ridgemont, recovered during the M1 Environmental Impact Assessment

chaeological landscape comprised 'a more or less continuous distribution of artefacts across the landscape, with highly variable density characteristics' (Boismier and Clark 1991, 13). It was a significant move away from the site-based analysis of earlier surveys and reflected the growing body of information from ethnographic analysis of contemporary hunter-gatherer societies. The Biddenham area comprised a gently sloping plateau, within a bend of the Ouse, with predominantly brown-earth soils on gravel beds. In all, eleven locations were attributed as short stay, permanent, and/or seasonal residential locations, though the artefacts densities were low where dates could be assigned to the early Mesolithic. Increasing density suggested to Boismier the possibility of increasingly sedentary activity towards the early/middle Neolithic (Fig 6.3).

In 1993, the M1 survey collection strategy reflected the linear area available (with collection points at 50m along three transects 5m, 30m, and 55m parallel to the motorway) and the varied topography of the route. The topography of the survey area contrasted with the homogeneity of the Biddenham Loop and explicit in the M1 strategy was the need to identify areas of Mesolithic potential for further investigation. Such a strategy concurred with the view that the archaeology of the Mesolithic landscape reflected a mobile society (Dawson 1993a, BCAS 1993/pt iv, 11). In the absence of significant quantities of tool types, the recognition of the landscape was dependent upon typological identification, in which Mesolithic activity was often identified with soft-hammer struck flint waste. Such an approach is probably invalid today as experimentation shows it is impossible to distinguish hard- from soft-hammer striking. Nevertheless some significant locations were identified including Beckerings Park where an axe and waste flakes were found.

The value of Ward's catalogue was in its quantification of Mesolithic assemblages known in the late 1980s, whilst the two later surveys explicitly shifted the balance of regional analysis away from site-specific distributions towards the formulation of a theoretical framework of landscape development in which not only is climatic change influential, but human process has a significant role. Models of human activity in the Mesolithic period have drawn on a wide range of analogues (Smith 1992) and the range and scale of work in the 1990s has broadened the scope of interpretation. There is, however, still considerable scope for advance.

The lower Great Ouse and Fenland

Mesolithic occupation has been extensively surveyed in the Fenland (Hall and Coles 1994, fig 15). In general the first appearance of evidence for Mesolithic activity has been assigned to the 7th to 6th millennia BC, concurrent with the initial stages of peat formation in pollen zone IV. In general this was a time of continuing change as woodland, ini-

tially birch, was replaced by pine, and ultimately by elm, oak, and hazel. Rising sea levels impacted upon the river valleys, increasing peat formation by the creation of large areas of salt flats and encroaching upon areas such as Doddington, Manea, Chatteris, and Ely (Seale 1979). In the eastern Fen, Mesolithic assemblages seem to have been concentrated on sand ridges close to water courses. A detailed survey in the Wissey embayment, based on the composition of lithic assemblages, has allowed activity areas to be distinguished from the more general spreads of lithic material. The eastern Fen sites may be characterised by the sand ridge location at Shippea Hill where, for a period of possibly up to half a millennium, a clearing was maintained and periodically occupied. In the southern Fen area where the postglacial course of the Ouse flowed into the fen at Earith, along Hammonds Eau and West Water before its confluence with the old Nene at Benwick, the distribution of sites favours the higher ground of March, Manea, and Chatteris, but with a preference for the fen edge. Some sites, such as Somersham and Fowlmere (Evans and Hodder 1987), produced large quantities of lithic material suggesting a correlation with the flint-rich sites on the upper Thames.

In the Fenland Survey, areas of Mesolithic activity have been equated with sites where tool kits including cores, flakes, and blades can be recognised. In general the Fenland Survey has taken a functional view of the Mesolithic. The discovery of axes at Bedlam Hill, for instance, has been taken as evidence of tree clearance, whilst fen-edge and river locations may be preferred sites for 'economic' reasons, providing 'easy routeways' (Hall and Coles 1994, 33, 37). Yet the problems of interpretation must not be underestimated; the survey makes clear that distributions of sites are far from complete and that still more work is required to understand the dynamic of changes occurring in the fen during the latter part of the Mesolithic. Nor is the problem of site definition overcome, with the absence of hearths difficult to reconcile with more than very short term occupation. Significantly, although over one hundred sites had been located in the Fenland, density of occupation was thought to have been low, with human activity heavily influenced by the effects of sea level change.

The middle Ouse Valley

In the middle Ouse Valley, from north Cambridgeshire to the Buckinghamshire border, Mesolithic sites occupy a greater variety of topographical locations. However the known density of sites is considerably reduced from the area north of Cambridge (Taylor 1979, 24–5, fig 5) and only 53 sites are known in Bedfordshire (Bedfordshire HER). Of the latter, there are two sites, at Clapham (Dawson et al 1988) and Kempston (Crick and Dawson 1996), where there is some evidence of structures, with small groups of Mesolithic flints found

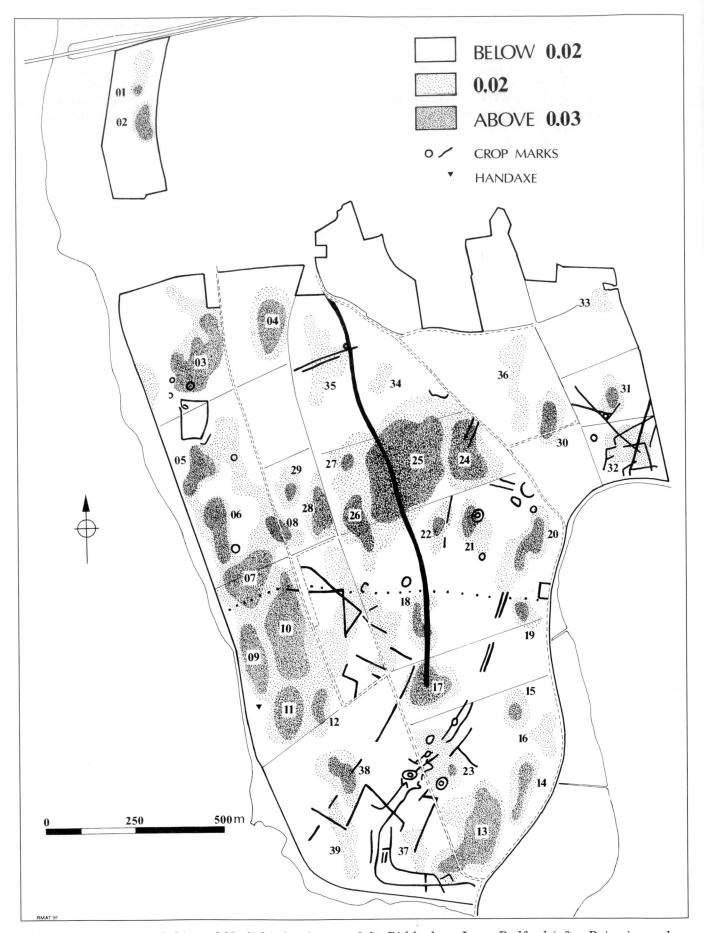

Figure 6.3   The Mesolithic and Neolithic landscape of the Biddenham Loop, Bedford (after Boismier and Clark 1991). Lithic artefact distribution plotted in relation to cropmark features showing identified artefact concentrations

in pits, although at neither site was there an extensive lithic assemblage.

Many of the Middle Ouse assemblages are qualitatively different to those of the Fenland. Many comprise incidental finds from excavations which focused on periods other than the Mesolithic. Recently, however, several field artefact surveys have identified locations which extend the range of topography from which Mesolithic material can be expected (Dawson 1993b; Atherton 1994). Presently, although riverside locations such as that at the Biddenham Loop, Bedford (Boismier and Clark 1991), or Octagon Farm, Willington (Maull 1995) may be preferred, the greensand ridge and areas of clay, such as Shillington, can be expected to yield evidence of Mesolithic exploitation.

Technological change is more difficult to distinguish through the present data. Ward has noted a predominance of larger cores on the chalk areas of the Chiltern hinterland when compared to the non-chalk areas, but the implications of this are far from clear. Also increasing is the potential within this area to begin to differentiate between sites on the basis of function. Although, as yet, no formal analysis has been carried out, there are now more than eleven tranchet axes from the area (Ward 1987) and several sites, such as Shillington (Dawson 1993c), have produced implements and waste flakes from restricted areas. An assemblage of 571 Mesolithic flints, recovered from Grove Priory in five concentrations, a pattern similar to that from the Biddenham Loop, suggests there may be a functional correlation between the middle Ouse and the larger assemblages from the upper Thames and Fen edge.

The upper Ouse

Evidence of Mesolithic activity in the valleys of the Ouse tributaries the Ouzel and the Loughton Brook (Milton Keynes) has been briefly described as originating, mainly in sealed riverine deposits (Zeepvat 1993, 52). No flint assemblages were recovered but a tranchet axe from Pennylands is assumed to indicate tree clearance, and it is clear that in common with the Fenland Survey a functional approach underpinned interpretation of the artefact distribution.

Discussion

This brief survey of the Mesolithic evidence from the Great Ouse Valley indicates several conflicting trends, both in determining a framework for the period and in gathering further data. Clearly data collection is increasing as more artefact collection surveys are undertaken, yet the quantity of reliable data that can be confidently assigned to the period is falling. The reduction in the quantity of data is a function of the erosion of earlier typologies as the hard/soft-hammer struck distinction is invalidated. Secondly, the occurrence of Mesolithic and Neolithic assemblages at the same locations, whilst properly eroding the artificial distinction between the periods (French 1992), focuses attention away from the flint evidence towards sequences based on independent, scientific, dating techniques. Together these factors place increased reliance on the identification of diagnostic tool types and on functional interpretation, but not on 'type' sites which are then used to characterise the wider region.

The erosion of the Mesolithic/Neolithic divide and the movement away from broad based typologies places greater reliance on the potential of statistical modelling over wider areas, but this approach once more reduces the amount of data available to such techniques, as a consistent fieldwalking strategy is a basic requirement. Some movement towards consistency in collection strategies during artefact surveys has been made, ironically driven not by archaeological principles but by development control specifications intended to provide comparison between commercial tenders (Medleycott and Germany 1994).

Closely related to the trends in data collection and recognition is the distinction in print between local approaches, which consistently stress function in interpretation, in contrast to broader based theoretical work. This is particularly evident in conventional attempts to define sites in terms of hunting and foraging strategies, which then omit, for instance, the role of phenomenological factors which may have resulted in site locations removed from practical/rational concerns (Tilley 1994).

Lastly, one of the most positive aspects of recent developments is in the area of environmental work. Pollen sampling from areas beyond the Fenland (Scaife this volume) is slowly beginning to redress the imbalance within the Ouse Valley and between the Ouse Valley and other regions. As for the future, one of the greatest challenges facing the region is the recovery of corroborative dating evidence, whether C14 or an alternative (Mellars 1976b), on which to formulate a framework for the Mesolithic. Until this is achieved the interpretation of the region's Mesolithic past will remain decontextualised and ahistorical.

Bibliography

Atherton, C, 1994 The Arleseley Stotfold Bypass: Boundary Farm, Bedfordshire County Archaeology Service Rep 1994/17. Unpublished, 11–12

Bigmore, P, 1979 *The Bedfordshire and Huntingdonshire landscape*. London: Hodder & Stoughton

Boismier, W, & Clark, R, 1991 Biddenham Loop Archaeological evaluation: stage 1 fieldwalking and earthwork survey, Bedfordshire County Archaeology Service Rep. Unpublished

Crick, J, & Dawson, M, 1996 Archaeological Excavations at Kempston Manor, 1994, *Bedfordshire Archaeol*, **22**, 67–96

Dawson, M, *et al* 1988 Excavations at Ursula Taylor Lower School, *Bedfordshire Archaeol*, **18**, 6–24

Dawson, M, 1993a M1 widening junctions 10–15. Archaeological Impact Assessment Stage 3A artefact collection survey, Bedfordshire Part IV, Bedfordshire County Archaeology Service Rep 1993/iv. Unpublished

Dawson, M, 1993b Arlesey-Stotfold Bypass: Archaeological Evaluation Stage 1 desktop, topographical survey and surface artefact collection, Bedfordshire County Archaeology Service Rep 1993/9. Unpublished

Dawson, M, 1993c Archaeological evaluation of the Shillington Upton End Sewer Line Bedfordshire. Bedfordshire County Archaeology Service Rep 1993/8. Unpublished

Evans, C, & Hodder, I, 1987 Between two worlds: archaeological investigations in the Haddenham level, in J Coles & A J Lawson *European wetlands in prehistory*. Cambridge: Cambridge University Press, 180–91

French, C A I, 1992 Fenland Research Priorities: Late Neolithic Transition, *Fenland Research*, **7**, 2–3

Hall, D, & Coles, J, 1994 *Fenland Survey: an essay in landscape persistence*, NS report 1. London: English Heritage

Holgate, R, 1995 Early prehistoric settlement of the Chilterns, in R Holgate (ed) *Chiltern archaeology. Recent work. A handbook for the next decade*. Dunstable: The Book Castle, 3–17

Maull, A, 1995 Octagon Farm, Cople. Archaeological Field Evaluation, Bedfordshire County Archaeology Service Rep 1995/39. Unpublished

Medleycott, M, & Germany, M, 1994 Archaeological fieldwalking in Essex, 1985–1993: interim results, *Essex Archaeol & Hist*, **25** (1994), 14–27

Megaw, J V S, & Simpson, D D A, 1979 *Introduction to British Prehistory*. Leicester: Leicester University Press

Mellars, P A, 1976a Settlement patterns and industrial variability in the British Mesolithic, in G de G Sieveking, I H Longworth, & K E Wilson (eds) *Problems in Economic and Social Archaeology*. London: Duckworth, 375–400

Mellars, P A, 1976b The appearance of narrow blade microlithic industries in Great Britain: the radiocarbon evidence, in S K Kozlowski (ed) *Les Civilisations du 8em au 5em milleniare avant notre ere en Europe*. Nice: International Union of Prehistoric and Protohistoric Sciences, 166–74

Schofield, J, 1994 Looking back with regret; looking forward with optimism: making more of lithic scatter sites, in N Ashton & A David (eds) *Stories in stone*, Lithic Studies Society Occasional Paper **4**. London : Lithic Studies Society, 90–8

Schofield, J, 1995 Order out of chaos: making sense out of surface Stone Age finds, *Conservation Bulletin*, March 1995, 9–11

Seale, R S, 1979 Ancient courses of the Great and Little Ouse in Fenland, *Proc Cambridge Antiq Soc*, **69**, 1–19

Smith, C, 1992 *Late Stone Age Hunters of the British Isles*. London: Routledge

Taylor, M, 1979 A survey of prehistoric sites north of Cambridge, *Proc Cambridge Antiq Soc*, **69**, 21–36

Tilley, C, 1994 *A phenomenology of landscape: places, paths and monuments*. Oxford/Providence USA: Berg

Ward, S S, 1987 The evidence for the Mesolithic in Bedfordshire south of the Ouse Valley. Unpublished BA thesis, St John's College, University of Cambridge

Zeepvat, R, 1993 The Milton Keynes Project, *Rec Buckinghamshire*, **33**, 49–63

7   The development of a Neolithic monument complex at Godmanchester, Cambridgeshire *by Fachtna McAvoy*

Introduction

This paper presents an interim summary of the principal structures associated with the origin and development of a Neolithic monument complex at Rectory Farm, Godmanchester (NGR TF 258712, Fig 7.1). This was recognised during the course of work initially directed towards the excavation of a Roman 'villa' (Frere and Tomlin 1991, 256) located to the north of the complex. The project was occasioned by an application for mineral extraction and was carried out by the Central Archaeology Service of English Heritage between 1988 and 1992, with excavation funded by Redland Aggregates Ltd.

The project area lies at *c* 9m OD on a flood plain of Pleistocene river gravels, partly covered by alluvium, to the north-east of Godmanchester. The area is bounded to the west and north by the River Ouse and its associated channels and streams, and to the east by a low range of hills formed from Boulder Clay.

Trapezoidal structure

The earliest element recorded within the monument complex, determined stratigraphically and by spatial referencing, was a large trapezoidal structure (reconstructed in Fig 7.2), the fundamental components of which were:

- an array of free-standing timber posts

- a boundary ditch with an inner bank

These were arranged symmetrically to form a trapezoidal shape, aligned north-east–south-west, with an opening at the north-east end. The area within the structure was *c* 6.3ha, the maximum width was 228m, the axial length was 336m, and the opening was 168m wide, the same as the minimum width. The timber posts, numbering 24 in total, were adjacent to the bank, except for a single post placed at the centre of the opening.

The post array

The postholes were set between 31.5m and 41.6m apart along the sides of the structure. The postpipes were generally oval in plan, (average dimensions: length 0.75m, width 0.63m, depth 0.92m), although two posts, both located at the opening, were D-shaped with the face of the timber orientated towards the north-east.

The posthole sections showed considerable variation in postpipe definition, but none clearly demonstrated that the posts had been replaced. Charcoal was found in every postpipe, suggesting that the posts had been burnt.

The boundary ditch

This was generally 3m wide and 1m deep (as excavated) and was recut along the northern and southern sides of the trapezoidal structure, but this recutting was not apparent at its south-west end. Significant deposits within the ditch were a cattle upper skull, on the base of the southern ditch terminal at the opening, and two cattle lower-jaw bones (left and right), on top of the primary fill in the northern ditch terminal.

The bank

No *in situ* remains of the bank were detected, but evidence for its location was provided by the fills of the segments excavated through the boundary ditch. The layer sequence consistently showed that the bank was situated internally, and presumably occupied the 5.5m interval between the inner edge of the ditch and the post array.

Dating

Artefactual dating for the structure is slight and consists of sherds of early to middle-Neolithic bowls found in the primary fills of the ditch. The fabrics are almost exclusively flint-tempered and some of the vessels are carinated, with the absence of decoration on the body or rim being a notable feature.

Table 7.1   Radiocarbon dates from postholes

SAMPLE NO	¹⁴C AGE BP	CAL BC: 1Σ	CAL BC: 2Σ
OxA-3370	5050 ± 80	3965–3780	4000–3700
OxA-3646	5035 ± 70	3960–3715	3990–3700
OxA-3367	4950 ± 80	3925–3645	3960–3535
OxA-3369	4850 ± 80	3780–3525	3905–3375

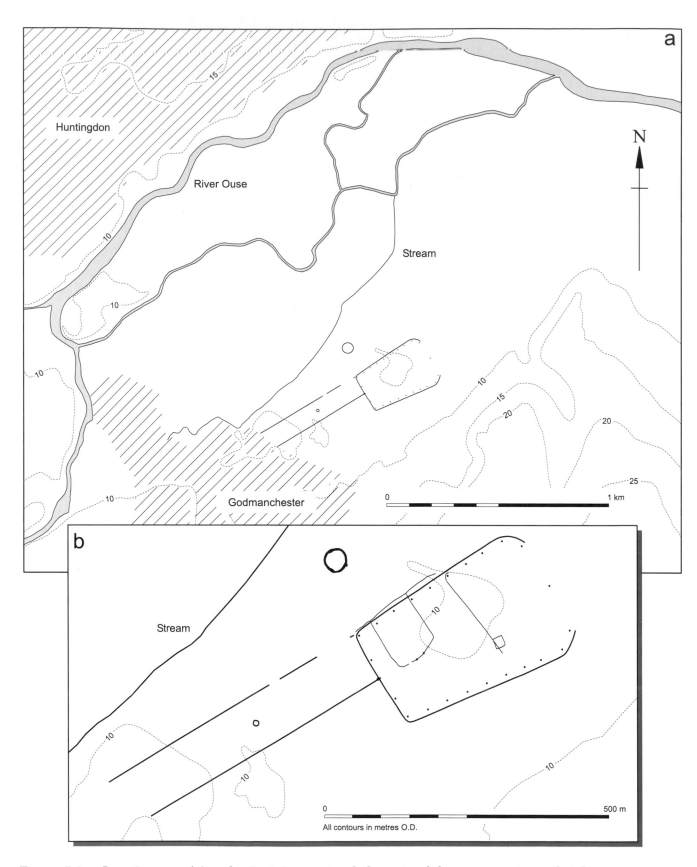

Figure 7.1   Location map (a) and principle structural elements of the monument complex (b)

Figure 7.2   Reconstruction of the trapezoidal structure

Scientific dating has, however, been obtained from charcoal associated with the post array (Table 7.1). These determinations form a reasonably close group, indicating a probable date of construction in the first half of the fourth millennium BC. Contemporary Neolithic structures would therefore have been funerary monuments and causewayed enclosures.

Archaeoastronomy

The assessment (Humble, nd) has demonstrated a correlation (Fig 7.3) between the position, on the horizon, of significant events in the lunar and solar cycles, and alignments to the horizon between key post-locations within the trapezoidal structure. If this proposition can be sustained then the size of the structure may be a result of the long sightlines required for accurate calibration, rather than a requirement to create a large area for assembly.

The nature of the trapezoidal enclosure

The components of the enclosure occur in other Neolithic monuments. The demarcation of a large internal space by ditches with internal banks is a feature of causewayed enclosures, whilst the trapezoidal shape and the use of timber posts can be found at a number of funerary monuments.

The enclosure at Godmanchester is, however, without parallel in both the combination of these elements and the sheer scale of the work. It demonstrates, at the least, an ability to devise a geometric design and translate this into a groundwork with considerable precision, even without the possible incorporation of celestial alignments.

The unique character of this enclosure presents a challenge in determining both its function and its place in the development of Neolithic society. One insight will, however, be provided by the consideration of its relationship to other structures detailed below.

Features external to the trapezoidal structure

Small ring-ditch

This was a slightly ovate ditch situated to the south-west of the trapezoidal structure. This feature, although relatively small in terms of size (enclosing an area 9.5m long and 8.5m wide), may have marked a location of considerable importance, perhaps associated with the setting out of astronomical alignments embodied within the trapezoidal structure (Fig 7.3). The central point within the enclosed area was exactly between the two side ditches of a cursus (see below), and these veered slightly to the south of the alignment needed to form a right-angle with the cursus terminal, as if to accommodate a pre-existing feature. The significance of the location of the site was also long-lived, evidenced by its having been respected by a field system of possible late-

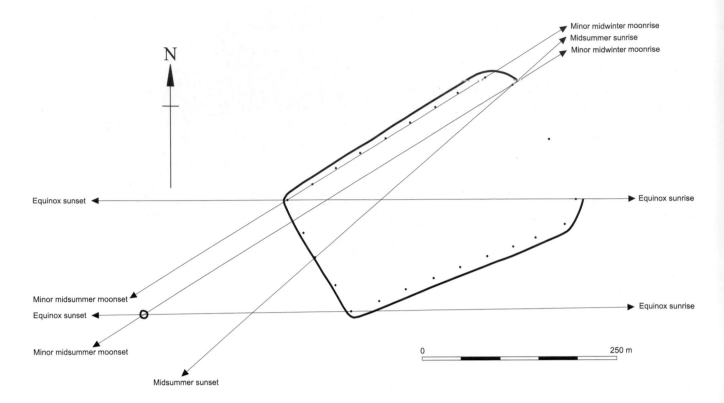

Figure 7.3   Possible correlation of post alignments and astronomical events

Bronze Age date and also by a small group of cremations, set in an arc alongside the outer south-west edge of the ditch. One of these cremations contained a single Romano-British sherd, but this might have been intrusive.

Large ring-ditch

This was situated almost midway between the trapezoidal structure and a stream to the north. The ditch was ovate and enclosed an area 37m long and 34m wide. The width of the ditch varied between 4.2m and 2.7m and there were also marked differences in the ditch profile and infill around its course.

The area enclosed by the ditch contained a low turf-built mound, *c* 26m wide, whose limits lay 3–5m from the inner lip of the ditch. No features were recorded at the centre of the mound but just to the west of this point was a small rectangular pit. The mound was also cut by twelve irregular features, some of which were recognisably tree-fall holes. The excavation of these features produced a number of flints but no other artefacts.

Cursus

This was orientated north-east–south-west and could be traced, from aerial photographs, for 0.5km after which its course is covered by the suburbs of Godmanchester (Fig 7.1). It is defined by two parallel lines of ditches, 90m apart, aligned on the centre

and western corner of the end of the trapezoidal structure, whose boundary ditch was cut by the terminal ditch of the cursus. Evidence for an internal cursus bank is provided by its ditch infills, and definite recutting of the ditch occurred at, and on both sides of, the southern corner of the terminal ditch.

All passages through the cursus were located on the northern side. The first, moving from south-west to north-east, was formed by a break of 18m which lay astride the shortest distance between the two ring-ditches. A further gap of 58m lay to the north-east but the terminal of one of the investigated ditch lengths was very abrupt and misshapen, as if unfinished, and the original intention may have been either to form a continuous link, or to create another, narrower, passage.

There is, however, no doubt that a 3m wide passage in the northern corner of the cursus was planned from the outset. This passage was next to the terminal of a gully or small ditch, which redefined the northern side of the trapezoidal structure and whilst these features may not have been contemporary in origin, it is entirely possible that they were in use concurrently. The configuration of the various terminals suggests that a new passage may have been established in the adjacent corner of the trapezoidal structure.

The ditches on the northern side of the cursus were extremely shallow in comparison with the southern side, whilst the broadest and deepest length of ditch was that which formed the terminal. This reflects the fact that the terminal ditch was cut through the loose infill of the boundary ditch of the trapezoidal structure. Nevertheless, the marked contrast in size between the northern ditch and the more substantial terminal and southern ditches, and thus in the amount of primary material available for bank construction, must have been intentional. It is conceivable that the banks were deliberately made higher at the cursus terminal and along its southern side as a means of screening the earlier trapezoidal structure.

Features within the trapezoidal structure

Rectangular enclosure

This was sited c 50m away from, and aligned parallel to, the southern side of the trapezoidal structure and was defined by a continuous ditch which enclosed an area 17.7m long and 16.3m wide. No contemporary features were recorded within the enclosure, whose ditch produced only a small number of ceramic sherds consistent with a Neolithic date.

Transverse ditch

This was a narrow feature which crossed the interior of the trapezoidal structure. The north-west terminal arced around one of the postholes and ran parallel to the boundary ditch. The transverse ditch can be regarded as respecting the position of the inner bank of the trapezoidal structure and the spatial relationship with the post location is unlikely to be fortuitous.

The ditch cut through the interior of the rectangular enclosure described above but its south-east limit was not established. A radiocarbon date of 3390 ± 75 BP (OxA-3366), corrected to 1870–1535 Cal BC (1σ), 1885–1525 Cal BC (2σ), was obtained from charcoal associated with a cremation cut into the transverse ditch where it crossed the rectangular enclosure.

Pit group

This is a cluster of pits (Fig 7.4), dug into the junction between the southern ditch of the cursus and the boundary ditch of the trapezoidal structure. The pit fills contained charcoal and burnt flint with a relatively large quantity of animal bone, some flint and stone objects, a few Neolithic ceramic sherds, perhaps from one bowl, and a single Beaker sherd. Additionally there were a few pieces of human bone from the upper pit fills. The lower pit fills were waterlogged and contained plant macrofossils and other biological material.

The biological remains in the individual pits were sufficiently diverse to suggest that they were infilled under differing habitat conditions and were not contemporary (Murphy, in prep). The pits were broadly sequenced on this basis, on the supposition

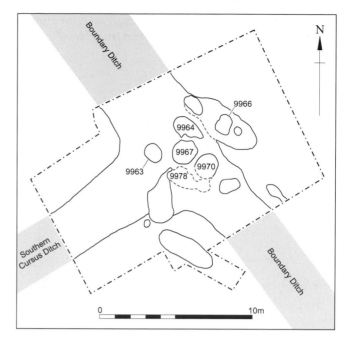

Figure 7.4   Pit group at the junction of the trapezoidal structure and cursus

that the habitat changed from wooded to open conditions. Once radiocarbon dates were available this assumption was tested and the results are shown in Table 7.2. The evidence for increased crop-processing in the later pits corresponds with the occurrence of quern fragments.

Rectilinear enclosure

This enclosure was situated on the northern side of the trapezoidal structure and was defined by a single ditch, encompassing an area 100m long and 76m wide (c 0.76ha). It was orientated north-west–south-east with an entrance located off-centre on the south-east side, adjacent to two oval pits which were either earlier than, or contemporary with, the ditch. The north-west side of the enclosure ditch was cut through a layer of bank material within the infill of the boundary ditch of the trapezoidal structure. This infilling occurred after the boundary ditch had been recut.

Evidence which would date the use of the enclosure is solely artefactual. Sherds of Food Urn and Biconical Urn were found in the ditch, and Food Urn and Beaker sherds were recovered from the pits. The construction of the enclosure may, therefore, fall within the date range suggested for the activities associated with the pit group.

This rectilinear enclosure may have been laid out with spatial reference to the trapezoidal structure and possibly also the cursus, as the enclosure appears to have been sited across the projected line of its side ditches. It may be the case that these ditches and/or their banks were extant at the time of enclosure construction, and, if the terminal ditch of the cursus had been infilled, this new enclosure would have lain at the end of a cursus 'corridor'.

Table 7.2   Pit sequence and summary of habitat change (after Murphy, in prep, with contributions from Robinson, nd, and Wiltshire, nd)

| FEATURE | RADIOCARBON DATING | | | INFERRED HABITATS AND HUMAN ACTIVITY | SAMPLE NO |
	CAL BP	CAL BC: 1Σ	CAL BC: 2Σ		
Cursus ditch	–	–	–	Conditions locally open with woodland in vicinity. Maintenance of open conditions by grazing	–
Pit 9963	4000 ± 60	2588–2465	2861–2369	Local woodland with scrub	GU-5266
Pit 9970	3830 ± 60	2456–2149	2470–2049	Local woodland with scrub but more open than above. Some disposal of charred cereals	GU-5267
Pits 9964, 9966, 9967,9978	3240 ± 50 (pit 9964)	1600–1450	1671–1420	Locally open conditions conditions. Disposal of charred and uncharred crop plant remains (cereals, flax, opium poppy)	GU-5213

Conclusion

Later events in the area around the monument complex include the laying out of field systems and enclosures and the construction of a Romano-British 'villa'. A comparison can be made between the structural evidence for the Neolithic and Roman periods at Rectory Farm. Both periods provide a major site, respectively the trapezoidal structure and a building complex, each approached from the south-west by a formal access; a cursus and a metalled road. Neither major site impinges upon the other although the access routes are superimposed. One aspect of analysis, therefore, will be to seek to determine whether the spatial distribution is simply a result of land suitability and availability or, more significantly, continued historical association.

Acknowledgements

The illustrations for this paper were produced by John Vallender of the Central Archaeology Service. Thanks are due to all the members of the Godmanchester project team for their work, either on-site, or in the assessment programme.

Bibliography

Frere, S S, & Tomlin, R S O, 1991 Roman Britain in 1990, *Britannia*, **22**, 256

Humble, J, nd Godmanchester (Site 432) Neolithic 'Enclosure': An Assessment of the Possible Astronomical Significance of the Posthole Alignments. Unpublished report

Murphy, P, in prep, Rectory Farm, Godmanchester, Cambs (Site 432): Plant macrofossils from Neolithic-Bronze Age, Roman, and Saxon contexts

Robinson, M, nd Assessment of Samples from Godmanchester for Insect Remains. CAS Archive, unpubl report

Wiltshire, P E J, nd Godmanchester (Site 432): Assessment of the Potential of Sediments for Pollen Analysis. CAS Archive, unpubl report

8 The ritual landscape of the Neolithic and Bronze Age along the middle and lower Ouse Valley *by Tim Malim*

Introduction

The Great Ouse River Valley was a centre of activity throughout the prehistoric period and its archaeological remains have the potential to contribute significantly to understanding the development of Neolithic and Bronze Age Bedfordshire and Cambridgeshire. Its national importance derives from the prominence of the Ouse as a corridor for continental contact. Although some pattern to the distribution and form of the major monuments has been recorded by air photography, the destruction of the archaeology over this century has been extensive, enhancing with particular value those rare areas as yet undisturbed. The archaeological response to destruction from aggregate extraction, extensive building programmes, road construction, and agricultural activities has been generally piecemeal and poorly funded. Consequently, publication of results is in a poor state and, until this volume, no synthetic statement has been produced.

The surviving evidence for the Neolithic and Bronze Age landscape shows that specific areas were chosen for ceremonial purposes and it is mainly the remains of these large monuments that are readily available for study. Evidence for farming and settlement is more ephemeral and thus its unambiguous identification has been rare along the Ouse, but a more systematic archaeological response in recent years has begun to define this aspect at certain locations.

This synthesis focuses on the variety and distribution of Neolithic and Bronze Age sites within the Ouse valley. It is the product of a rapid survey of easily consulted sources, set against a more general archaeological background relating to these periods. The information contained here must be regarded as a preliminary (but long overdue) statement which would amply reward a greater investment of time than is presently available. It is based in the main on work up to 1994, along with a rapid revision of recent published material in 1998. A complementary paper has also been written for a book on cursus monuments (Malim 1999).

The present paper synthesises the ceremonial complexes along the middle and lower Ouse, from Biddenham to Chatteris. There are no definite Neolithic monuments listed along the upper Ouse, west of this area, in Bedfordshire or Buckinghamshire. It concentrates on the ceremonial landscape, focusing on the morphological similarity and distribution pattern of these rather than of settlement remains. Co-axial field systems which relate to the pattern of the ceremonial monuments visible in the landscape are not included here.

A series of ceremonial complexes, which developed over several centuries, are distributed relatively evenly along the river valley, 5–6km apart. Each contains a number of different types of monument, including long (mortuary) enclosures, cursuses, hengiform monuments, pit alignments, territorial marker ditches, and barrows/ring-ditches. These complexes appear to have had significance as burial places and locations for communal ceremonies, and as such they might have acted as focuses for distinct groups occupying clearly differentiated sectors of the Ouse. The continuing importance of these sites in later times is evident in the lack of Iron Age and Romano-British disturbance and by the positioning of Celtic temples at several earlier prehistoric ceremonial complexes.

Within SMRs the distinction between cursus and long mortuary enclosure is unclear, as can be seen for the descriptions given to the Octagon Farm 'mortuary enclosures' as opposed to remarkably similar monuments at Eynesbury described as 'cursuses'. In archaeological literature mortuary enclosures as a term can imply timber, earth, or stone structures for collective storage of the dead; they may have become included within other monuments such as long barrows or oval barrows at a later date in their development. Thus at Brampton I have interpreted the monument at the end of the cursus as a mortuary enclosure, perhaps a long barrow. Long barrows and oval barrows are terms that are also loosely used, generally with the idea that oval barrows are a variant of long barrows.

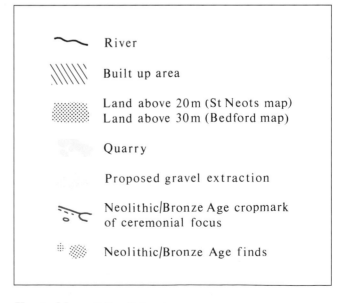

Key to Maps 8.1 – 8.4

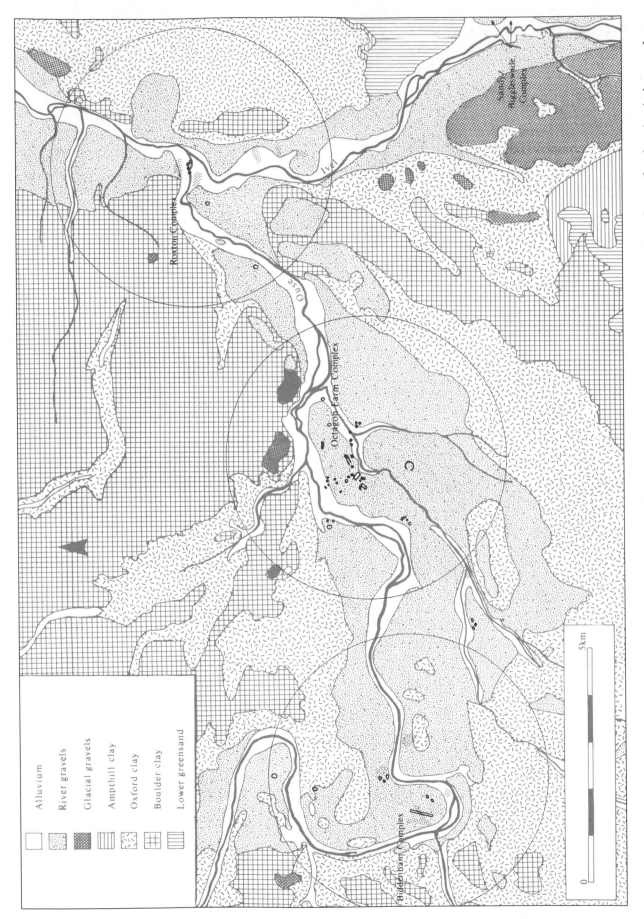

Figure 8.1   Bedfordshire: Geological background; Neolithic and Bronze Age monuments are shown in red (circles = 6km 'territories' centred on the ceremonial complexes)

Alluvium
River gravels
Glacial gravels
Ampthill clay
Oxford clay
Boulder clay
Lower greensand

Roxton Complex
Ouse
Octagon Farm Complex
Biddenham Complex

5km

0

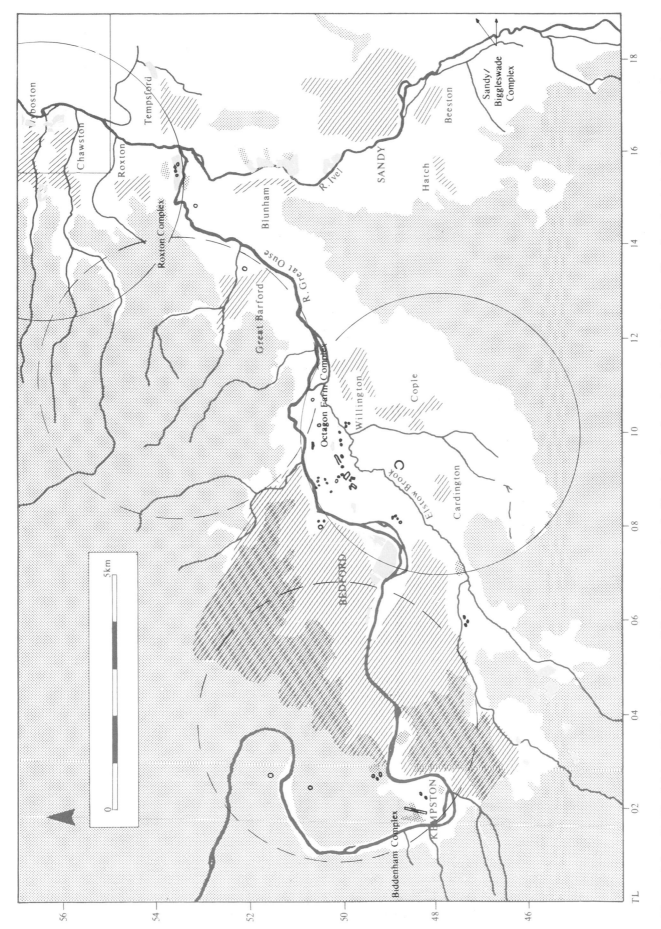

Figure 8.2   Bedfordshire: Relief above 30m OD; with quarries (yellow) and archaeology (red) (circles = 6km 'territories' with ceremonial complexes located at river boundaries)

Table 8.1   List of Neolithic monuments and associated ring-ditches

Site		Length (m)	Width (m)	Exc'd	Ditch dimensions		profile	Orientation	Interpretation	Ring-ditch
					width (m)	depth (m)				
Biddenham		?450	70	no				NNE–SSW	mortuary enclosure	to N and E
		?750	?10–20	no				NNE–SSW	cursus	-
		?227	?10–14	no				NNW–SSE	long/oval barrow	-
Brampton (SAM 121)		90	17–20	yes	1.0	0.3	U-shaped	NW–SE	mortuary enclosure	E end
		?300	25	yes	?	?	?	NW–SE	cursus	2: N side
Huntingdon Race Course		20	14	yes	1–1.6	0.45	wide V-shape	SE entrance	rectangular enclosure	to S 100m
Buckden-Diddington		?700	?15	no				NW–SE	cursus?	to S
		35	15	no				NNE–SSW	mortuary enclosure?	to N
Cardington		(2.5–4.2 ha)		no				-	causewayed enclosure	-
Cardington-Cople (Octagon Farm)	Site 2	95	35	yes	?	?	?	NNE–SSW	mortuary enclosure	E side
	Site 4	75	15	yes	?	?	?	NE–SW	mortuary enclosure	-
	Site 7	70	20	no				N–S	mortuary enclosure	to W
	Site 8	175	50	yes	?	?	?	NW–SE	mortuary enclosure	to E
	Site 28	?125	20	no				NE–SW	cursus	E end
Chatteris		?350	?250	no				-	enclosure	to S, SE
Eynesbury, St Neots		314	80	yes	1.29	0.37	U-shaped	NNE–SSW	cursus	to S
		>100	66	yes	1.1	0.2–0.57	U-shaped	NNE–SSW	cursus	long bw(?) S end
		132	52	no				W–E	cursus	to S
		58	25	no				NNE–SSW	long barrow?	-
		300–420	175	yes	1.4–1.55	0.62–0.8	-	N–S (enclosure)	pit alignments (8.5ha)	to S, E
Fenstanton		?650	30–60	no				NW–SE	cursus?	to NE
Godmanchester Rectory Farm		?500	90	yes	1.5–4.45	0.3–1.27	flat-rounded base	NNE–SSW	cursus	NE end or mid
		336	180–230	yes	3.0–4.45	1.0	flat base	NNE–SSW	horned enclosure (6.3ha)	to W
		17.7	16.3	yes	1.25	0.7	narrow flat base	-	square enclosure	
		100	76	yes	1.7	1.25	narrow flat base	NW–SE	rectilinear enclosure	
Haddenham	Site 10	(8.5 ha)		yes	1.5		U-shaped	-	causewayed enclosure	to W
Sutton	Site 6	52	11–16	yes	2.5	1.5	U-shaped	NE–SW	long barrow	to NE
	Site 11	50	21	no	3.5	0.8	?	NE–SW	long barrow	-
Stonea		400–500	20	yes	3.7	1.0	U-shaped	NW–SE	cursus	SE end & W side
Willington Plantation Quarry		27	25	yes	1.8–2.2	1.0–2.2	narrow flat base	-	mortuary enclosure	-

Evidence, threat, and response

The Ouse has seldom been the focus of structured archaeological investigation, and most of what we know has been recovered as a consequence of an *ad hoc* response to gravel and sand quarries, the archaeological funding of which was often minimal. There are a host of names who did what they could in these conditions (amateurs such as J R Garrood, G T Rudd, and C F Tebbutt, or archaeologists involved in Community Programme work schemes during the 1980s such as M Alexander, C Evans, A Herne, and F Wilmot, see Table 8.3). It is not surprising that this approach has resulted in a lamentably poor record of publication. In the same way that the geology and topography of the river valley clearly influenced Neolithic and Bronze Age activity, these factors also dictated the nature of the evidence (Figs 8.1 and 8.3). The ease of cultivation on the river terraces has meant that prehistoric earthworks have not survived the plough of later generations. In contrast, it is ironic that widespread activity in modern times has allowed a greater range of evidence to be accessible. Predominant amongst these is aerial photography, which highlights the cropmarks that are formed on gravel terraces with shallow plough soils capping them. When the palimpsest of features is untangled, this method of survey gives the single most comprehensive overview of the landscape for individual periods. Physical evidence in the form of artefacts exists in a more haphazard form, and records of excavated features are even rarer. It is a paradox familiar to archaeologists that where an abundance of archaeological remains exist, their very existence is often only known as a consequence of a process of destruction such as ploughing or quarrying (Figs 8.2 and 8.4).

Archaeology

Travelling up-river from the fens, a sequence of spectacular Neolithic and Bronze Age monuments is found, concentrated on low areas in close proximity to the Ouse and its tributaries (Figs 8.2 and 8.4). The microtopography and underlying geology are all important in understanding their locations, and in general terms they are situated in liminal areas prone to flooding. The interpretation of these monuments, their date and function, is based on morphological evidence provided by air photographs, and on excavated data (see Tables 8.1 and 8.2).

Stonea

In the Cambridgeshire fens, near March, lies the island of Stonea, Wimblington, on which a cursus has been tentatively identified from air photographs and limited excavation (Jackson and Potter 1996, 25, 68). Its orientation is north-west–south-east and it runs for 400m to meet with a Bronze Age barrow excavated in the 1960s (Potter 1976), beyond which

an undated rectilinear enclosure is also visible on air photographs (eg CUCAP NH17). Ring-ditches are apparent within the area to the west of the possible cursus, and the area continued to be an important place in later times, with construction of Stonea Camp and the presence of a Romano-Celtic temple.

Chatteris

The ancient course of the Ouse flowed to the west of Chatteris, *en route* to a confluence with the Nene near Benwick (Seale 1979, 2). To the north lies early-prehistoric peat fen with little evidence of occupation, but Chatteris itself was mainly dry land, with the best soils on Horseley Fen. Here the Fenland Survey identified a D-shaped enclosure (Hall 1992: Chatteris site 38) potentially of Neolithic date because of its low altitude and overlying occupation remains. It appears to be of a similar size to the Haddenham causewayed enclosure a little way upstream. Like many of the other Ouse Valley monuments it remained a significant location after the Neolithic. A triple ring-ditch, 46.5m in diameter, located from air photographs (site 32: Cambridgeshire SAM 43) lies immediately south of the enclosure and is probably a large multi-phase barrow. A further four ring-ditches and one surviving barrow in the same field make this group the largest cluster within Hall's Chatteris barrowfield, which extends away from the river towards Mepal. The ring-ditches reflect a continued ceremonial focus on the area of the enclosure in the Bronze Age.

Haddenham

At Haddenham, several sites were identified from fieldwork and from air photography during the Fenland Survey. These included a causewayed enclosure, three long barrows, a number of round barrows, and a Romano-Celtic temple, all located on gravel terraces near to ancient meanders of the Ouse.

Excavations of the causewayed enclosure were undertaken during the 1980s. It was 8.5ha in area, delineated by a single ring of interrupted ditches and by an internal palisade. Although irregular in plan, the alignment of the western ditch may have been constructed to reflect the line of the contemporary Ouse. Possible formalized entranceways were identified to the north and west (Evans and Hodder 1987; Hodder 1992). The ritual significance of the monument is seen in the placed deposits found in many of the ditch segments, and the lack of settlement features within the enclosure.

Three kilometres to the north-east, in Foulmire Fen, a sub-rectangular long barrow was excavated which contained a wooden mortuary structure, 7.9m long and 1.6–1.9m wide. The surrounding ditch was 2–3m wide and 1m deep, with a timber facade at its eastern end (Shand and Hodder 1987). The total size of the mound was 49 × 19m and it was orien-

Table 8.2 Dating evidence

Table 8.2 Dating evidence
Radiocarbon determinations have been calibrated using OxCal (v2.18) (Bronk Ramsey 1995) using data from Stuiver et al (1998) (INTCAL98.14C). The calibrated date ranges for the samples have been calculated using the maximum intercept method of Stuiver and Reimer (1986), and are quoted in the form recommended by Mock (1986) with end points rounded outwards to ten years.

a: List of C14 dates (post-Bronze Age dates omitted)

Site		Monument	Lab No	Date BP	Context	Calibrated date range (66%) BC	Calibrated date range (95%) BC
Brampton (SAM 121)		mortuary enclosure	GU-5264	3910 ± 70	oak charcoal from pit outside west end	2480–2290	2580–1240
			GU-5265	4140 ± 140	oak charcoal from pit cutting southern ditch	2900–2470	3090–2300
Buckden - Diddington		Site III 'ring-bank'		3575 ± 40	cremation 503, predating ring-ditch IV	2010–1830	2030–1770
Godmanchester Rectory Farm		horned enclosure	OxA-2323	4220 ± 90	deposit in post-hole	2910–2640	3080–2500
			OxA-3367	4950 ± 80	post-pipe charcoal	3890–3650	3960–3540
			OxA-3369	4850 ± 80	post-pipe charcoal	3710–3530	3790–3380
			OxA-3370	5050 ± 80	post-pipe charcoal	3960–3710	4040–3650
			OxA-3491	4360 ± 75	post-pit charcoal	3090–2890	3340–2870
			OxA-3646	5035 ± 70	post-pipe charcoal	3960–3710	3980–3650
			GU-5266	4000 ± 60	pit cutting infilled enclosure ditch	2620–2460	2840–2340
			GU-5267	3830 ± 60	pit cutting infilled enclosure ditch	2410–2140	2450–2040
			GU-5213	3240 ± 50	pit sequence cutting infilled enclosure ditch	1600–1440	1680–1410
Haddenham	Site 6 (selection)	long barrow	Har-9173	4730 ± 80	forecourt pavement	3640–3370	3660–3350
			Har-9175	4950 ± 70	wood from floor of mortuary structure	3800–3650	3950–3630
			Har-9176	5050 ± 60	facade post	3960–3770	3980–3700
			Har-9178	5770 ± 140	bone	4780–4450	4940–4340
	Site 10	causewayed enclosure	Har-8093	4560 ± 90	ditch segment, base of shell marl platform	3500–3100	3630–2920
			Har-8096	4630 ± 80	ditch segment, charcoal from basal fill	3520–3340	3640–3090
			Har-10520	4690 ± 90	ditch segment, burnt post in secondary fill	3640–3360	3650–3120
Roxton		ring-ditch B	Har-997	3620 ± 80	Collared Urn burial	2140–1830	2200–1740
			Har-998	7700 ± 170	primary fill (Mesolithic occupation)	6690–6400	7060–6220
		ring-ditch C	Har-999	3800 ± 130	Collared Urn burial	2470–2030	2620–1830
			Har-1000	3660 ± 80	Collared Urn burial	2140–1920	2290–1770
			Har-1001	3130 ± 60	secondary cremation	1490–1310	1520–1220
			Har-1002	3620 ± 80	Collared Urn burial	2140–1830	2200–1740
			Har-1003	3200 ± 50	secondary cremation	1520–1410	1600–1320
Willington (Cardington - Cople)		square mortuary enclosure	OxA-4553	4530 ± 130	human skeleton from single central pit	3500–3020	3640–2880
		ring-ditch 403	Beta-87190	3410 ± 60	ditch,charcoal from secondary cremation	1860–1620	1880–1520

Table 8.2   Dating evidence (continued)

b: List of diagnostic Neolithic pottery from primary excavated contexts

Site		Monument	Ware	Context
Brampton (Huntingdon Race Course)		rectangular enclosure	Plain Bowl, Grooved Ware	eastern enclosure ditch, placed on base
Cardington-Cople	Site 4	'paperclip' enclosure	Mildenhall (plain)	enclosure ditch
Eynesbury		ring-ditch	Grooved Ware, Mortlake	old land surface
Godmanchester		horned enclosure	Plain	enclosure ditch primary fills
		rectilinear enclosure	Food Urn	pits associated/contempory with enclosure
Haddenham	Site 6	long barrow	Mildenhall	ditch terminal
	Site 10	causewayed enclosure	Mildenhall	ditch segment

tated south-west–north-east (Hall and Coles 1994, 51–4).

Carbon dating has shown the long barrow to be of early-Neolithic date and the causewayed enclosure slightly later (Table 8.2), but the relationship between them may be evidenced by the activities occurring at each. Hodder (1992) argues that patterns of digging and deposition in the causewayed enclosure ditches parallel events at the long barrow. However, the monuments may also refer to each other through a set of oppositions which imply complementary roles within the ceremonial landscape (Last pers comm):

Enclosure:	**Barrow:**
facade to west (facing river)	facade to east (away from river)
interrupted ditch	continuous ditch
activity focused on edges (ditches)	activity focused on centre (mound and mortuary structure)

The sites went out of use during a period of increasing wetness, when the regional water-table was rising (Waller 1994, 179). A date of 3950 ± 95 BP for this phase was gained from directly below marine incursion deposits, and the maximum extent of fen clay in this area occurred during the 2nd millennium BC. In common with Chatteris, the continuing significance of both sites is evident from later activity. Some of the causewayed enclosure ditches were recut in the later Neolithic, associated with pottery of Ebbsfleet and Mortlake type (Evans and Hodder 1985), and dozens of Bronze Age round barrows have been identified around the area. The Haddenham-Over barrowfield alone consists of at least 25 monuments covering a 7km stretch of the eastern flanks of the river Ouse between Over and Hermitage Marina at the Haddenham/Earith boundary (Hall and Coles 1994, 81). Their placement, however, indicates different responses to the two Neolithic sites: while a group of three round barrows clusters around the southernmost of the Foulmire Fen long barrows; further south the barrows are found positioned alongside the river at a

distance of 1km from the causewayed enclosure. One exception to this group, which contained a Collared Urn burial, forms an easterly outlier of the main barrow group and is found much nearer the enclosure (Evans and Hodder 1984).

At the end of the 2nd millennium BC a rectangular enclosure was constructed within the old Neolithic monument (Evans and Hodder 1988), with Iron Age domestic occupation extensively recorded in the vicinity. Later still a Romano-Celtic shrine was built suggesting a renewal, if not continuity, of the area's ceremonial importance. All of these monuments reflect a continuation of the ceremonial landscape largely based upon burials (eg the long barrows and their successors at the Haddenham-Over barrowfield) (Hodder and Evans forthcoming).

Fenstanton

If these complexes occur at regular intervals along the Ouse valley, one would expect an intermediate group between the excavated sites at Haddenham and Godmanchester. Interestingly, there is a possible cursus and ovoid mortuary enclosure north-east of Fenstanton (Cambridgeshire SMR 8826: Wait and Butler 1993). Air photographs show a palimpsest of cropmarks including a linear feature running north-west–south-east about 1km south of the modern Ouse. A group of ring-ditches is visible to the north of this. Whatever the status of this uninvestigated site, it seems to reflect the different character of the monument complexes beyond the Fen edge, which include a number of mortuary enclosures and cursuses.

Godmanchester (McAvoy, Chapter 7)

A unique and massive enclosure at the end of a cursus was identified and scheduled from air photographic evidence at Rectory Farm (Fig 8.5). The site was investigated by English Heritage from 1988–91. It comprised a huge rectilinear 'horned' ditched enclosure approximately 6.3ha in area, with an internal bank and 24 internal posts ranged regularly along the perimeter. The single ditch was 3m wide and 1m deep, delimiting a level area at 10.3m

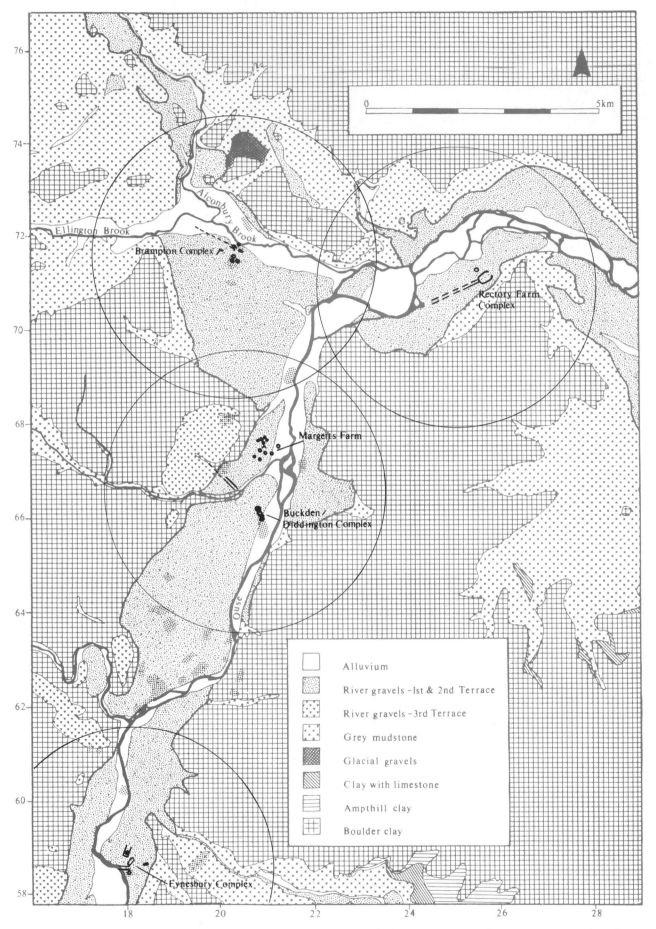

Figure 8.3   Cambridgeshire: Geological background; Neolithic and Bronze Age monuments are shown in red (circles = 6km 'territories' centred on the ceremonial complexes)

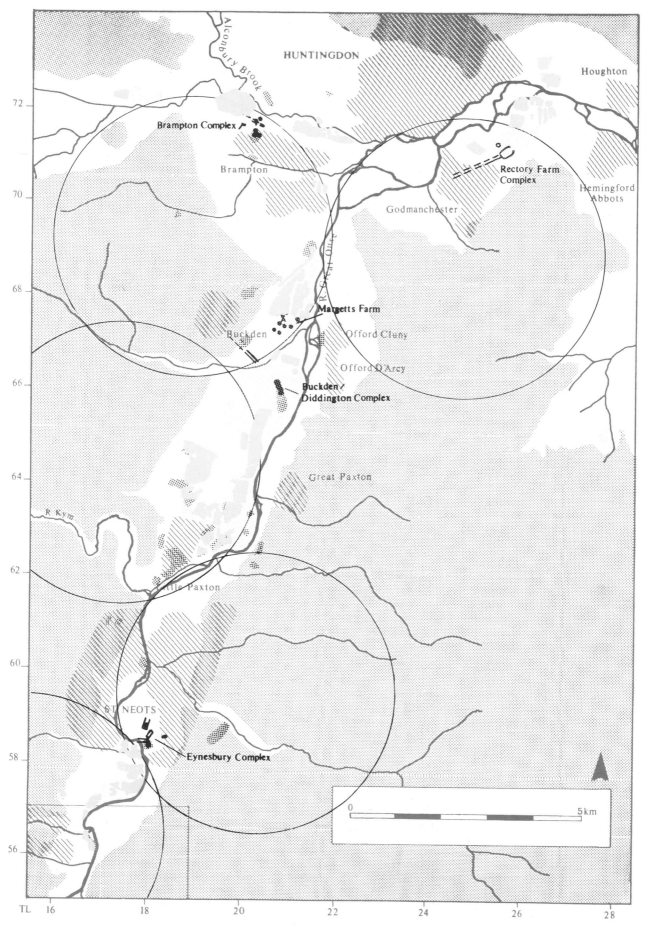

*Figure 8.4   Cambridgeshire: Relief above 20m OD; with quarries (yellow) and archaeology (red)
(circles = 6km 'territories' with ceremonial complexes located at river boundaries)*

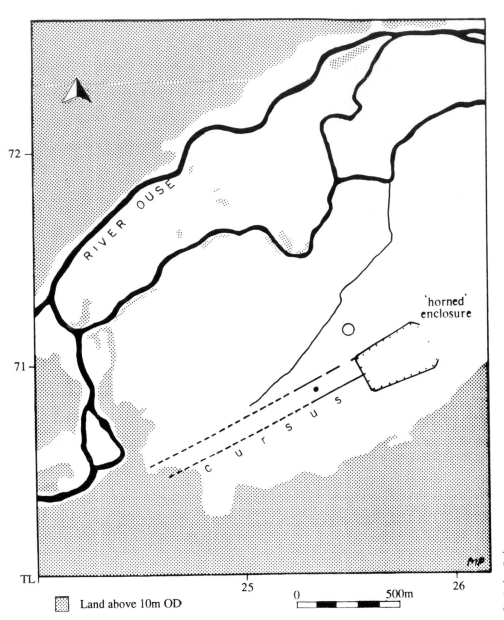

Figure 8.5
Godmanchester: Rectory
Farm ceremonial complex
('horned' enclosure and
cursus; based on McAvoy)

☒ Land above 10m OD

OD (McAvoy interim reports).

Although very few Neolithic artefacts were found, carbon-dating provided dates for the monument broadly contemporary with causewayed enclosures (5050 ± 80 – 4850 ± 80 BP (see Table 8.2) which calibrates to a period in the early-4th millennium BC) and it is clear that this enclosure continued to act as a focus, with later monuments (cursus, single ring-ditches, and small enclosures) respecting the earlier enclosure. A sequence of late-Neolithic and early-Bronze Age pits were found to have been cut into the ditch of the horned enclosure at its juncture with the cursus. Similar pitting was found to the south of the complex in 1997 (Hinman and Kenney 1998), suggesting that this activity was of a widespread nature, but one that would have been tightly focused on attributes of the horned enclosure and post alignments. The Iron Age and Romano-British field systems appear to have avoided the interior of the enclosure and to have respected the earlier monuments.

Brampton

A complex of late-Neolithic and early-Bronze Age ceremonial monuments, spanning several hundreds of years, is situated north-west of Brampton village, on the south side of Alconbury Brook at approximately 12m OD. A mortuary enclosure, cursus, hengiform monuments, and ring-ditches have been identified, the latter consisting of simple and multiple forms, with some having been palisaded (Figs 8.6 and 8.7). Land-use of later generations appears, by its layout and the distribution of finds, to have respected the location of these monuments, thus suggesting some continuity of appreciation of the earlier monuments. It also suggests that the site may have survived as an earthwork for thousands of years.

The complex is similar in form and development to the Octagon Farm complex at Cardington-Cople, Bedfordshire, and to Dorchester-on-Thames (Whittle *et al* 1992).

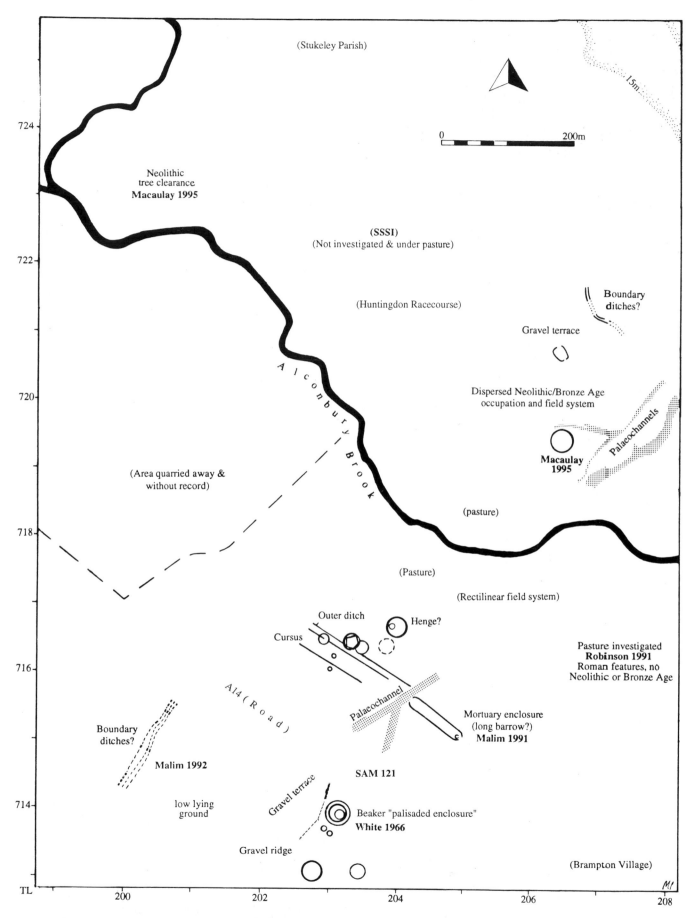

(Stukeley Parish)

0   200m

15m

Neolithic
tree clearance
Macaulay 1995

(SSSI)
(Not investigated & under pasture)

(Huntingdon Racecourse)

Boundary
ditches?

Gravel terrace

Dispersed Neolithic/Bronze Age
occupation and field system

Palaeochannels

724

722

720

718

716

714

A l c o n b u r y   B r o o k

(Area quarried away &
without record)

**Macaulay
1995**

(pasture)

(Pasture)

(Rectilinear field system)

Outer ditch   Henge?
Cursus

Pasture investigated
Robinson 1991
Roman features, no
Neolithic or Bronze Age

A14 (R o a d)

Palaeochannel

Mortuary enclosure
(long barrow?)
Malim 1991

Boundary
ditches?   **Malim 1992**

SAM 121

low lying
ground

Gravel terrace

Beaker "palisaded enclosure"
White 1966

Gravel ridge

(Brampton Village)

TL

200   202   204   206   208

*Figure 8.6   Brampton: plan of ceremonial complex and general area including Scheduled Ancient
Monument Cambridgeshire 121 (cursus, mortuary enclosure, ring-ditches) and Huntingdon Race Course
(The Stukeleys)*

Figure 8.7 Brampton: (a) air photograph of SAM 121 from south (AFY90, July 1962). White's ring-ditches are in the foreground, other features are evident north of the road (but the cursus and mortuary enclosure are not easily visible), and beyond the sinuous course of the Alconbury Brook can be seen Huntingdon Race Course.

Figure 8.7 Brampton: (b) air photograph showing detail of above from north (YW 49, June 1959). The fine lines of the cursus and mortuary enclosure can be seen between the ring-ditches and the road (Cambridge University Collection of Air Photographs: copyright reserved)

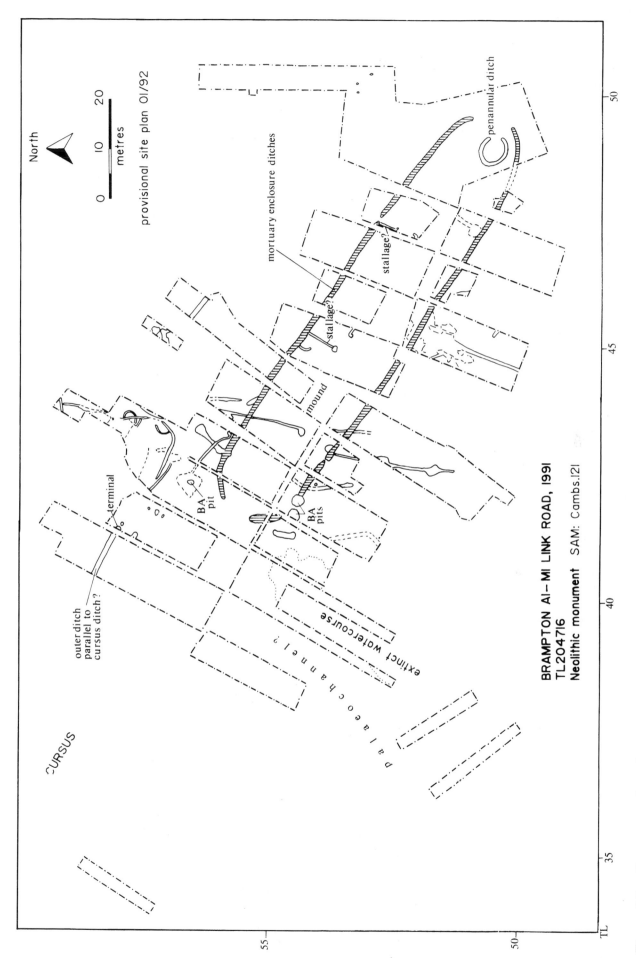

North

provisional site plan 01/92

0   10   20

metres

penannular ditch

mortuary enclosure ditches

stallage?

stallage?

stallage?

mound

terminal

outer ditch
parallel to
cursus ditch?

BA
pit

BA
pits

extinct watercourse

CURSUS

palaeochannel?

BRAMPTON AI–MI LINK ROAD, 1991
TL204716
Neolithic monument   SAM: Cambs.I2I

Figure 8.8   Brampton: plan of mortuary enclosure / long barrow from excavations in 1991

In 1966, D A White undertook excavations on behalf of the Ministry of Public Buildings and Works in an area which had been granted housing permission, and is now known as the Miller Way estate (White 1969). Severely hampered by depth restrictions set by Huntingdonshire County Council, he investigated several ring-ditches situated on a gravel terrace slightly higher than the surrounding low land. He concentrated on a triple ring-ditch complex containing a cinerary urn and an important Beaker burial, which were both found in pits within the phase 1 barrow, and also excavated an Iron Age settlement. No further work in the area occurred until 1990 when an evaluation excavation carried out in advance of the A1–M1 link road demonstrated the survival of a discrete monument, previously unidentified, at the eastern end of a cursus (Malim 1990). Fuller excavations followed in summer 1991 which confirmed the initial interpretation of this monument as a Neolithic mortuary enclosure with a possible long mound. Salvage excavations in the pasture fields immediately to the east of the scheduled area were conducted in the autumn of 1991, revealing an extensive spread of Romano-British features, including possible timber-built structures associated with crop-processing activities.

In 1992, the fields west of White's excavations were evaluated prior to detailed planning permission for extension of the Miller Way housing estate. The expected continuation of the Iron Age enclosure and settlement was found, but also parallel ditches of probable Neolithic date were discovered leading southwards from the main concentration of monuments (Malim and Mitchell 1992). However, it was not until 1993 that occupation evidence for the Neolithic and Bronze Age was found as part of a large scale evaluation programme over Huntingdon Race Course, north of Alconbury Brook (Welsh 1993a). A single pit, with sherds from more than four Beaker pots, was also found to the south of Brampton, between two streams (Welsh 1993b). Further work at Huntingdon Race Course (Stukeley) during 1994–5 has demonstrated the nature of Neolithic and Bronze Age activity north of Alconbury Brook and north of the ceremonial complex at Brampton. The elements include definite evidence for tree clearance (in the form of burnt-out tree boles), occupation (consisting of pits with Neolithic pottery and flints, which have been related to contemporary watercourses and gravel terraces), and other features such as multiple sinuous (boundary?) ditches, a Bronze Age co-axial field system, a large ring-ditch, and a sub-rectangular enclosure (Macauley unpublished). The latter features suggest some extension of the ceremonial landscape from Brampton to the north of Alconbury Brook.

The mortuary enclosure at Brampton (Fig 8.8) is interpreted as such because its form is similar to examples such as the Long Enclosure (Site VIII) at Dorchester-on-Thames (Whittle et al 1992, 148–52), or Belas Knap in Gloucestershire (a more detailed description of the Brampton monument can be found in Malim 1999). Parallel ditches aligned north-west–south-east enclosed an area 90m long by 17–20m wide. The enclosure ditches curved in at both ends leaving openings of 5m and 7m respectively. A shallow horseshoe-shaped penannular ditch was located within the eastern terminals, but no obvious monumental details were noticed at the western end. However, a number of narrow gullies crossed the monument, spreading out from it as antennae ditches, and these appeared to terminate internally as large postholes. These features might represent bays or 'stallage' as seen in other monuments of this type such as Giants Hill, Skendlebury (Phillips 1935), or maybe remnants of an earlier structure in the same location. Soil assessment within the monument suggests the presence of a buried land surface and vestiges of a mound towards the western end.

The main ditches were cut into gravel natural to a depth of 0.3m, and were generally U-shaped in profile and 1m wide at the top. They seem to have been cut in segments, as occasional narrow causeways and abrupt changes in direction were noted. Several pits with evidence of burning in them were found on the west side, two of them cutting the original (middle- or late-Neolithic) main ditch of the monument. Carbon dates from these pits came out at 4140 ± 140 BP Gu-5265 and 3910 ± 70 BP Gu-5264 confirming Bronze Age continuity. A similar pattern of events was noted at Godmanchester, with early-Bronze Age pits cutting into the in-filled ditches of the 'horned' enclosure and east ditch of the cursus. A palaeochannel was found adjacent to the south-west corner of the enclosure at Brampton. Finds were few and, as such, significant in their absence, suggesting deliberate removal or a policy of avoiding the leaving of pottery, flint flakes, or animal bone in the vicinity.

It is clear that microtopography played an important part in the siting of the different elements of the complex where these lay adjacent to wet areas/palaeochannels, as the monuments were on slight rises in the gravel terraces. A sequence of development at the Brampton complex similar to that proposed for Dorchester-on-Thames (Whittle et al 1992) is suggested:

phase I   = mortuary enclosure
phase II   = cursus and boundary ditches
phase III = Beaker burials and palisaded barrow
phase IV   = secondary rings, cinerary urn burial, and other barrows, with possible henge to north of cursus.

Buckden-Diddington

A possible cursus running from Stirtloe (Buckden) towards a complex of ring-ditches within the junction of the Ouse and Diddington Brook has been interpreted from air photographs by Professor St Joseph (Cambridgeshire SMR No 2484C). The air photograph plot shows the feature orientated to-

Figure 8.9   Diddington: plan of cropmarks and air photograph from the north-west (AFW 95, July 1962) of ring-ditches and temple; note the fine lines of the small 'paperclip' enclosure to the south-east of the temple, with a ring-ditch at its northern end (Cambridge University Collection of Air Photographs: copyright reserved)

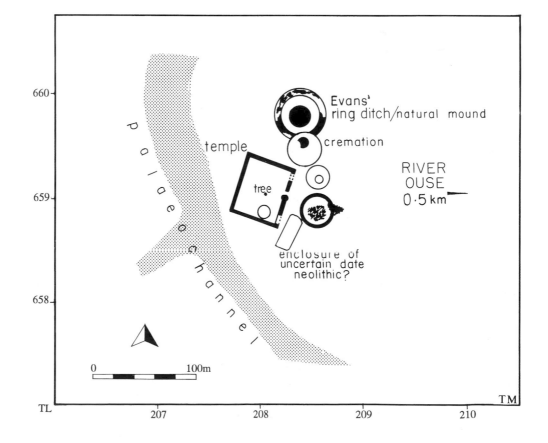

wards a small valley at its (squared-off) north-west-ern end, but shows no definitive eastern end or any continuation of the monument on the south-east side of Diddington Brook, although its alignment leads towards ring-ditches near the Ouse at Diddington. A Romano-Celtic temple enclosure, with circular shrine and a tree-hole central to the enclosure, were found close to the ring-ditches during rescue work in the 1980s, and limited excavation of these features was undertaken in 1985–7 (Fig 8.9). Four main phases of activity were recorded starting with a 2nd-millennium ring-ditch complex (see below), followed by middle-Iron Age, then late-Iron Age/Romano-British occupation, and the Romano-Celtic shrine. To the north a further scatter of ring-ditches can be seen on air photographs near to Margetts Farm, Buckden, and a second Romano-Celtic temple may be visible at NGR TL 202680 (CUCAP ZD 87–8).

Air photographs and cropmark plots (Fig 8.9) would tend to imply that a second ring-ditch, or 'ring-bank', cut across the southern side of the wide ring-ditch in the northernmost barrow (site IV). However, excavation evidence reversed this interpretation and suggested that the south-eastern part of the wide ring-ditch (IV) was laid out with a much reduced ditch, which arched around earlier features (site III). (These relationships are fully discussed in Evans 1997.)

In 1986, excavations of a ring-ditch situated on a 0.3m high natural knoll were undertaken after severe truncation of archaeological features had occurred during topsoil stripping in advance of quarrying. Ring-ditch IV was 42m in diameter and appeared to postdate a 'ring-bank' (site III) which contained a cremation pit and large (totem?) post located externally to its south. It was the northernmost of a line of ring-ditches and it contained a 10m square burnt mound in the centre. The ditch was 4m wide and originally up to 1.25m deep, with a causewayed entranceway to the west. Patterns of sequential cleaning-out and recutting of the ditch have left it with a pronounced U-shaped profile. Very few artefacts relating to the ring-ditch or external cremation were discovered, but a 2nd-millennium date has been assigned to it on its spatial morphology (Evans 1987). Initial results from C14 dates associated with the cremation pit (modern contamination) and the primary fill of the recut ring-ditch terminal (1910 ± 50 BP) were unhelpful. However, a subsequent sample from the cremation gave a result of 3575 ± 40 BP which can best be calibrated within a tight date range of 1840–1780 cal BC (Evans 1997, 19).

It would seem probable in such a landscape that the ring-ditches were not the earliest phenomenon at Diddington; indeed the ceremonial complex may have included the cursus recognized at Stirtloe-Buckden, which would represent an earlier phase. This cursus might not have been isolated, as many cursuses orientated themselves on earlier monuments, such as mortuary enclosures, and later ring-ditches often cluster about cursuses. Further Neolithic monuments may have existed near to the ring-ditches and temple, but the nature of the rescue excavations during gravel extraction was such that the evidence for any remains would have been difficult to identify. However, in addition to the ring ditches and temple a palaeochannel and a small sub-rectangular enclosure are evident on air photographs. The enclosure is distinctly reminiscent of the 'paper-clip' enclosure at Octagon Farm, Cardington-Cople (Bedfordshire SMR 1480.4) and may therefore be of Neolithic date. Its southern side appears to differ in alignment from the later rectilinear field system' also showing on the air photographs, which intersect it at this point. Unfortunately it was not investigated during the excavation, when priority was given to more prominent features such as the temple and ring-ditches.

Eynesbury, St Neots

Two or three short cursuses, a long oval barrow, ring-ditch, pit alignments, and hengiform monuments have been recognized (by Palmer and Cox of Air Photo Services) from air photographs taken between 1959–76 and in more recent years (see Figs 8.10 and 8.11, and also shown in Kemp 1997, 4–5). The distribution pattern of these cursuses is similar to those excavated at West Cotton, Northamptonshire, (Windell 1988; Parker Pearson 1993, 81) and in size and form they are similar to the mortuary enclosures at the Octagon Farm complex, Cardington (Table 8.1). Their co-axial alignments suggest at least two phases, the southernmost one runs west–east and is very short and is intersected at its eastern end by the southernmost of the north–south cursuses. The long barrow might have acted as the original focus of the complex, the northernmost cursus laid out around it with a possible entranceway to the south. This may have channelled movement towards the earlier monument, as is suggested at Brampton and Godmanchester. Pit alignments can be seen to form a rectilinear enclosure spreading out from the south and west of the cursus.

This area of Neolithic activity at Eynesbury lies between the River Ouse and Barford Road, and to the north of the A45(A428) bypass. Construction of roads and commercial buildings, with associated borrow pits, has damaged parts of this complex of monuments, but other parts were investigated in 1983–4, 1993–4, and 1997.

Neolithic pottery and flint tools were found in association with the large ring-ditch and buried soil beneath the barrow. A complex pattern of development, with Mortlake pottery found in association with pits, postholes, and charcoal represents a possible phase of domestic occupation. This was followed by an enclosure of Grooved Ware date, which was later developed into a single-ditched early-Bronze Age barrow with a c 20m diameter mound and a 36m (external) diameter ring-ditch (Herne 1984). The site was ploughed in the Iron Age and

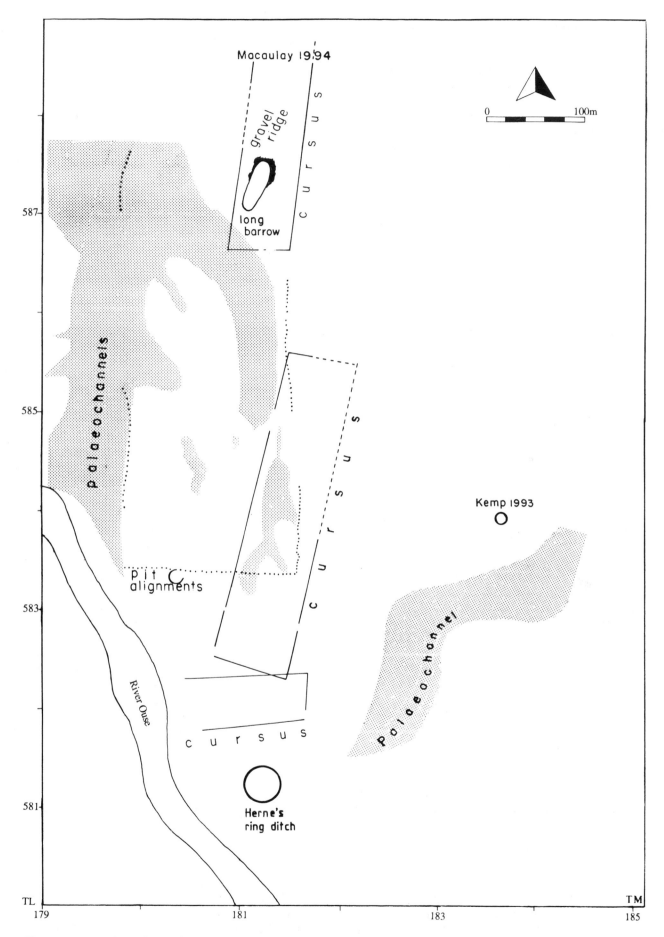

Figure 8.10   Eynesbury, St Neots: plan of ceremonial complex from air photographs (after Cox and Palmer) and excavated evidence (a more detailed plan can be found in Malim 1999)

Figure 8.11 Eynesbury, St Neots: air photograph (ACA 90, July 1960) of complex from south with Herne's ring-ditch in foreground; the very faint lines of the east-west 'cursus', and beyond it the southernmost of the north-south ones, can just be discerned to the north of the ring-ditch (Cambridge University Collection of Air Photographs. copyright reserved)

Roman period, demonstrating that the importance of the monument was lost during the later Bronze Age or early Iron Age. This may have been due to flooding, as alluvial deposits were found in the ring-ditch from a secondary phase of infill.

Further investigations to the north-east of the ring-ditch in 1993 located the remains of two smaller ring-ditches and other features, but little artefactual material with which to date them was recovered (Kemp 1993, 1997). A palaeochannel was also identified running south-westwards, which appears to have come very close to the east side of Herne's ring-ditch. This may represent an extinct course of the Ouse.

In 1994 recording work was undertaken at Ernulf School, where alluvially filled U-shaped ditches were found surviving to a width of 1.1m and a depth of 0.3m. These were correlated with the ditches of the northernmost cursus as plotted from air photographs (Macaulay 1994). A gravel ridge ran north–south between the ditches, and it appeared that this ridge extended into the field to the south where a possible long barrow was situated inside the cursus, utilizing the ridge for the marginal extra height it provided.

A more intense phase of evaluation of the main complex of monuments including the cursuses and pit alignment was conducted in 1997 covering some 41ha. Although no dating information was found for

the earlier features the character of the cursuses were defined with U-shaped ditches of 1.1–1.45m in width and 0.3–0.57m in depth (Kemp 1998). Five pits from the pit alignment were excavated and proved to be variable in form ranging from 1.4–1.55m in diameter and 0.62–0.8m in depth. They only produced a sherd of sandy Iron Age pottery, and a gritty prehistoric sherd, whilst an isolated pit of very different nature (4.6m in diameter by 0.84m deep) produced an assemblage of late-Bronze Age/early-Iron Age pottery, burnt sandstone, and animal bone. It is not sensible to attribute an Iron Age date to the pit alignment on this evidence alone as the sherd could be intrusive. Indeed, an Iron Age gully was found to cut one of the infilled pits, whilst the fact that the pit alignment intersects with one of the ring-ditches would tend to suggest relative contemporaneity between them, and a date earlier in the sequence of monuments would seem reasonable for the initiation of the pit alignment, although later additions may have been made to it over the centuries.

In summary, a group of ceremonial monuments have been identified which were located in a low-lying area close to the present day Ouse, as well as the palaeochannel mentioned above and those seen from air photographs (see Fig 8.10), and which utilized the local microtopography of a gravel ridge to maximize their height. The relationship of the western edges of the pit alignment and middle cursus seem largely to respect extinct watercourses which may have been contemporary with them. A possible phasing could be suggested for the development of this complex as follows:

phase I = long barrow
phase II = northernmost cursus
phase III = pit alignment forming rectilinear enclosure
phase IV = progression of monuments southwards (although middle cursus might be aberrant); ring-ditch final phase

(A more detailed discussion of this complex of monuments at Eynesbury can be found elsewhere – see Malim 1999)

Roxton

The complex at Roxton comprises five univallate ring-ditches (from 30–38m in diameter) and a timber arc-shaped structure with an associated burial, situated on a slight rise of the gravel terrace (Fig 8.12). This is bordered to the south by the River Ouse and to the north by the flood course of the river. The site may well have occupied a piece of land which was virtually an island during wetter periods. Two phases of alignment can be defined, dividing the cemetery into two distinct groups. Carbon dating for primary cremations gives an early-2nd millennium date (with a mean date range of 2270–1850 cal BC: see Table 8.2) whilst dates in the later 2nd millennium were obtained for secondary cremations (mean date range of 1590–1430 cal BC: ApSimon in Taylor and Woodward 1985). The former date would suggest that the charcoal dated came from an earlier context than the Collared Urns in which the cremations were found, but this may be due to the use of timbers from pre-existing structures on site as part of the cremation pyre. The 'ring-barrows' would therefore appear to have been constructed between 2270–1850 and 1590–1430. Significantly, the evidence also indicates that human activity took place on the site prior to the Bronze Age barrow construction, including the building of timber structures possibly of Beaker date. The arc of posts with internal inhumation, structure B7, might have been a precursor to the barrowfield, a series of barrows which the excavators showed to have developed, and become more elaborate, throughout the Bronze Age. As such, this free-standing timber mortuary structure would fit well with the ideas of Neolithic burial practices and later monumental remodelling (eg Aldwincle) as expounded by Kinnes (1976) and Clare (1987).

A complex of barrows was excavated in advance of gravel extraction during the early 1970s (Taylor and Woodward 1985). Subsequent work in the area has found scatters of flint a little distance to the north of the barrow complex, and it has been noted that the ring-ditches were situated on a gravel ridge, as deep alluvium is found immediately to the north-east (Shotliffe, pers comm).

The barrows were ploughed out during the late-Iron Age/Romano-British period when a field system and later habitation was constructed over them. This suggests that the importance attached to the location of the barrow-field was lost during the Iron Age, but there are two pieces of evidence which indicate some continuity. A 1st-century BC 'defensive' ditch was constructed which separates the barrows from encroaching fields, possibly showing respect at this late stage, and in addition, as finds of Venus figurines hint at, the possible existence of a Romano-Celtic shrine (Jenkins in Taylor and Woodward 1983).

Cardington, Cople, Willington

A series of Neolithic and later monuments was identified during the 1970s from air photographs at Octagon Farm, south of the present course of the Ouse, immediately south-east of Bedford. This complex was investigated during 1990–92, in advance of the Bedford southern bypass.

The complex consists of a cursus with five mortuary enclosures, hengiform monuments, and several ring-ditches of single and multiple type (Figs 8.13 and 8.14). A causewayed enclosure is found to the south-east of these monuments. Several of the mortuary enclosures appear to have been situated on islands between palaeochannels of the Ouse or Elstow Brook. Rectilinear cropmarks within two of the ring-ditches (Bedfordshire SMR 1480.12 and 20746) suggest the possible presence of earlier mortuary structures, a stratigraphic relationship confirmed by geophysics and excavation (Clark 1992; Dawson 1996, 44). The early mortuary structure and ring-ditch are on line with the entrance of one of the mortuary enclosures (Bedfordshire SMR 1480.8). Fieldwalking, geophysical survey, and evaluation excavation have identified few additional features to those seen from air photographs, and flint scatters were absent from mortuary enclosures. About 1 km to the south of the complex lies a causewayed enclosure, and to the north of the complex a line of rectilinear enclosures hugging the edge of the gravel terrace has been identified with late-Iron Age and Romano-British dispersed settlement. In addition, three square enclosures, one double-ditched with corners on the cardinal points, are candidates for possible Romano-Celtic temples/funerary enclosures (Bedfordshire SMR 20748, 1480.16, and 1480.17: the latter because of the larger, double-ditched enclosure). The smallest square feature (1480.16) has an entranceway on its eastern side and, when trenched as part of the evaluation work, a posthole was found on the interior, close to the west side opposite the entrance. If the enclosure was for a shrine, this 'posthole' could suggest the presence of a tree or totem. However, it is also remarkably similar to an excavated example of a Neolithic mortuary enclosure at Plantation Quarry, Willington, which was situated 'isolated in the landscape' on a small gravel ridge (Dawson 1996, 11). This contained a central pit with a crouched prone

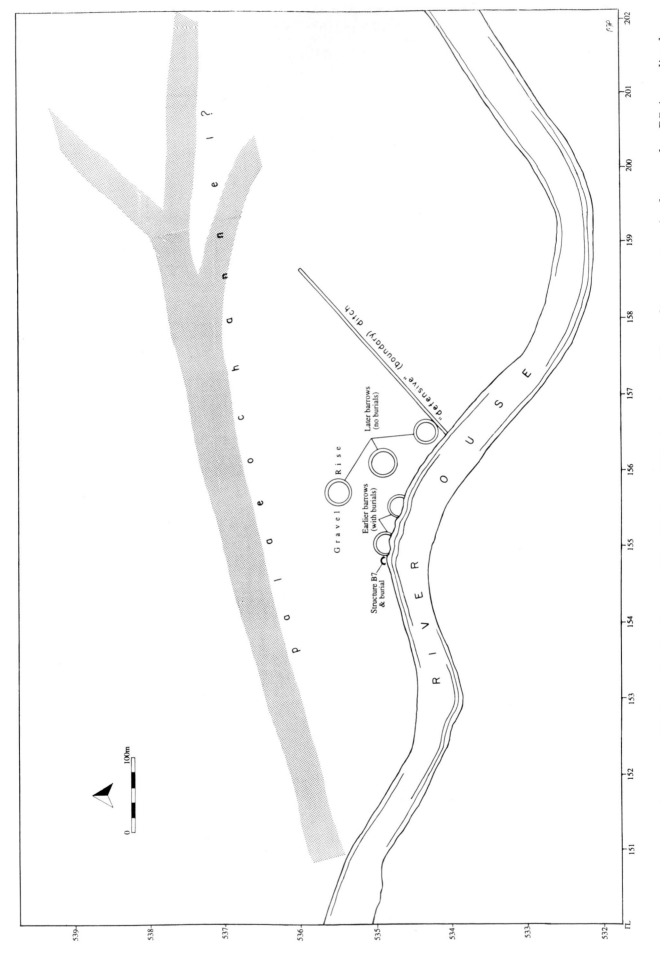

Figure 8.12   Roxton: plan of ring-ditches and other features (after Taylor and Woodward); note the earliest structure in the complex, B7, immediately west of the early barrows

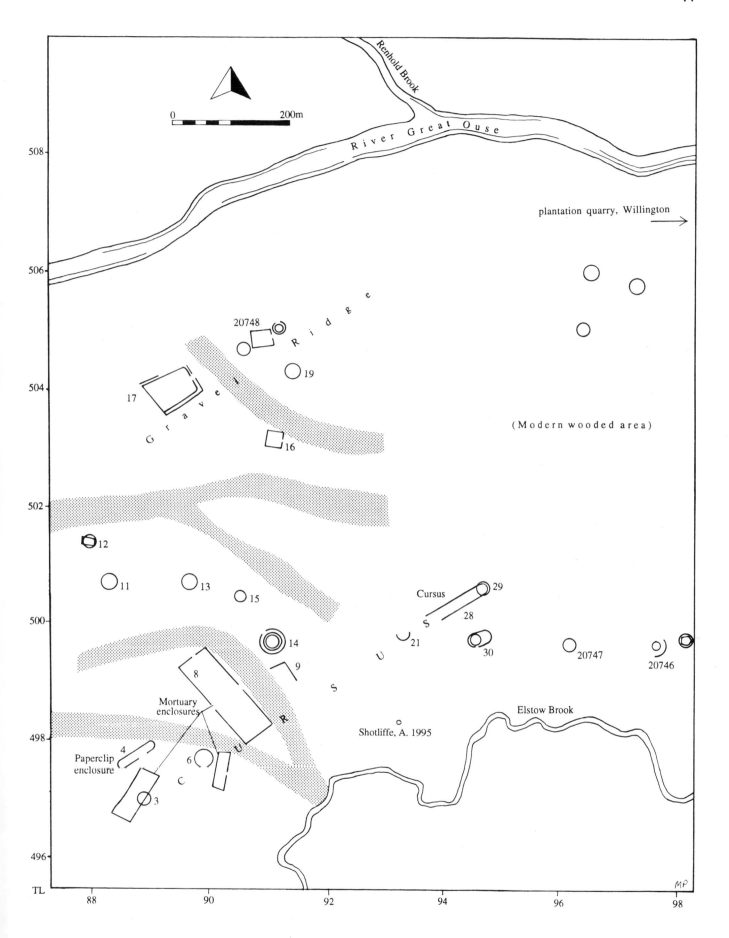

Figure 8.13   Cardington-Cople: plan of Octagon Farm ceremonial complex from cropmarks (numbers 1-30 are all part of Bedfordshire SMR 1480)

Figure 8.14 Cardington-Cople: air photograph (BXU 98, June 1976) of main area of complex from north-east; note the various mortuary enclosures, including the 'paperclip', interspersed with ring-ditches and the dark bands of palaeochannels (Cambridge University Collection of Air Photographs: copyright reserved)

inhumation of a young woman buried with an antler, and dated to 3526–2917 cal BC OxA–4553 (*ibid*, 9). Continuity of this ritual landscape into later times was witnessed at Willington by a ring-ditch containing a secondary cremation dated 1884–1601 cal BC, and by a second ring-ditch which was utilised in the Iron Age for construction of a 'unique' rectangular timber structure appended to its circuit and focused on a pit with pig bones located within the ring-ditch (*ibid*, 16–32); the structure is interpreted as an Iron Age shrine. This relationship between a later rectilinear structure and earlier ring-ditch is mirrored to the south of the cursus at Octagon Farm where a small square palisade cut a ring-ditch associated with a Beaker pit (Shotliffe 1995).

The cursus is apparent on air photographs at its north-east end, at 23.5m OD, but after about 100m it ceases to be visible. Its extent can perhaps be deduced from an alignment of four ring-ditches which start at the eastern end of the cursus (Bedfordshire SMR 1480.29) and end with a ring-ditch situated centrally along the eastern side of a mortuary enclosure (1480.2); this would give it a total length of 700m. This ring-ditch (1480.3) blocks the eastern entranceway to the mortuary enclosure (Clark 1992), mirroring the pattern of the ring-ditch alignment in that a ring-ditch is also constructed over the eastern end of the cursus (1480.29).

In summary, a complex group of structures and ceremonial monuments are evident which, although undated, probably cover a wide time span. They are linked into a series of relict water courses that were probably extant during their construction, indicating the location of this complex in a wet area with individual monuments positioned on slight islands of higher ground.

The sequence would involve construction of mortuary enclosure(s) in the early–middle Neolithic; later alignment of the cursus to meet this at its central eastern side during the later Neolithic; possible henge (1480.14 – triple ring-ditch with entrance to north-west, the same orientation as entrance in enclosure 1480.8); and a Bronze Age continuation of this alignment by the construction of the four barrows. The 'paperclip' enclosure (1480.2) is orientated parallel to the cursus (or *vice versa*). Thus a possible phasing for the development of this complex could be suggested as follows:

phase I = 'paperclip' and other mortuary enclosures
phase II = cursus
phase III = mortuary structures at Bedfordshire SMR 1480.12 and 20746; henge? constructed
phase IV = barrows/ring-ditches built over/around these structures, along the cursus, and in relation to existing mortuary enclosures

Figure 8.15 Biddenham: (a) air photograph (BXV 3, June 1976) of possible oval barrow (centre next to river) and other features from south-west (Cambridge University Collection of Air Photographs: copyright reserved)

Figure 8.15 Biddenham: (b) air photograph (VT 36, June 1959) of southern part of complex from south-west; note the sinuous course of the possible 'cursus', and associated ring-ditches (Cambridge University Collection of Air Photographs: copyright reserved)

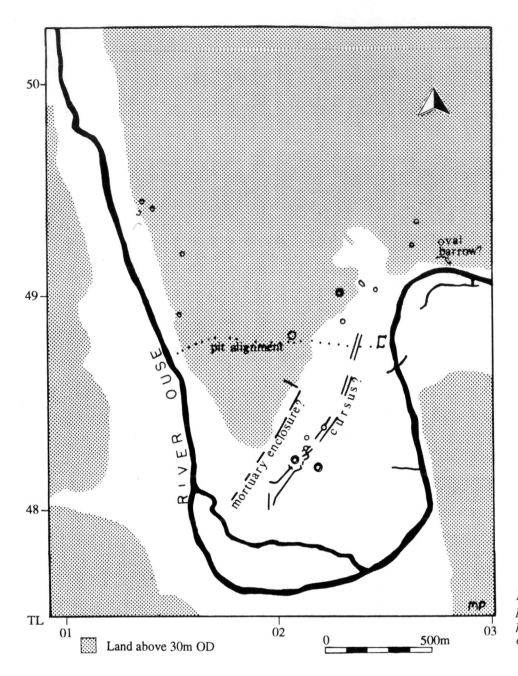

Figure 8.16 Biddenham: plan of cropmark features from possible ceremonial complex

Biddenham

Immediately west of Bedford the Ouse loops to the south, enclosing an area of land which is rich in prehistoric evidence, including a number of interesting cropmarks which appear to form a cursus (Fig 8.15b) and (possibly more than one) mortuary enclosure, an (oval?) long barrow (Fig 8.15a), round barrows, and pit alignments.

In spite of much fieldwork in recent years (Boismier and Clark 1991) the air photographs have unfortunately not been rectified and plotted, possibly due to a dearth of good control points available on the pictures (see Fig 8.15). The pattern of these cropmarks is hard to decipher but from the south northwards it seems to consist of parallel ditches curving from the south-west to the north-east, accompanied by double and single ring-ditches, with a possible mortuary enclosure running parallel on the west side (Fig 8.16). These features are terminated to the north by a west–east pit alignment, beyond which lie isolated ring-ditches, and to the east, near the river Ouse, by an enclosure containing a cropmark not unlike a long (oval) barrow or hengiform monument.

The complex is not respected by Iron Age/Romano-British trackways and settlement in the south, but it is interesting to note that south of the Ouse a Roman road runs up to the river and presumably crossed to the settlement. The 'cursus' to the north may have been located here because the river was also forded at this point in prehistoric times, and the correlation of some cursuses with river crossing points has been noted for the upper Thames Valley (Brereton 1990).

Discussion

The dating and phasing of the monuments described in this paper has been proposed by the analogy of morphological similarity with well-dated examples from other regions, or by direct archaeological evidence (Table 8.2). Functionally these complexes are composed of burial places and communal monuments associated with the ceremonial aspects of social interaction (Table 8.1). From this analysis it is clear that the ceremonial complexes or landscapes along the Ouse indicate a temporal continuity over hundreds, even thousands, of years for discrete areas where specific locations with primary monuments have acted as the focus for secondary construction. Reuse, if not continuity, of some of these areas can be seen occurring in the later Iron Age and Roman period with the setting of temples in the same general area as the earlier ceremonial centres.

There is also a clear spatial continuity along the Ouse, apparent in the similarities to the pattern and development of these ceremonial centres throughout the Neolithic and Bronze Age (Table 8.1 and Figs 8.1–8.4). Microtopography and the existence of palaeochannels played major roles in their exact locations, and orientation may have been of significance. Most monuments between Biddenham and Godmanchester occur on the north and west sides of the present Ouse (Figs 8.2 and 8.4), whilst further downstream they occur on the east. Those complexes that appear not to conform to this generalisation, Cardington-Cople and Eynesbury, may have been influenced by palaeochannels which could represent contemporary courses of the River Ouse, their original locations possibly being to the north and west of the river. If this pattern is true, the only exceptions remaining on the south side are the Cardington causewayed enclosure and the Godmanchester complex, which are both atypical because the first has no parallel amongst other complexes between Cardington and Haddenham, whilst the complex at Rectory Farm (Godmanchester) contains a type of monument that is altogether unique. Such a pattern emphasises the possibility that the Ouse itself, although a thoroughfare in some respects, would also have been a barrier to communication and may have served as a natural boundary to the communities on either side of the river.

Linear features dominate the complexes along the middle Ouse, whilst on the lower river other types of monument are pre-eminent, possibly limited by their location on fen islands. At Haddenham there may be complementary roles between discrete monuments such as the long barrow and causewayed enclosure, and such associations may also exist for other monuments. The large enclosure at Godmanchester is similar in size to causewayed enclosures, but in design and date is perhaps contemporary with long barrows, such as Haddenham and Brampton. For example, the patterns of secondary monuments, later additions, at both God-

manchester and Brampton are very similar, both have cursuses aligned on them containing small internal ring-ditches and larger external ones to the north. Late-Neolithic/early-Bronze Age pitting occurs in the ditch infills of both original monuments. This latter feature is also found in the ditches of the causewayed enclosure at Haddenham, and the interiors of all three monuments contain enclosures which are presumed to be Bronze Age in date (squarish features at Godmanchester and Haddenham, and a penannular ring-ditch at Brampton) further emphasising their general similarity in concept.

The frequency of the complexes, at c 6km apart (Figs 8.1–8.4), suggests a regularity in spatial patterning beyond that determined purely by the topography – the appropriateness of the location was important but the frequency of the complexes was derived from social need. How this hypothesis relates to other issues, such as possible 'tribal' grouping, sedentary as opposed to transhumant populations, and demography, is tantalizing. Green (1974) has previously explored the issue of communal territories and his adroit use of statistical data from ring-ditch clusters along the upper and middle Ouse also addresses questions of economy and population size. The apparent distance between these clusters is approximately 10km ('a diameter of this size fits the territorial models of Higgs and Vita-Finzi': Green 1974, 128–9) but when factors such as modern pasture and built-up areas are taken into consideration Green argues for a distribution closer to 5km. Such a distribution conforms to that proposed for the distribution of ceremonial complexes along the Ouse, a pattern that may continue along one of its tributaries, the Ivel, at Sandy-Biggleswade. The possible extent of the 'territories' to which they relate are plotted as circles of 6km diameter on Figures 8.1–8.4: 8.1 and 8.3 show ceremonial complexes at centre of circle; 8.2 and 8.4 show the complexes on the boundaries, which also coincide with streams/rivers at many points.

Thus, if specific monuments relate to specific communities, and these monuments are situated in marginal land, is it possible that their locations represent territorial boundaries? The placing of barrows and cemeteries at the boundary between one community and another has been remarked on for later cultures such as the Anglo-Saxons. The development of those monuments by additional features over the generations, which resulted in the 'ceremonial complexes' described in this paper, would suggest great longevity for such boundaries. The 'defensive' ditch built during the Iron Age at Roxton, the pit alignments at Biddenham, and the triple ditches and sinuous ditches noted at Brampton all have boundary connotations, whilst the Ouse and its tributaries, so often found in close association with these monuments, would have acted as clear physical barriers (see Figs 8.2 and 8.4).

Green argues that the ring-ditches/barrows along the Ouse were built for a very small number of individuals (perhaps 2% of the population), and that they were probably dynastic mausoleums (Green 1974, 133, 136). On the spatial patterning of the ring-ditch clusters he argues for 18 'territories', of which 1.44 barrows per generation were built in each territory. He suggests that these barrows represent the 'home-base' for communities engaged in transhumant pastoralism, but his statistics argue against the exclusive siting of barrows on marginal areas by rivers or on poor agricultural land. Nonetheless, the case for repetitive monument clusters representing communal territories, at the centre of the home-base or at the boundaries between two communities, is a strong one. A wider territorial (perhaps 'tribal') division of the landscape may be evident in the distribution of larger and infrequent monuments such as causewayed enclosures, as at Cardington and Haddenham. This has been argued elsewhere, for example for Wessex by Renfrew (Joussaume 1988, 32) where he suggests five groupings of long mound types based around five causewayed enclosures (Dorset – Maiden Castle; Cranborne Chase – Hambledon Hill; eastern Salisbury Plain – Whitesheet Hill; western Salisbury Plain – Robin Hood's Ball; and Wiltshire – Windmill Hill/Knap Hill).

Diversity of monument type within the ceremonial complexes displays many variants on common themes: mortuary enclosure, long barrow, oval barrow; henges and hengiform monuments; single and multiple ring-ditches/barrows, but they also display common characteristics (Table 8.1). An example of this common factor is seen in cursuses which definitely lead to specific points of specific monuments (eg Godmanchester, Brampton, and Cardington-Cople); a similar pattern has been noted for some of the Thames valley monuments (Brereton 1990; Whittle *et al* 1992). They form part of the continuing development of the ceremonial complexes, linking together significant features of earlier monuments, and thus taking their alignment from the relationships of those monuments.

Alignments may be the result of astronomical observations, as proposed for Godmanchester, and their construction may reflect standstills, equinoxes or solstices. The general levelness of the land on which the ceremonial complexes described above are sited would prove invaluable for affording views of the celestial events connected with the ceremonies presumably conducted at the monuments. Some of the alignments may have more prosaic origins, with topographical features, such as gravel ridges, hills, or confluences of rivers, providing a focus for the monuments. There is, for instance, similarity in the alignment of the Cardington cursus with that of Godmanchester (Figs 8.5 and 8.14), and perhaps Biddenham and Eynesbury display affinities of alignment (see Figs 8.10 and 8.16). Both Godmanchester and Biddenham appear to run parallel to the line of higher land to their side, and Brampton runs parallel to the line of a low spur to the north of Alconbury Brook. Any northern extension

to the Buckden cursus would take it into a valley of boulder clay between higher land of third terrace gravels (Fig 8.3). Much further research with good ground observation is needed before generalized statements about alignments/orientations can be successfully made.

Field (1974) noticed a lessening in the number of barrows/ring-ditches the further up-country the river travels. A comparable lessening of other ceremonial monuments in the upper Ouse can also be noted (Buckinghamshire SMR has no Neolithic sites listed along the Ouse), and this may be attributable to a narrower river valley as the river nears its origins. Figures 8.1–8.4 show that ceremonial complexes and flint scatters conform very closely to the gravel terraces and alluviated valley floor of the Ouse and are absent from the higher land all around. The widest areas of alluviated valley bottom are those chosen for construction of the ceremonial complexes, and these areas are usually coincident with braiding and confluences of rivers.

The lack of evidence suggests that the heavy clay uplands around the Ouse valley were little used during the Neolithic and Bronze Ages for settlement or for ceremonial purposes (Figs 8.1–8.4); unless, perhaps, the types of activity undertaken in those regions were of a kind that left little physical trace. The heavy clays would have been difficult to cultivate with an ard, and water sources are scarce on the plateau to either side of the Ouse. The traditional view that these areas would have remained largely wooded until Saxon or medieval times seems extremely likely (Fox 1923). Stray finds which might indicate other activities such as woodland management or the existence of routeways seem to be rare, although access to the resources of the upland would have been readily available to communities living in the river valley. The latter were never more than 2–3km distance from the edge of the higher claylands.

Where are the earlier monuments? The relative absence of causewayed camps is remarkable (Cardington and Haddenham being the only two confirmed along the Ouse). It might be argued that the date and function of the massive horned enclosure at Rectory Farm, Godmanchester, was similar to that of causewayed enclosures, but possibly their relative absence from the record may be due to lack of detection. If placed in very wet locations close to rivers, alluvial deposition may have so hidden or obscured their appearance that they have so far not been recognized from air photographs. Alternatively, the location of causewayed enclosures may have occurred on the high ground, in the wooded periphery of the river valley as with some of the Wiltshire monuments (Whittle *et al* 1993), and perhaps the heavy clays of these areas have precluded their identification from aerial survey and therefore the identification of sites revealed by these methods might be skewed. However, their potential role in regard to wider territories extend beyond the limitations of river valleys. Mercer (1990) shows a fair-

Table 8.3 List of prehistoric sites between Bedford and Huntingdon/St Ives (*see Figs 8.1 – 8.4*) *(continued over next two pages)*

Bedfordshire

SMR	Parish	NGR	Evidence	Prehistoric	Later	Publication
1965	Bedford (Bury Farm, Goldington)	TL 078 504	Excavation	1 – Neo/BA henge, cremations, 2 – field system		E Baker & R Mustoe 1988 Goldington Bury Farm, Bedford, Bedfordshire, S Midlands Archaeol, 18, 7–11
						R Mustoe 1988 Salvage excavation of a Neolithic and Bronze Age ritual site at Goldington, Bedford: a preliminary report, Beds Archaeol J, 18, 1–5
302	Cardington (Mill Farm)	TL 081 489	Excavation	BA/IA ring-ditches, drainage		D Johnston 1959 Excavations at Newnham and Mill Farm, Beds Archaeologist, 2, 16–19
						R Clark 1989 Excavations at Mill Farm, Beds. Unpub'd interim report
1797	Felmersham (Radwell Quarry)	TL 011 575	Excavation (1972–5, 1983)	BA/IA ring-ditch, enclosure, hut circle	Ro settlement	D Hall 1973 Rescue excavations at Radwell gravel pits, Beds Archaeol J, 8, 67–91
						D Hall & P Woodward 1977 Radwell excavations, 1974–75: the Bronze Age ring ditches, Beds Archaeol J, 12, 1–16
						A Pinder 1986 A ring ditch at Radwell Quarry, Beds Archaeol J, 17, 10–14
1786	Felmersham (Moorend)	TL 0106 5880	Excavation (1974–5)	BA/IA ring-ditch		Hall & Woodward op cit
2419	Harrold	SP 941 555	Cropmarks	BA/IA ring-ditches, cinerary urns, settlement		B Eagles & V Evison 1970 Excavations at Harrold, Beds, 1951–53, Beds Archaeol J, 5, 17–55
						Field 1974, 72 (note)
543	Odell	SP 956 568	Excavation (1974–8)	BA ring-ditch, IA settlement	Ro/AS settlement, wells	B Dix 1979 Odell: a river valley farm, Curr Archaeol, 6 (66), 215–18
						B Dix 1980 Excavations at Harrold Pit, Odell, 1974–78: a preliminary report, Beds Archaeol J, 14, 15–18
						Field 1974, 66 (note)
617	Roxton	TL 156 535	Excavation (1972–4)	BA ring-ditch.	Ro settlement, temple(?)	Taylor & Woodward 1985
14455	Willington	TL 1072 5056	Excavation (1984)	BA ring-ditch.		A Pinder 1986 Excavations at Willington 1984: 1 – the Bronze Age, Beds Archaeol J, 17, 15–21
		TL 101 504	Excavation (1988–91)	Neo mortuary encl, ring-ditches, burials	IA temple	Dawson 1996

Table 8.3 *(continued)*

Cambridgeshire

SMR	Parish	NGR	Evidence	Prehistoric	Later	Publication
02117	Brampton (SAM 121)	TL 204 716	Excavation (1966 – 2117 & a; 1990 – 1 – c) Cropmark (b & 02578)	BA barrow, ring-ditches; 02117a – IA settlement; b – uncal date ring-ditch, enclosure; c – Neo enclosure 02578 – uncal date ring-ditch, enclosure	02117 d – Ro field ditches, pot e – med f – post-med	White 1969; Malim 1990, 1999 CUCAP APs: 9/7/1962 – AFY 90–93; 11/06/1959 – YD 69–74; 19/6/1962 – AFO 4–9; 23/6/1959 – YW 46–51; 30/6/1970 – BCS 69–73; 2/7/1966 – AOT 53–5; 21/6/1967 – ARZ 64; 11/7/1963 – AHN 77, 78
10704	Brampton (Thrapston Road)	TL 201 715	Excavation (1992)	IA roundhouse, enclosure; 10704a – Neo ditch		Malim & Mitchell 1992
11176	Brampton (Park Road)	TL 2025 7085	Excavation (1993)	BA pot, bone in pit		Welsh 1993b
00861	Buckden	TL 202 680 OS No 13 NW	Excavation (1963–4)	00861a – Neo pot in gravel pit; b – IA pits with pottery and bone weights; d – prehist flint flakes; e – uncal date rectilinear enclosure complex, ditches, trackway, field boundary	Ro settlement, pits, ditches; pottery, whetstone, window glass; 00861c – AS settlement, post-holes, sunken houses.	C Tebbutt 1965 Neolithic pottery from Buckden, Huntingdonshire, Prcc Cambridge Antiq Soc, 58, 141–2. P Addyman 1961 MPBW Excs Ann Rep, 10 (note) C Tebbutt 1963, 1964 CBA Grp 7, Bull Arch Discoveries 10, 11 (notes) D Wilson & D Hurst 1962 Med Archaeol, 6, 307 (note) CUCAP APs: 30/6/1959 – ZD 87–8; 13/7/1957 – VR 44; 23/6/1959 – YW 55–7; 15/6/1960 – V-D 40–1; V-E 28–31, 75, 77
02484	Buckden	TL 2007 6687 OS No 09 NW	Excavation (1941 – a), Cropmark (b & c)	02484a – BA flints; b (TL 205 669) – enclosure system; c (TL 201 666) – rectilinear enclosure, trackway (cursus?), ring ditch; b & c – uncal date	Ro settlement, ditches; pottery, millstone, spear.	G Clayton 1947 Pottery, etc. from Buckden, Hunts, Trans Camb and Hunt Archaeol Soc, 6, 257–9 OS Corr 6ins 1949 (C Tebbutt); 1958 CUCAP APs: 15/6/1960 – V-D 37-9; b – 22/6/1976 – BXX 46A–49; c – also NMR APs: TL 2066/2/8, 9
02531	Buckden	TL 215 687 TL 216 689 OS No 24 NW	Excavation	Meso, Neo/BA worked flints: a – Meso flints: 1 core, 11 blades & flakes, 43 microliths		J Wymer 1977 A Gazetteer of Mesolithic Sites in England and Wales. CBA Res Rep 20, 134 (note)
02532	Buckden	TL 208 689 TL 210 690 OS No.07 NW	Excavation	Pal mammal bones in gravel pits, flint flakes, blades,		D Roe 1968 A Gazetteer of British Lower and Middle Palaeolithic Sites. CBA Res Reps 8, 129 (note) OS Corr 6ins 1951 (Tebbutt); 1953 (J Garrood)

No.	Place	Grid reference	Investigation	Description	Period / finds	References
	(… Farm)		Excavation (1985)	ditches (…), linear trackway, field boundary		Field 1974, 69 (note)
11660	Diddington		Excavation (1985–7, 1992–8)	IA settlement; b – BA ring-ditch	a – Ro shrine	CUCAP APs: 13/7/1957 – VR 8–10, 12–14; 24/6/1959 – YX 80; 30/6/1959 – YX 20, 83; 22/6/1972 – BIX 28–30; 5/7/1971 – BJE 93, 94
00381	Eynesbury/ St Neots	TL 202 651– 209 659	Cropmark, Excavation (1994)	linear ditches, barrow		Evans 1997 ; Jones and Ferris 1994 *Proc Cambridge Antiq Soc*, **82**, 55–66; Jones 1995 *Proc Cambridge Antiq Soc*, **83**, 7–22; Jones 1998 *Proc Cambridge Antiq Soc*, **86**, 5–12
06150	Eynesbury (Barford Rd)	TL181 587	Excavation (1993)	Neo cursus, ring-ditch.		Macaulay 1994; CUCAP APs: ADO 53
10198	Eynesbury	TL 184 583	Excavation (1983–4)	BA ring-ditch, flint, pottery; 10198a – Meso; b – Neo; c – IA	10198d – Ro; e – AS; f – med; g – post-med	Kemp 1993, 1997, 1998; Malim 1992; CUCAP AP's: YK 9–11; Herne 1984 (unpublished)
00589	Little Paxton	TL181 584	Excavation (1967)	Neo post-holes, hut, Peterborough ware sherds, worked flints	Ro settlement, ditches; pottery, animal bones, coin, millstone, bracelet, key	G Rudd 1968 A Neolithic hut and features at Little Paxton, Hunts, Proc Cambridge Antiq Soc, 61, 9–13
00633	Little Paxton	TL 183 627 OS No 35 SE	Excavation (1958), finds scatter	a – IA settlement	Ro settlement	E Greenfield 1969 The Romano-British settlement at Little Paxton, Hunts, Proc Cambridge Antiq Soc, 62, 35–57; CUCAP APs: LZ 34
00663	Little Paxton	TL 195 625 OS No 17 SE	Excavation (1944–6)	a – BA flints, ring-ditch; b – IA pits, ditches	c – Ro pits, ditches, well, hearth; animal bones, timber, quern. sandal	C Tebbutt 1969 Gravel pit finds in the neighbourhood of St Neots, Hunts, Proc Cambridge Antiq Soc, 62, 55–7
02486	Little Paxton	TL 198 632	Excavation	BA pottery, flint implements	02486a – Ro pottery	Clayton 1947, op cit; OS Corr 6ins (C F Tebbutt)
00524	Offord Darcy	TL 218 668	Excavation	BA(?) ritual pit with butchered cattle, horse bones; scraper		G Rudd 1969 CBA Grp 7, Bull Arch Discoveries 16 (note)
00568	St Neots (Crosshall, Eaton Ford)	TL 1727 6099 OS No 79 SE	Excavation	Pal flint implements, flakes, scraper, animal bones		C Tebbutt 1927 Palaeolithic industries from the Great Ouse gravels at and near St Neots, Proc Prehist Soc E Anglia, 5 (2), 166–73
08405	St Neots	TL 186 602	Excavation	Meso flint working site; 08045a – Neo occupation; b – BA barrow	08405c – AS burials	A Taylor 1985 Report of the County Archaeologist, *Cambs Archaol Comm Ann Rep 1984–85*, 4–6 (note)
11134, 11740	St Neots	TL 180 600	Excavation (1993–5)	Neo/BA pits, ditches, enclosure, ring-ditch		Welsh 1993a, Macaulay archive
11135	Stukeley (Huntingdon Racecourse)	TL 206 720	Excavation (1993)	Neo flint, axe		Welsh 1993a, Macaulay archive
	Stukeley (Huntingdon Racecourse)	TL 200 723				

ly even distribution across the east Midlands and
East Anglia in contrast to the Thames, and the only
other known causewayed enclosures in Bedfordshire and Cambridgeshire are Maiden Bower,
Etton/Maxey, Great Wilbraham, and possibly Mel-
bourn. At Upton a large rectilinear enclosure near
Ermine Street has been shown to be Neolithic in
date (Challands 1991).

Where is the evidence for later prehistoric ceremony? The middle and lower Ouse appears to have
no record of river finds of skulls or prestige metal
artefacts, as have been found in rivers such as the
Thames, Trent, or Witham. Prehistoric structures
such as those identified at Fiskerton, Lincolnshire,
by N Field (Hillam 1985) or Fengate/Flag Fen, Cambridgeshire (Malim 1989; Pryor 1992), are absent
from the archaeological record. In contrast, Iron Age
and Romano-British ceremonial sites are to be
found, such as the Romano-Celtic shrines/temple
enclosures which appear regularly at the ceremonial sites of earlier periods (eg Haddenham, Diddington, Roxton (?), and Cardington-Cople/Willington).
This is not surprising, as the location of Gallic
shrines (or in Britain altars to Condatis) has been
noted to occur at the confluences of streams and
rivers (Jenkins in Taylor and Woodward 1983) and
therefore does not argue for continuity but simply
reuse of the same locations, perhaps for similar reasons as their predecessors.

In conclusion, it can be seen that major monuments of early date exist in profusion along the
Ouse, together with evidence for their associated
environmental and settlement context, but that
there has been a massive attrition of the archaeological record since the war through development
and mineral extraction. This has had a severe impact on the fragile preservation of important evidence relating to the prehistoric period. Immediate
action is needed to address the problems that have
been left to us and to prevent further large-scale destruction. However, it might already be too late to
reverse planning decisions for more mineral extraction, in which case recording excavations will need
to operate within well defined research strategies
and overall frameworks to optimise the surviving
resource and target work appropriately. Apart from
the lacunae discussed above the paucity of well documented settlement evidence is one area that must
be explored and linked to the existing pattern of ceremonial centres, and the distribution and relationship of the Bronze Age monuments to their predecessors must be more extensively studied. Such research will help to elucidate the nature and extent
of the earlier prehistoric communities of this region.
Full publication of past and future excavations of
these monuments will allow us to see discrete detailed sequences and examine how their landscapes
developed, which would then facilitate further synthesis and a broader discussion. For too long the archaeological community has allowed the Ouse to be
a backwater for prehistoric research, and thus the
archaeological resource of the area has been greatly
underrated (see Table 8.3).

Acknowledgements

Thanks are given to all those who have helped in
preparing the background data for this paper, most
notably the SMR officers of Bedfordshire and Cambridgeshire, Stephen Coleman and Nesta Rooke.
Melodie Paice has executed the majority of the illustrations which have presented the raw data in a
clear and aesthetic form, and many thanks are
owed to her and Caroline Malim for their patience
in dealing with the many updates given to the maps
and plans as the work progressed. Mike Dawson
has helped throughout by his role as conference fa-
cilitator, and Nick Shepherd and Royston Clark
have provided invaluable information about Octagon Farm. Andy Herne has made the results of his
work at Eynesbury freely available. Adrian Axinte,
Rose Desmond, and Jen Goode assisted in compiling
and drafting disparate information, Erika
Guttmann in editing a first text, Jonathan Last in
commenting on the final text and suggesting fresh
ideas, and many other colleagues within the Archaeological Field Unit have contributed by their
fieldwork and comment. I am grateful to Drew
Shotliffe, Rog Palmer, and Chris Cox, all of whom
have provided useful extra information on a number of the sites mentioned in the text, and to Ian
Hodder who kindly provided details of Haddenham
C14 dates. Thanks also go to Peter Marshall and
Alex Bayliss, of English Heritage, for their help in
supplying the calibrated radiocarbon dates.

Bibliography

Bedfordshire Sites and Monuments Record
Boismier, W, & Clark, R, 1991 Biddenham Loop
    Archaeological evaluation: stage 1 fieldwalking
    and earthwork survey, Bedfordshire County
    Archaeology Service Rep. Unpublished
Brereton, S, 1990 *Cursuses in the Upper Thames
    Valley*, In-Service project No 1. Oxford
    Archaeological Unit
Bronk Ramsey, C, 1995 Radiocarbon Calibration
    and Analysis of Stratigraphy: The OxCal
    Program, *Radiocarbon*, **37**, 425–30
Buckinghamshire Sites and Monuments Record
Cambridgeshire Sites and Monuments Record
Challands, A, 1991, in G J Wainwright (ed) *English
    Heritage Annual Review 1990-911*, 25–6
Clare, T, 1987 Towards a reappraisal of henge mon-
    uments: origins, evolution and hierarchies, *Proc
    Prehist Soc*, **53**, 457–77
Clark, R, 1992 Geophysical survey in a ceremonial
    landscape, in A Challands, Magnetic susceptibili-
    ty surveys on Fenland archaeological sites.
    Unpublished conference proceedings:
    Environmental and Industrial Geophysics Group
    of the Joint Association for Geophysics, 15
    December 1994, Burlington House
Dawson, M, 1996 Plantation Quarry, Willington:
    Excavations 1988–91, *Bedfordshire Archaeol*, **22**,
    2–49
Evans, C, 1987 The excavation of a major ring-ditch

complex at Diddington, nr Huntingdon. Unpublished archive report

Evans, C, 1997 A Ring-ditch Complex at Diddington, near Huntingdon, *Proc Cambridge Antiq Soc*, **85**, 11–26

Evans, C, & Hodder, I, 1984 Excavations at Haddenham, *Fenland Research*, **1**, 32–5

Evans, C, & Hodder, I, 1985 The Haddenham project, *Fenland Research*, **2**, 18–23

Evans, C, & Hodder, I, 1987 Between the two worlds: archaeological investigations in the Haddenham Level, in J M Coles & A J Lawson (eds), *European Wetlands in Prehistory*. Oxford: Clarendon, 180–91

Evans, C, & Hodder, I, 1988 The Haddenham project – 1987: the Upper Delphs, *Fenland Research*, **5**, 7–14

Field, K, 1974 Ring-Ditches of the Upper and Middle Great Ouse Valley, *Archaeol J*, **131**, 58–74

Fox, C, 1923 *The Archaeology of the Cambridge Region*. Cambridge: Cambridge University Press

Green, H S, 1974 Early Bronze Age burial, territory and population in Milton Keynes, Buckinghamshire, and the Great Ouse Valley, *Archaeol J*, **131**, 75–139

Hall, D, 1992 *The Fenland Project, Number 6: the south-western Cambridgeshire Fenlands*, East Anglian Archaeol **56**. Cambridge: University of Cambridge, Cambridgeshire Archaeological Committee

Hall, D, & Coles, J, 1994 *Fenland Survey: an essay in landscape persistence*, NS report 1. London: English Heritage

Herne, A, 1984 Eynesbury excavation. Unpublished summary

Hillam, J, 1985 Recent tree-ring work in Sheffield, *Current Archaeol*, **96**, 21–3

Hinman, M, & Kenney, S, 1998 *Prehistoric and Romano-British Remains on Land Adjacent to Cow Lane, Godmanchester*, Cambridgeshire County Council Archaeological Report 150

Hodder, I, 1992 The Haddenham causewayed enclosure – a hermeneutic circle, in I Hodder, *Theory and Practice in Archaeology*. London: Routledge

Hodder, I, & Evans, C, forthcoming *The Haddenham Project: The Emergence of a Fenland Landscape*, MacDonald Institute of Archaeology Research Series

Jackson, R, & Potter, T, 1996 *Excavations at Stonea Cambridgeshire 1980–85*. London: British Museum Press

Joussaume, R, 1988 *Dolmens for the Dead*. London: Batsford

Kemp, S, 1993 *Prehistoric and Roman Archaeology at Barford Road, Eynesbury*, Cambridgeshire County Council Archaeological Report 90

Kemp, S, 1997 *Prehistoric, Roman and Medieval Landuse at Barford Road, Eynesbury, St Neots*, Cambridgeshire County Council Archaeological Report 134

Kemp, S, 1998 *Neolithic and Bronze Age Ritual Landscape at Barford Road, Eynesbury, St Neots*, Cambridgeshire County Council Archaeological Report 148

Kinnes, I, 1976 Monumental function in British Neolithic burial practices, *World Archaeol*, **7**, 16–29

Macaulay, S P, 1994 *Archaeological Investigations on a Proposed Synthetic Pitch at Ernulf School, Eynesbury*, Cambridgeshire County Council Archaeological Report A41

Macauley, S P, nd Huntingdon Racecourse: Draft archive report, unpublished

Malim, T, 1989 A Prehistoric Timber Avenue at Fengate, Peterborough, *Fenland Research*, **6**, 5–10

Malim, T, 1990 *Brampton 1990: A1–M1 Link Road*, Cambridgeshire County Council Archaeological Report 16

Malim, T, & Mitchell, D, 1992 *Neolithic Ditches and Iron Age Settlement at Thrapston Road, Brampton*, Cambridgeshire County Council Archaeological Report 81

Malim, T, 1999 Cursuses and related Monuments of the Cambridgeshire Ouse, in A Barclay & J Harding *Pathways and Ceremonies: The Cursus Monuments of Britain and Ireland*, Neolithic Studies Group Seminar Papers **4**. Oxford: Oxbow

McAvoy, F, nd Rectory Farm Godmanchester: assessment report and updated project design. Unpublished internal English Heritage report

Mercer, R J, 1990 *Causewayed Enclosures*. London: Shire Publications

Mook, W G, 1986 Business meeting: Recommendations/Resolutions adopted by the Twelfth International Radiocarbon Conference, *Radiocarbon*, **28**, 799

Parker Pearson, M, 1993 *Bronze Age Britain*. London: English Heritage/Batsford

Phillips, C W, 1935 The excavation of the Giants' Hills Long Barrow, Skendlebury, Lincolnshire, *Archaeologia*, **85**, 37–106

Potter, T W, 1976 Excavations at Stonea, Cambs, *Proc Cambridge Antiq Soc*, **66**, 23–54

Pryor, F, 1992 Current research at Flag Fen: The Fengate/Northey landscape, *Antiquity*, **66**(251), 518–31

Seale, R S, 1979 Ancient Courses of the Great and Little Ouse in Fenland, *Proc Cambridge Antiq Soc*, **69**, 1–19

Shand, P, & Hodder, I, 1987 Haddenham Project – the long barrow, *Fenland Research*, **4**, 36–8

Shotliffe, A, 1995 *Archaeological Evaluation at Octagon Farm, Bedford*, Bedfordshire County Archaeology Service report 1995/39

Stuiver, M, & Reimer, P J, 1986 A computer program for radiocarbon age calibration, *Radiocarbon*, **28**, 1022–30

Stuiver, M, Reimer, P J, Bard, E, Beck, J W, Burr, G S, Hughen, K A, Kromer, B, McCormac, G, van der Plicht, J, & Spurk, M, 1998 INTCAL98 Radiocarbon age calibration, 24,000–0 cal BP, *Radiocarbon*, **40**, 1041–83

Taylor, A, & Woodward, P, 1983 Excavations at

Roxton, Bedfordshire, 1972-4; the post-Bronze Age settlement, *Bedfordshire Archaeol*, **16**, 7–28

Taylor, A, & Woodward, P, 1985 A Bronze Age barrow cemetery, and associated settlement at Roxton, Bedfordshire, *Archaeol J*, **142**, 73–149

Wait, G, & Butler, R, 1993 An earlier Neolithic settlement near Fen Drayton, Cambridgeshire, *Fenland Research*, **8**, 51–2

Waller, M, 1994 *The Fenland Project No 9: Flandrian Environmental Change in Fenland*, East Anglian Archaeology **70**. Cambridge: University of Cambridge, Cambridgeshire Archaeological Committee

Welsh, K, 1993a *An archaeological assessment at Huntingdon Race Course (Areas A and B)*, Cambridgeshire County Council Archaeological Report 86

Welsh, K, 1993b *A Beaker pit at Park Road, Brampton*, Cambridgeshire County Council Archaeological Report A21

White, D A, 1969 Excavations at Brampton, Huntingdonshire, 1966, *Proc Cambridge Antiq Soc*, **62**, 1–20

Whittle, A, Atkinson, R J C, Chambers, C, & Thomas, N, 1992 Excavations in the Neolithic and Bronze Age complex at Dorchester-on-Thames, Oxfordshire, 1947–1952 and 1981, *Proc Prehist Soc*, **58**, 143–201

Whittle, A, Rouse, A J, & Evans, J G, 1993 A Neolithic downland monument in its environment: excavations at the Easton Down Long Barrow, Bishops Cannings, north Wiltshire, *Proc Prehist Soc*, **59**, 197–240

Windell, D, 1988 West Cotton, *South Midlands Archaeol*, **18**, 51–60

9 A Fenland delta: Later prehistoric land-use in the lower Ouse reaches *by Christopher Evans and Mark Knight*

Life in the delta – small terrace-islands, backwaters, and pools. Sluggishly meandering and braided, before its canalisation the river would have been difficult to tie down or identify as a 'constant'. A landscape in flux, the Ouse would have had many roles – an environmental niche, landscape corridor and potentially a territorial divide – variously a *zone*, *path*, and *border*.

Since 1990 the Cambridge Archaeological Unit (CAU) of the University of Cambridge has been working within ARC quarries in the study of early prehistoric landscapes along the lower reaches of the Great Ouse. Following excavations at Fen Drayton and St Ives, investigations are currently focused downstream, closer to its junction with the fen-edge, at Barleycroft Farm and now directly across the river at Over (Fig 9.1). At Barleycroft, following earlier watching-brief cover, the area of formal investigation extends over 85ha; at Over, some 550ha in total. If all proceeds accordingly, this is a case of archaeology and landscape study coming full circle – progressing from work at Haddenham in the 1980s, to upstream on the west bank of the Ouse at Barleycroft (three years) and, crossing the river, for 25 years at Over; eventually returning to the Old West riverside where the researches began. The scale of the ARC workings permits in-depth investigation on a scale unimaginable if restricted to public resources, and the exposure of 'deep' fen/floodplain landscape they allow may never occur again. From the outset, they have been approached within a broad research framework and, in effect, as a *wet-landscape laboratory* – an arena for experimental techniques and new approaches – and an opportunity to explore broad landscape usage and not just 'sites'.

The area is renowned for its monuments, primarily the Haddenham causewayed enclosure on the

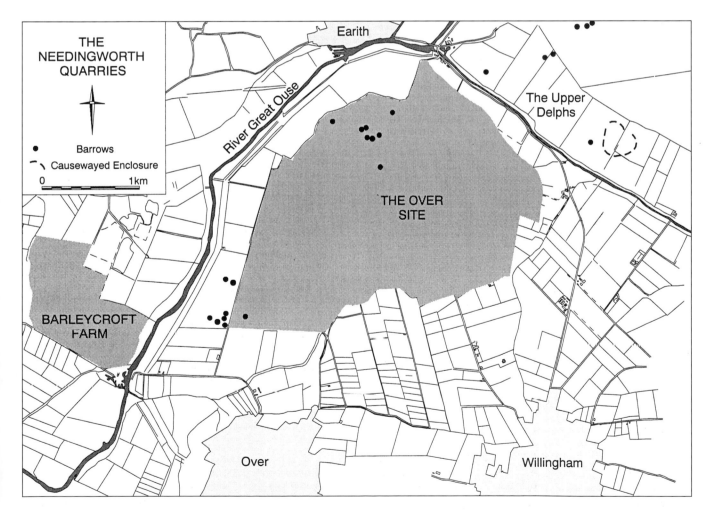

Figure 9.1 Area of study

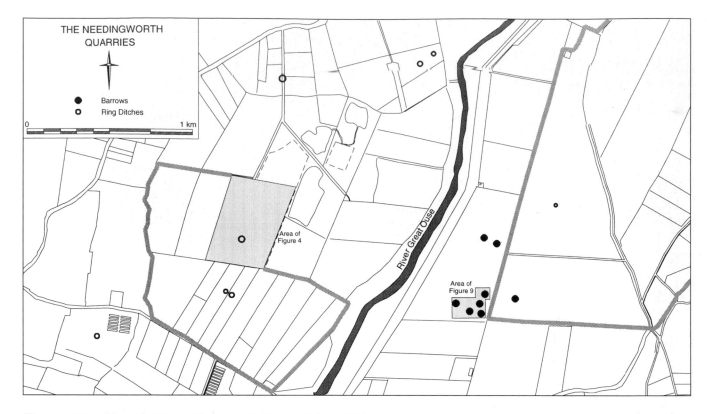

Figure 9.2   Distribution of barrow fields and ring-ditches

Upper Delphs terrace to the north-east and, further out in the fen towards Sutton, three long barrows (Hodder & Evans forthcoming). Nearby, clusters of alluvium-sealed round barrows lie upon the terraces along the western margin of the Over site (Figs 9.1 and 9.2; Hall and Coles 1994, fig 52; Hall 1996, figs 33 and 83). Yet blanketed by peat and flood clays, it is the emptiness of the immediate investigation area that is most challenging. Whereas find spots and long-known sites dot the surrounding 'uplands', the archaeology of the riverside and fen-edge evades easy detection through standard methodologies. In response, an array of unconventional techniques have already been applied: air-flown radar, large-scale test pitting, and even field-walking following commissioned ploughing of buried soils after the stripping of alluvium. Due to the depth of overburden cover, reconstruction of buried topography coupled with the study of environmental sequences is a major component of the research programme. While at 2.70–4.50m OD the current Barleycroft 'site' lies relatively high within the Ouse floodplain, at Over the buried ground surface drops below sea level and there is as much as 4m of cover. The prehistoric landscape has already been modelled employing Geographic Information Systems (GIS) computer imagery drawing upon ARC's many borehole logs (Fig 9.3; Burton 1995). From this, the course of a major palaeochannel of the Ouse has been distinguished running across the middle of the site, *c* 1km east of its present course (the approximate line of Over Lode, this channel

was also mapped by Holmes; see Phillips 1970). Across the northern half of the area the topography fragments into a delta-like pattern and, prone to silting, the low-lying river system would have frequently carved new channels.

The chronology of the Ouse's channels within the environs will be established over the coming years. A substantial berm has, of course, been left between the two quarries and the present course of the river. Nevertheless, palaeo-topographic survey to date would give no indication of a natural channel on this line (the highest ground is in the immediately riverside fields at Barleycroft) and it is possible that adjacent to the village of Over, as it flows today, the Ouse is canalised. Investigations within the Barleycroft floodplain would indicate that a north-western palaeochannel system must have been a backwater tributary without upstream connection with the main course. However, the eastern Over-side course could have met with it. Aerial photographs reveal a myriad of small channels adjacent to the Holywell 'bend', probably a subsidiary watershed from the Swavesey high ground. It is with these that the near-Over route would seem to join and, if so, it may have been a major channel in later prehistory. Only extensive coring within the immediate riverside zone of the present course will determine if the line of the river between the quarry sites is 'late' and/or artificial.

Investigation on this scale (and duration) has already altered our own sense of immediate landscape cognition. Approached from the outset with

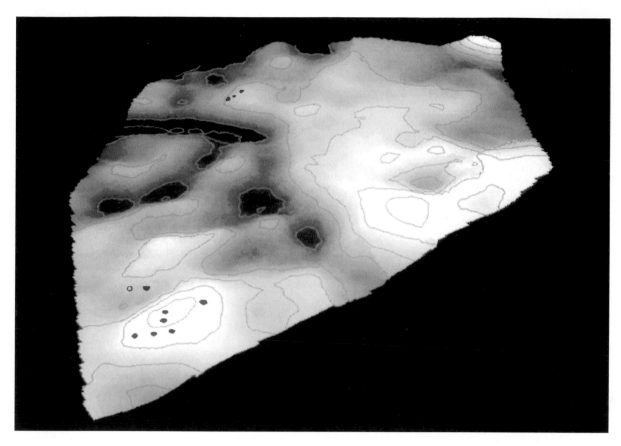

Figure 9.3   GIS plot of the Over site looking north-eastwards: the red circles, round barrows; the eastern Ouse palaeo-channel is visible along the left side (N Burton & C A Shell)

vaguely realised 'fenland-use' models, the work has entailed coming to terms with low-lying floodplain topography. This is, of course, essentially what the earlier fen basin was. Yet it has been envisaged as something more – an ever-receding succession of 'edges' from which, if only investigations could go deep enough, the elusive chimera of an extensively waterlogged prehistoric wetland would be forthcoming. Sadly, this seems not to be the case. Against expectations, to date absolute depth has not proven a critical factor and there are few low locales with suitably drained subsoils to attract settlement. 'Viable' topography was essentially determined by Pleistocene deposits, with more than half the area consisting of the heavy clays of glacial channels. Generally the clay/drained terrace divide is marked and relatively high (2.50–3.00m OD). Although utilised, nobody was living on the clays, and the lesson thus far at Over is that the instances where the gravels go deep are few – when discovered they must be intensively sampled.

The southern fen-edge did not get seriously 'wet' until the later Bronze Age, and only after *c* 1200–750 BC did marsh develop on any scale. Within the Over environs the ensuing back-up of the river system led to the formation of Willingham Mere. Starting as a marsh in the first half of the 1st millennium BC, it eventually became a large freshwater lake extending over 32ha that was only drained in the mid-19th century. Given the depth of cover throughout the Over site and its many buried 'wet' edges (mere/riversides), there is still considerable potential for the recovery of both waterlogged remains and wetland-specific sites (eg fishing stands and jetties). In recognition of this, English Heritage is sponsoring a programme of groundwater level monitoring (French *et al*, forthcoming).

Whilst both Barleycroft and Over sites lie in the floodplain and share the same broad environmental sequence and geology, their topography differs. On the Barleycroft side the low rises of the gravel terraces predominate, are only divided by the clays of the glacial channels. Thus far, of the 110ha evaluated on the eastern Ouse bank the inverse holds true – clays extend (uninterrupted) across the northern half of the immediate area with gravels confined to the south-western margin, from where spines extend east to the Ouse palaeochannel. This produces a more linear relief with sites 'bunching up' upon these terrace corridors. Although background artefact densities are thus far generally lower on that side (only a quarter of the total area has there been investigated), this pattern would have determined more 'strategic' land-use; there would have been fewer routes to traverse it if restricted to the dry gravels. (Despite extensive trenching at critical points, no timber causeways seem present across the wet clay ground.)

Floodplain strategies

Integral to the spirit of the investigations is the premise that there is no necessary distinction between fieldwork within a research and developer-funded environment. The latter can be theoretically informed and problem-oriented. The corollary must be that it is appropriately prioritised and not driven by an agenda of uniform excavation nor total recovery, rather *coherent sampling*. The days of vast 'Fengate-style' open-area stripping to expose dispersed features seem over, especially if the information locked into buried soils is also to be addressed (eg finds densities and chemical traces). Accepting financial constraints, certain aspects of some 'things' will have to be sacrificed, or at least more summarily dealt with, if landscape-scale phenomenon are also to be considered. In the case of the Barleycroft investigations, it has been realized that it is the Roman field systems which (after much chasing) can only be dealt with at the coarsest level. Enormous resources would be expended tracing what would otherwise warrant only summary excavation if alluvium did not impede cropmark recognition.

The measurement of 'non-occurrence' is equally essential and amongst the major aims of the work is the provision of *solid negative evidence*. Far too much field archaeology is driven by a positivist 'discovery(-only)' agenda and it is just as imperative to know at what period which areas of landscape were not utilised as when they were. Fieldwork of this kind blurs the often all-too-neat distinction between evaluation and excavation. Stages of investigation need to enfold into, and complement, each other, encompassing patterns of *landscape movement* (or at least less tangible patterns of activity) and not just 'the settled'. Some phenomena can only be appropriately addressed through intensive landscape sampling rather than open-area excavation. Neolithic and earlier Bronze Age scatter sites are a prime case in point. Largely apparent as only buried-soil artefact spreads, the 'site' often disappears through area-stripping. Equally important is the artefact definition (by type and density) of such sites from 'background', or broader, land-use traces (Evans 1993); employment of compatible large-scale sampling and formal excavation units are necessary if site and landscape patterns are to be studied in unison. Finally, in pursuit of this theme, the study of monuments and settlement must be interrelated. It can be questioned whether the concept of their being somehow isolated or pristine 'ritual landscapes' is an appropriate research framework and if, instead, it simply reflects an inability to tease-out and 'capture' more ubiquitous modes of contemporary settlement. Just because they are readily apparent, it little advances our understanding of the past to treat monument complexes as 'islands' displaced at such-and-such an interval through a landscape like so many ant hills. Whilst not advocating research proscription, it is the immediate history of monuments, their landscape interaction and the relationship between domestic and ritual contexts that now demands attention – *monument 'play' alone is inadequate*.

Throughout the investigations to date, the same pragmatic methodology has been consistently employed. Whilst open to elaboration as necessary, it is essential that this be maintained if key variables are to be measurable throughout. In evaluation of artefact densities, the 'base-line' is the hand-sorting of standard 90 litre samples from the buried soil horizon on a 100m grid. These 'test pits' are thereafter machine-enlarged into 5m² 'test stations'. Essentially opened to permit in-depth topographic/environmental recording, the latter also provide 'incidental' prospection for features/sites, which are otherwise tested for through 50–75m long trenches excavated in the centre of each test station-defined hectare (oriented according to the buried topography). Beyond this, there is judgmental cover to further trace features, define sites, and investigate specific landscape phenomenon (eg 'wet-edges', palaeochannels, etc). Increasingly the fieldwork has shown that it is the recovery of sufficiently large landscape-samples that is paramount, and the methodology has been augmented by reducing the interval with 'test point' grab samples (again 90 litres).

Arising out of basic methodologies developed in the course of the Haddenham Project and subsequently modified by the CAU, the basic strategy of test station-expanded 'pit' sampling was adopted by English Heritage's Fenland Management Project (Evans forthcoming). Not particularly sophisticated (especially given the paucity of sieving, which in-field experiments shows exponentially increases labour demands), its virtue lies in its simplicity. Employing the National Grid throughout, 73 test pit samples were processed at Barleycroft and, to date, 52 at Over (plus 49 'point' samples, see below) – absolute methodological consistency on both sides of the river being the key research directive. In fact, the results across the southern swathe of the Barleycroft fields (60ha) were such that during the 'excavation phase' the bucket-sample density was doubled throughout and, locally, further increased to a 25m interval (271 additional sample points in total; Fig 9.4). This is an unprecedented scale of landscape-artefact investigation; such techniques are essential in an attempt to consider broader patterns of land-usage and non-feature-defined modes of activity.

This tiered approach to sampling allows for site resolution through artefact density. Whereas the 100m grid sampling gives indication of broad areas of high density usage (such as is the case in the three riverside fields at Barleycroft), at the 50m interval individual scatters emerge; only at the 25m level does their 'shape' resolve (see below, Fig 9.4). Whilst certainly not absolute, these approaches also provide a degree of statistical control of retrieval rates. The number of axe fragments recovered through the various 'pit/point' sampling gives, for

Test Pitting

1- 2 flints

3- 5 flints

6+ flints

Figure 9.4 Barleycroft Farm (the southern fields) - Artefact/landscape densities (worked flint per 90 litre sample)

0   400m

example, insight of their total population in the landscape, and the pattern of trenching an indication of what is 'missed' (ie site-type recovery rates). Of course, there are problems with this kind of sampling programme. Foremost is extrapolating pattern from low absolute numbers and the willingness to take appropriate action. A case in point is the northern Barleycroft field system reported below (Fig 9.5). Whilst high artefact numbers were recovered from specific features during the evaluation, the site complex was only 'announced' by one occurrence of six flints per 90 litre sample and three pieces from another (otherwise only 'ones'). Unlike other instances, its excavation was not based upon buried soil density, but feature recovery. Nevertheless, prior to excavation the area was stripped of alluvium, the buried soil ploughed and then fieldwalked (10m grid collection; Evans et al 1999). The results largely confirmed the pattern of sample test pitting – specific feature-complexes aside – this was not a high density site.

Amongst the most obvious broader distributional patterns to date is the contoured recovery of early-Neolithic material. Occurring sporadically throughout the area of the higher dry terraces, it concentrates along their edges with the heavier Pleistocene channel deposits. Presumably the latter would have carried thick forest cover (and a high groundwater-table); the former, pockets of early clearance. Equally distinct is the paucity of later Mesolithic finds – only a tranchet axe and two/three other possible pieces. The earlier Neolithic obviously saw much more extensive patterns of floodplain usage, with the Mesolithic presumably largely confined to the corridor of the river channel proper. (Mesolithic scatters are known on the Ouse-side terraces at the north-western margin of the Over site and downstream at Foulmire Fen – Evans and Hodder 1987; Hall 1996, 147.) At the time of writing this is what is being tested in the Over investigations and, more specifically, whether the earliest Neolithic also adhered to this pattern of corridor (-only) usage.

Amongst the opportunities the quarries offer is the testing of Fenland Survey distributions. Much has been made of the general contrast between prehistoric densities along the eastern and south-eastern fen-edge when compared to its western margins. The latter has major early monument complexes which seem conspicuously absent from the southern and eastern sides, but which locally have extraordinary densities of later Neolithic/earlier Bronze Age sites (eg the Wissey embayment or the Isleham peninsula; Hall and Coles 1994; Edmonds et al 1999). Whilst such a neat patterning seems somehow complementary, how real is it in terms of the relative paucity of scatter sites given the extensive alluviation of the western fen margin? With its burnt-flint pot-boiler sites, the eastern margin does seem quite specific in its patterning. Nevertheless, the density of, especially, later Neolithic sites being discovered beneath the peat and alluvium at Barl-

eycroft Farm/Over suggests that, at least to some degree, this dichotomy between the respective edges is distorted by environmental factors.

Riverside communities

Consider Figure 9.5 – in the main, an early-Neolithic pit cluster overlain by a 2nd-millennium BC settlement strung-out along the edge of a co-axial fieldsystem, with a ring-ditch complex at its southern end. It succinctly encapsulates a major issue within later British prehistory – modes of landscape mobility and settling down – trails and clearances, monuments and plots ...

Much pottery and flintwork had been deposited within the cluster of some twenty early 4th-millennium BC pits. With Mildenhall-type wares, it is comparable, albeit on a much reduced scale, to Clark's renowned Hurst Fen site (1960). Within that scatter of approximately 200 pits, individual clusters of 10–15 features each could be distinguished around its periphery. Equated with separate households, the Barleycroft cluster may represent a similar grouping – a family unit (Clark 1960, 241; Pollard forthcoming). The quantity of material within the Barleycroft pits contrasts with the contemporary buried soil artefact distributions. A near-void zone surrounds them that suggests a 'boy scout-like' ethos of refuse burial (though possibly effected by subsequent truncation of the old ground surface). A now common negative recovery pattern, no substantial contemporary building remains per se were found, only the traces of 'light' stakehole structures (wigwam/tent-like: Evans et al 1999). A key issue is whether it represents a short-lived permanent settlement or a repeat-visit campsite within an annual round – were the pits infilled en masse with midden-derived refuse or with material selectively discarded before moving on each year? Certainly, bulky Neolithic bowls would have inhibited mobility and could have either been smashed or cached between trips. Yet there is only limited evidence of any pit-intercutting and the former interpretation would seem the more plausible given that sherds from a number of different vessels are represented in most (only in one case did all the sherds derive from a single vessel). Of course, this is not absolutely conclusive in as much as middens could have been maintained at a seasonally visited base that were either successively backfilled into features or dumped in upon the final abandonment.

In two instances tree-throws appear to have been 'utilised', with great quantities of ceramics and worked flint recovered from their hollows (255 and 319 pieces of worked flint and 157 and 238 sherds respectively). As distinct from the pit-cluster material, the pottery is of an earlier plain-bowl style. This is a phenomenon recorded on other early-Neolithic 'clusters' in the region (Mortimer and Evans 1996). Dotting the floodplain, up-turned tree-bowls would surely have served as landscape markers, acting in the lowland in much the same manner as rock-face overhangs in uplands (Evans *et al* 1999). Whilst the resultant hollows may just have been employed as a convenient middening locale, this abundant deposition could attest to something 'more' – the up-ended roots possibly providing a ready mass-wall from which to drape tent-skins for temporary shelters. Such living 'in wood' would have obvious affinities with the use of 'mass timber' construction in Neolithic ceremonial complexes such as was evident in the Haddenham long barrow (Hodder and Shand 1988). Pit/artefact clusters such as this at Barleycroft appear to provide whatever domestic base-line there is for the major Neolithic ritual monuments in the vicinity. Full comparison between this complex and the Haddenham cause-wayed enclosure (Evans 1988; Hodder and Evans forthcoming) will provide insights concerning the interrelationship between these 'centres' and the annual round behind them. The insubstantial nature of contemporary (unenclosed) settlements may, in fact, call for some reappraisal of the ritual attribution of such enclosures based essentially on a paucity of domestic remains.

During the course of the 1994 watching-brief trenching in Field I at Barleycroft, a previously 'unannounced' ring-ditch was discovered (Fig 9.5; Site A). Dictated by circumstances, its excavation had to be summary, though fortunately it proved uncomplicated. However, in the summer of 1996 the opportunity arose to carefully excavate a double-circuit ring-ditch, lying on Butcher's Hill, in its entirety, and subsequent trenching in the vicinity led to the discovery of another small ring-ditch on its western side (Figs 9.6 and 9.7). The double-circuit ring had been detected through recent aerial photographic cover (by R Palmer; the only pre-Roman feature to be so) and further reconnaissance has shown that two other such 'monuments' fall immediately beyond the borders of the quarry zone. Moreover, another small ring-ditch has been discovered through trench-sampling during the first phase of evaluation in the Over quarry (Fig 9.2). This is a remarkable recovery rate. Situated on the crowns and edges of terraces/floodplain knolls, their distribution seems quite regular – part of the fabric of the lowland land-use – and could suggest landscape parcelling. This is not to suggest that their layout was uniform or in any way 'geometrically' regular, but (as opposed to the clustering of the barrow-fields) their dispersion has a sense of underlying interval (c 800–1000m).

Of the ring-ditches investigated within the quarries, whilst they may have been embanked, none seem mounded. They are circular *ditch* complexes and not ploughed-out barrows. Most telling of this is that found on the Over side. Lying 400m north-east of the main barrowfield (whose mounds are still upstanding by *c* 1m), apart from its much smaller diameter and that the ditch is of a markedly different profile, there would be no mechanism to explain its complete reduction and the survival of the adjacent

barrows. Sealed by late-Roman alluvium, it would be equally difficult to imagine that earlier arable practices could have eradicated substantial mounds. This is a crucial result. Far too often the distribution/function of ring-ditches and barrows are considered equivalent, the former as poorly surviving versions of the latter (eg Field 1974, 58; Taylor in Lawson *et al* 1981). Their floodplain survival (and distribution) attests that they were a quite different category of ceremonial monument than barrows; their function not exclusively mortuary. The Barleycroft ring-ditches all seem to be of early-Bronze Age date. Whilst there is evidence of 'henge-like' activity, in their primary phases they are variously associated with Food Vessel and Collared Urn. Their (primary) land-use context is, therefore, the ubiquitous flint scatters of the period and it is here that the apparently regularity of their distribution becomes crucial as it may relate to later patterns of 'block' allotment and contemporary movement.

An intriguing point of comparison with the Haddenham investigations is the relative paucity of Beaker thus far from the western Barleycroft side. At Haddenham, it was recovered in association with the round barrows, in the upper fills of the cause-wayed enclosure, and in pit groups. Whilst Grooved Ware has been widely recovered on both sides of the Ouse, very little Beaker has been identified at Barleycroft Farm. Does this correlate with the lack of barrows *per se* within the immediate area of investigation? Until the west bank investigations are completed this cannot be stated with certainty (and in some ways it is a distribution pattern too neat to be readily true). Nevertheless, it could suggest different histories of landscape usage (eg mortuary traditions) on the opposite banks of the river and possibly territorial division. Alternatively, the opposite could be true. It may be the social unity of lower Ouse communities that is expressed through bank-shared landscape zoning, with the immediate eastern Ouse-side terraces as 'dead-ground' during the earlier Bronze Age – one shared by groups on both sides of the river. If, however, the Ouse then flowed in an eastern channel and not along its present route, then the southern barrow group would directly relate to the Barleycroft side.

In some respects, the lower Ouse system is obvious or 'classical' in terms of its Neolithic/early-Bronze Age expression: a massive causewayed enclosure with neighbouring long barrows; the line of the riverside terraces picked out by extensive early-Bronze Age barrowfields. Within the region the only comparison is the lower reaches of the Welland. Having mortuary enclosures instead of long barrows, its interrupted Neolithic enclosures are far smaller and barrowfields less extensive. But what the Welland does have are major henge monuments which, at least to date, are lacking from the lower/middle Ouse (Pryor and French 1985). This may relate to the fact that the ring-ditches recovered seem just that – earlier/middle-Bronze Age *ring-ditches* – and not later Neolithic hengiforms.

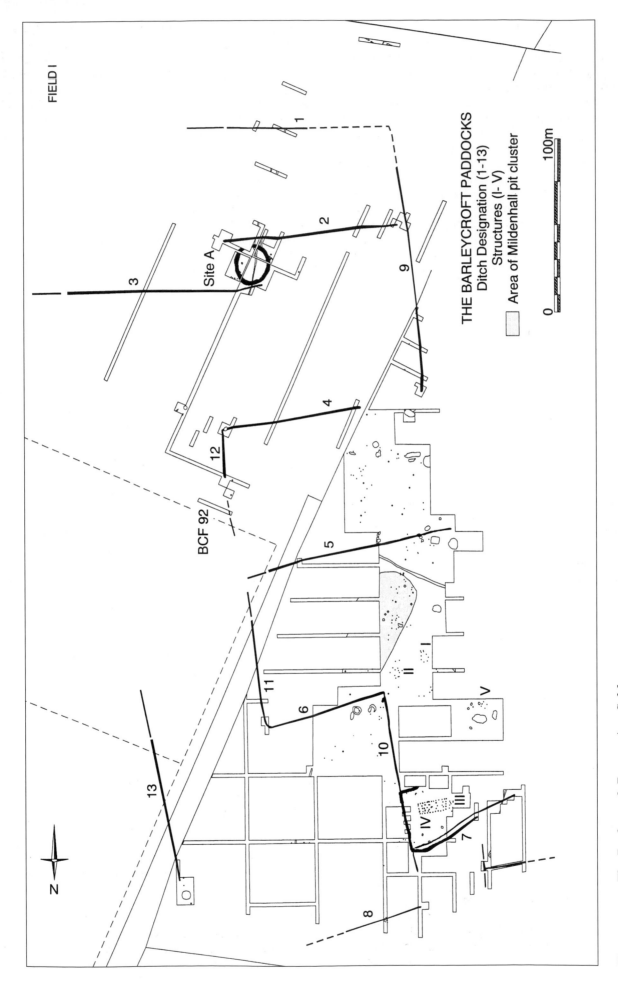

FIELD I

Site A

BCF 92

THE BARLEYCROFT PADDOCKS
Ditch Designation (1-13)
Structures (I- V)
Area of Mildenhall pit cluster

0   100m

N

Figure 9.5   The Barleycroft Bronze Age fieldsystem

The implications of these diverse patterns are beyond the scope of this paper, but they do suggest that river valley systems are perhaps more appropriate analytical entities than arbitrary or broad environmental zones (eg 'the fenland').

In total, the main Bronze Age field system in the northern arm of the Barleycroft site has now been traced over 10ha. Whilst prehistoric ditch systems have now been found in the riverside strip of the quarry (see below), the southern end of the immediate system would seem to fall within Field I. Continuing north, beyond the immediate limits of the quarry, its eastern extent is also unknown. Although a line of 'cross-axis' has been recovered, how far the ditch on the northern side of the Field I ring-ditch runs east has not been established. In the course of the Plant Site evaluation pre-Iron Age ditches were found on the same alignment. If part of the same layout, it would indicate that the entire terrace-top was thus allotted and the system must extend over more than 35ha and could conceivably have been substantially larger (100ha? – unfortunately, the intervening area was lost to extraction with only minimum watching-brief cover; within ongoing quarry workings it proved impossible to detect such dispersed ditch patterns). If so, only a very limited portion of this field system has been investigated. Alternatively, the Field I ring-ditch may mark a 'seam' or eastern divide, with the ditch which extends east being part of a larger linear ditch system which may even predate the monument whose northern circuit appeared to flatten in relationship to it. Whatever the case, the staggered arrangement of the boundary ditches on either side of the ring-ditch suggests that it served as a *nodal point*, integrating portions of the system. Whilst the work demonstrates that the investigation of such systems requires large-scale response, landscape will always be open ended – excavation cover will never suffice and something will always escape.

By its scale and formality of layout, the Barleycroft system invites comparison with that at Fengate, Peterborough. However, the absence of droveways within the portion investigated at Barleycroft may be a telling difference (Pryor 1996) and, on the whole, it seems more 'reeve-like', dividing up large parcels of land in which a broad range of activities evidently occurred (pits were found scattered throughout). What makes this Ouse-side system truly remarkable is the interrelationship of its components – the incorporation of the ring-ditch and associated contemporary settlement. Strung-out between the foot of the field system and terrace-edge, access to (ground-)water would seem to have determined the immediate situation of the settlement. The main occupation zone includes roundhouses, four-poster granaries, large wells, and processing pits; the latter two presumably for watering herds and human supply. Deeper features were still waterlogged. The recovery of an *in situ* timber clamp within one pit might relate to tanning and quantities of burnt flint in others, probably cooking

processes; fragments of loomweights, crucibles, and bronze-working moulds attest to craft activity. Amongst the latter have been recognised pieces probably from mid-rib spearhead production (Needham pers comm), which provides a sense of domestic context for a middle-Bronze Age basal-looped socketed spearhead recently recovered from one of the Ouse palaeochannels at Meadow Lane (C14 dated from shaft wood to 3045 ± 55 BP OxA-5187; a spearhead tip was also recovered from the Fengate fieldsystem proper; Pryor 1980, 125–9, fig 75.7).

A rare discovery was a substantial longhouse (5.50 × 16.50m), found set within is own 'C'-shaped compound which recut one of the main field boundaries, its setting and layout is reminiscent of that at Down Farm (Barrett *et al* 1991, 183–211, figs 5.27 and 5.43). Its plan was actually slightly trapezoidal with the southern side longer by two posts, perhaps denoting an imposing facade-like front (no doorway was otherwise apparent; the round buildings all share this orientation; Figs 9.3 and 9.8). With more than forty major timber uprights set in five rows, the post pattern suggests a simple ridged roof carried by a line of central posts, with further internal support from more widely spaced aisle-posts. (There was no evidence of eaves-supporting posts as suggested in Taylor and Pryor's reconstruction of buildings as represented by structural timbers from Flag Fen; 1990, fig 3.) The building would certainly have appeared monumental when compared to the much smaller roundhouses (Fig 9.8), and the interrelationship between the two construction styles raises intriguing interpretative possibilities – were they distinguished by household status (headperson *vs* commoners), function (hall *vs* houses/barns) and/or sequence (the longhouse appears to have directly superseded a round structure)?

Associated in the main with Deverel-Rimbury ceramics, the field system would seem to date from the latter half of the 2nd millennium BC. This being said, that sherds of post-Deverel-Rimbury wares were recovered from the ditch enclosing the longhouse suggests it was utilised during the first centuries of the 1st millennium BC. Awaiting absolute confirmation, this dating remains provisional and there are sufficient quantities of earlier Bronze Age ceramics (eg Collared Urn) that might indicate the field system's earlier layout. However, the flint assemblage would further support a later Bronze Age attribution and recent reappraisal of the Fengate system suggests that c 1500 BC was a regional watershed in fieldsystem layout (Evans and Pollard nd).

A small cluster of roundhouses and a longhouse, set at the terrace side with processing pits/wells dotting the clay edge – a remarkably complete picture of a settlement. Yet, although having the attraction of a ready 'window' onto the past, the site obviously did not frame the inhabitants' entire social world. Depending on its total dimensions, the fieldsystem could have been traversed in anywhere from fifteen minutes to half an hour. A day's journey

Figure 9.6   Photo of Butcher's Hill ring-ditch (Mon.2)

The Butcher's Hill ring-ditch complex

Great quantities of earlier Bronze Age flintwork had been
deposited within the outer circuit of the main ring-ditch, requir-
ing the chequerboard-excavation of the buried soil (the density of
lithics varied from 0–14 pieces per metre square; Fig 9.6). One of
a pair of ring-ditches on the eastern side of the terrace knoll, the
double-circuit monument proved complex and subject to considerable remodelling: an inhumation (1) was the focus of a pair of
antennae-like troughs superseded by a deep horseshoeshaped
ditch from which a large sherd of decorated Collared Urn was
recovered (Fig 9.7, A & B; sherds of Collared Urn were also present within a broadly contemporary ditch running north-eastwards). These primary features seemed to orient/open upon the
smaller western ring-ditch (Mon 3) where a complete Food
Vessel had been set within a pit in its interior. Thereafter, within
the eastern monument the inner and outer circuits were subsequently cut (C & D). There is no way of knowing with certainty
which the central cremation pyre (2) was directly associated
with; the 35 'secondary' cremations confined within its southern
sector were certainly contemporary with the exterior and some
had been set within its fills (of the total, ten were urned:
Deverel-Rimbury). A 'satellite' cremation cluster in the south-
western end of their distribution is suggestive of a secondary
focus, perhaps another 'significant' ancestor/individual.

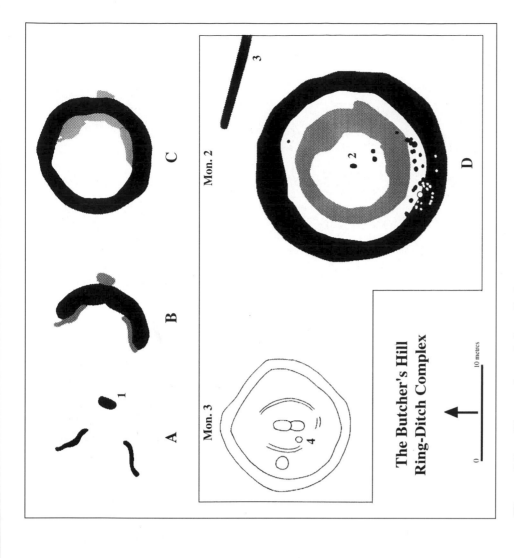

Figure 9.7   Phase plan of ring-ditch

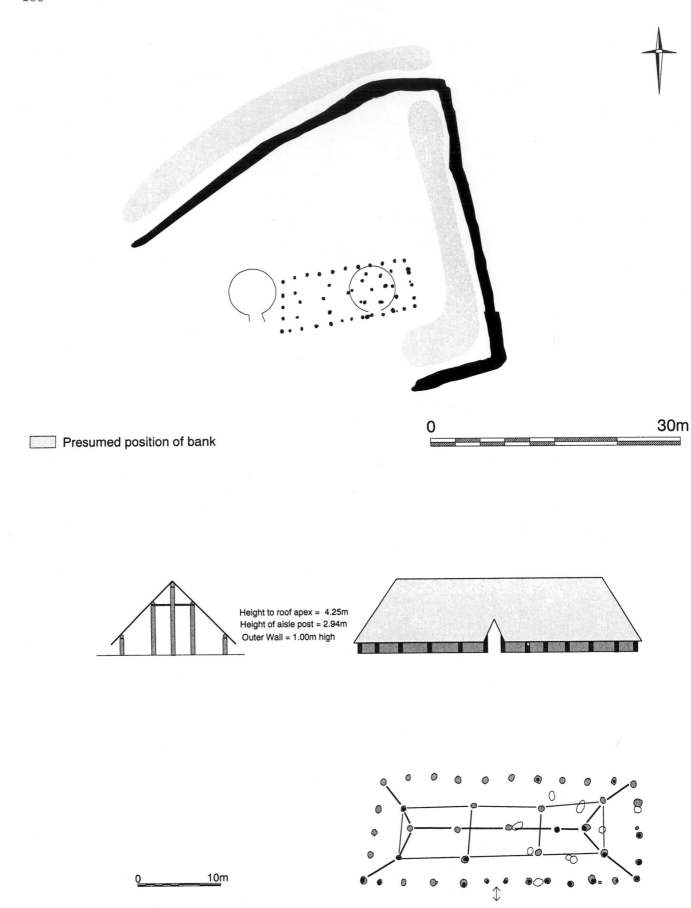

Presumed position of bank

0   30m

Height to roof apex = 4.25m
Height of aisle post = 2.94m
Outer Wall = 1.00m high

0   10m

Figure 9.8   Top, Barleycroft Farm, longhouse paddock (see IV Fig 9.5); note that the longhouse appears to replace a pair of round houses; another such pair lay to the south (see Fig 9.5, I & II). Bottom, aisled-hall reconstruction with southern entrance

(by foot) could have brought their inhabitants in contact with a number of such hamlets. This begs the issue at what level community resided – at a face-to-face level or in larger territorial units?

The correspondence of the longhouse/hall and the recovery of spearhead moulds (with the occurrence of contemporary weaponry nearby) could evoke traditional images of a warrior's household. Yet given its relationship to the field system – of which it must be presumed that only a portion has been investigated – it would be remarkably fortuitous to think that a chieftain's/headperson's residence has been found, if such existed. Beyond this, there is as yet no control of how many families shared a field system block such as at Barleycroft, and the number of other such hamlets that may be scattered around its fringes is unknown. However, applying the population figures used by Green in his analysis of early-Bronze Age territories along the Ouse (10 persons per square kilometre; 1974, 129–36), the excavated Barleycroft 'hamlet' could be the only such settlement associated with a field block of the size recovered. Until other such settlements are investigated within the area, there is little basis to assess its status – are longhouses relatively commonplace, their paucity to date only relating to the frequency of later Bronze Age settlement excavation, the dispersed nature of contemporary occupation, and 'techniques'? Nevertheless, it squarely raises the issue of the character of social relations/stratification during the latter half of the 2nd millennium BC. While widespread field systems suggest an 'authoritative' layout, generally there is little obvious evidence of such distinction by household, and 'power' seems to have rested within a broader community.

Albeit probably short-lived (?25–150 years), there is every reason to think that the settlement was permanent. Given the apparent low density of terrace-top occupation, there is no *de facto* need to evoke models of migratory lowland transhumance (see Evans 1987). Yet, to some degree, this contrasts with the evidence of the houses themselves. Although characteristically for the period they lack encircling eavesgullies to catch finds, the buildings were relatively 'clean', with negligible artefact densities in their (indisputable) postholes and only few finds within the overlying buried soil. This would correlate, for example, with the evidence of the roundhouses scattered throughout the Fengate system; low finds densities promoting their attribution as barns (Pryor 1980), an interpretation which could now be questioned in the light of the Barleycroft evidence. What the relative cleanness of the Barleycroft houses would, however, support is the evidence of organised middening. Whilst not so grand as at Runnymede or Potterne (Needham and Sorensen 1988), the uniform burnt clay-flecked fill matrix, locally shared by a number of adjacent pits, could indicate their backfilling from a single midden source.

In the light of recent researches (Bruck 1995), it is relevant that no human bone was recovered from the main Barleycroft settlement complex. Cremated, their dead (at least a substantial portion thereof) were possibly interred within a secondary elaboration of the eastern ring-ditch on Butcher's Hill, to the south. Presumably initiated by a ring-central pyre pit, 35 cremations were recovered in its southern sector. Concentrating and intercutting within this zone's margins, their clustering suggests interment within a demarcated area; ringing the periphery of the inner ditch, their distribution probably indicates that a low mound had been upcast over the central cremation (the manner of its firing suggesting 'clamping' in an oxygen-reduced atmosphere). As far as can be established, the central pyre related to the digging of the outer ditch circuit and the decision to site the cemetery upon the earlier small ring-ditch probably reflects ritual reference. A southern placement of secondary cremations was also found within the two round barrows investigated during the course of the Haddenham Project. When read in combination with the south-facing doorways of the Barleycroft Farm roundhouses, this could suggest a main axis of cognitive Bronze Age landscape orientation.

Whilst the Barleycroft ring-ditch complex generally appears pivotal in relationship to the field systems (see below), the distance at which it apparently lay from contemporary settlement may have been a critical factor. Its remove, and the relationship of the satellite cremations to the central pyre-pit, could suggest that burial was according to *lineage* rather than individual settlement. Small settlement clusters of the type recovered at Barleycroft could not have been so isolated, nor their inhabitants sufficiently numerous, to have been self-reproducing. The settlement-/field system-liminal situation of the southern Barleycroft ring-ditch may therefore be telling of the interaction between dispersed communities (ie 'inter-hamlet'). Given that it requires at least three lineages for social reproduction, its 35 cremations implies a minimum total population of at least 100 – a reasonable figure contingent upon the ultimate duration of the field system(s) complex (50, 100, 200 years?). Of course, too many 'ifs', 'unknowns', and presumptions undermine detailed population modelling. These, nevertheless, are appropriate questions if field archaeology is to contribute to a more thorough understanding of later prehistoric social life.

The most striking absence in the investigations to date is the Iron Age. Although a middle/later-Iron Age settlement was discovered during evaluation for the Barleycroft Plant Site (and subsequently preserved; Gdaniec 1995), across the 200ha thus far standardly sampled at Barleycroft/Over no material of this date has been recovered. From the Willingham Mere and other pollen cores it is known that the area first got seriously 'wet' during the early–1st millennium BC (Waller 1994) and the recovery of 'marsh-fast' timber structures (eg causeways and the Flag Fen platform) and metalwork elsewhere in the region indicates that the fen-edge effectively came into being during the later Bronze Age. This does not, however, explain the Iron Age distributions. A series of middle/later-Iron Age farmstead enclosures dotting the flanks of the Upper Delphs terrace were investigated during the course of the Haddenham Project (Evans and Serjeantson 1988). Generally lying at 2.50m OD – the same height as the Barleycroft Plant Site complex – in both instances major feature fills proved to be waterlogged and the sites appear to have been located at the wet/dry divide (between low-lying flood meadow and up-terrace arable). Ditch-associated upcast banks survived on both the Barleycroft Plant and Upper Delphs sites, and these lay directly upon the (dry) buried soil – there is no indication of pre-Iron Age flooding above the 2–2.50m OD contour. Accepting this environmental datum, all the area of the Barleycroft quarry and most of the Over-side terraces thus far investigated fall above this level, yet there seems little contemporary occupation. The ramifications of this are two-fold. On the one hand, it suggests a locational propensity at the 'wet-edge', presumably to allow ready access to marsh resources whose exploitation were so extensively attested to on the Delphs sites (Evans and Serjeantson 1988). Whilst on the other hand, the fact that the approximately 100ha of raised or 'usable' terrace thus far investigated at Barleycroft/Over saw only limited Iron Age usage suggests a very low overall density of settlement. Although flooding and marsh encroachment would have fragmented the landscape, seasonally isolating terrace islands and making cross-floodplain communication more difficult, many 'optimum' locales were evidently not utilised.

Seeming very dispersed communities, it is difficult to envisage the mechanisms or networks of extra-settlement interaction. Yet their topographic situation should not be misread as attesting to social isolation. It has, for example, been argued in the case of the Upper Delphs sites that the intensive exploitation of marshland wildlife related to trade in furs (beavers) and feathers (swan, pelican, and crane; Evans and Serjeantson 1988). More telling of 'meetings' was the excavation in 1994 of a series of Iron Age pit alignments in the ARC Quarry at Meadow Lane, St Ives (Pollard 1996). Waterlogged, they were found deeply buried beneath alluvium along the western edge of a major palaeochannel of

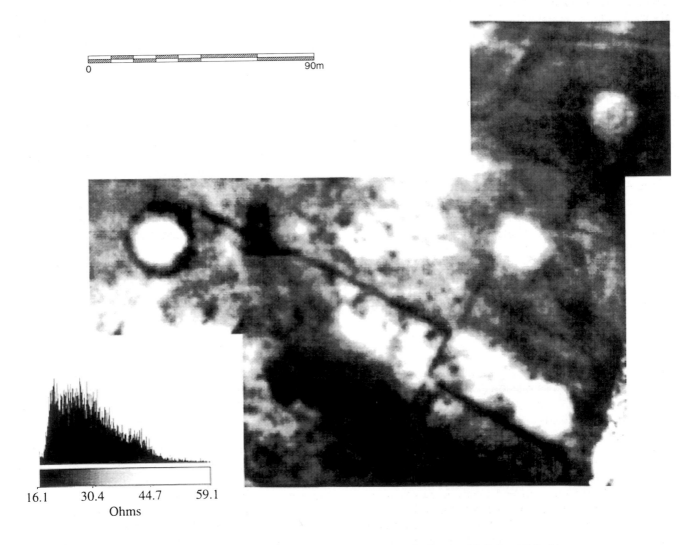

Figure 9.9   The Over-side barrows and fieldsystem (geophysical plot by M Cole, AMlab)

the Ouse that was evidently then in flow. A non-functional delineation of an obvious 'edge' (not in this instance ancestral to the layout of contemporary field systems), their existence suggests the establishment of territorial bounds as a larger (inter-)community 'project' and documents the river as a social divide.

Landscape themes

Given the bias of large-scale archaeological exposure within river valley quarries, it is relevant that recent work in the immediate uplands, on the heavier soils of Needingworth Ridge, failed to identify any substantive prehistoric presence (Schlee 1995) – the floodplain does indeed seem a distinct zone. The most extraordinary findings to date of the Barleycroft/Over campaigns are the character and extent of its Bronze Age usage, and its field systems add to a growing corpus recently discovered in the region (eg see papers in *Fenland Research* 8). Many must still evade aerial photographic recognition and their frequency suggests that much of the lowlands were then 'allotted'; in terms of pre-medieval land-use, the density of their coverage is probably only comparable to that in Roman times. Their recovery begins to provide a reasonable level of background context for the quantities of contemporary metalwork known from off-site sources, and markedly contrasts with the handful of sites known of that period from the region twenty years ago.

With excavation still underway in the southern fields at Barleycroft, notice of these results must be provisional. Nevertheless, there seems to be two other Bronze Age field systems. Although truncated by Roman features and only producing finds of Bronze Age date (unless found in direct association with settlement evidence), it is notoriously difficult to attribute such systems with certainty given problems of residuality. Consisting of large reeve-like strips, that in the south-western corner is reminiscent of the system in the north (described above). What is particularly relevant is that between excavation and cropmark evidence, the full extent of its north-east to south-west axis is known – *c* 1km – running from the cropmark ring-ditch at White Bridge Farm to that excavated on Butcher's Hill. Yet whilst the ring-ditches seem to roughly frame its limits, and in both instances field boundaries terminate in relationship to them, they do not set the exact axial alignment: no field-line runs from monument-to-monument, but rather they fall on adjacent boundaries. The relationship of the field system to the ring-ditches would seem one of respect, not dictatorship. The system found in the south-eastern riverside fields at Barleycroft differs in as much as it includes a number of minor paired double-ditches, probably either marking small droves or embanked hedge-lines, and seems much more similar to that found along the south-western margin of the Over site. The latter continues west into

the area of the riverside barrowfield, where it has been traced through geophysical survey by the Ancient Monuments laboratory (Fig 9.9). Given that within the area of the quarry this system extends down to 1.40m OD – well below the Iron Age fen-edge contour – there can be no doubt of its pre-Iron Age attribution. Sharing the same alignment, the marked similarity of the riverside-flanking field systems could suggest that the Ouse's course on its present line postdates them and that they could be one continuous system (later bisected). If so, the barrowfields, at least the southern Over group, would directly relate to the archaeology of the Barleycroft-side floodplain.

As absolute dating of these field systems is still awaited, it would obviously be foolhardy to speculate at length. Nevertheless two points are worth stressing. Firstly, that the three early field systems at Barleycroft are mutually exclusive by area (ie no spatial overlap) and, although there are 'stylistic' differences (droveway *vs* reeve-like pattern), this suggests their broad contemporaneity. Secondly, none seem subject to extensive recutting and, therefore, appear quite short-lived. Such an inference should only be made with caution, for hedge-lines could have been the mechanism of remnant field system survival (hedge trimmings were recovered from the waterlogged pits of the Meadow Lane Ouse-side alignments; see Taylor in Pollard 1996). Nevertheless, given their extent, at least superficially this field system horizon seems of limited duration.

The intensity of 2nd-millennium BC usage on the lower Ouse reaches contrasts with the relative paucity of late-Neolithic monuments. In comparison with the Welland, no major henge sites are known along the river, nor, for that matter, have any hengiforms been found in the course of the current investigations. Yet the critical factor may be that the distinction between late-Neolithic hengiforms and early-Bronze Age ring-ditches is entirely arbitrary – a purely chronological distinction of 'type'. These small monument forms may have hosted comparable ritual/ceremonial activity and fulfilled similar roles in the block parcelling of landscape. This issue obviously warrants further study and any observations must be tentative at this stage. However, through Pryor's researches on the Welland and Nene, with the Over/Barleycroft investigations there may soon be the opportunity for detailed comparison of long-term (pre-)history of land-use and allotment along the lower reaches of these respective river systems. Study of this kind cannot occur by comparing only specific/obvious monuments without reference to their immediate landscape context – this only comes from long-term campaigns of investigation – commitment within landscape.

Amongst the most remarkable aspects of the broader Barleycroft/Over investigations to date is the immediate recovery of almost the full range of prehistoric ceramic types (apart from Iron Age wares) – from Mildenhall and Grimston, to Peterborough, Grooved Ware, Collared Urn, Food Vessel, and Deverel-Rimbury. It is essential that the sequence of material culture change be considered within a landscape framework – what does it imply in terms of discrete or overlapping assemblages, ritual/domestic contexts, and their landscape situation? Although at risk of recourse to immediate localism to explain broader developments, it is imperative that, at least in some cases, the pattern of material distributions and assemblage variability be considered within a single landscape context. In a rush towards excavation, few large-scale programmes of landscape sampling are sustained within Britain. Far too often 'named' site-types are excavated in isolation (ie Grooved Ware pits), with their results proving either disappointing or inexplicable within the immediate context. As a consequence, analogy is too quickly drawn to 'national' exemplars (eg Durrington Walls in the case of Grooved Ware), which in the end does little more that reinforce the dominance of the Wessex sequence. With excavation just beginning at Over, it is crucial that the sampling be sustained to allow patterns to emerge before drawing ready explanations. There is little potential to now 'explain', for example, the north field Mildenhall cluster at Barleycroft without further comparative context (which the evaluation sampling shows is forthcoming). Whilst not a matter of 'the Ouse without Wessex', other contemporary sites must be investigated within the immediate floodplain environs before there will be a sufficient interpretative pattern – patience is needed if the 'landscape is to speak'.

Given the nature of the evidence, the main emphasis of the southern Barleycroft excavations at this time is upon the operation and layout of the field systems, their contemporary settlements and interrelationship with ring-ditches. 'Open' later Neolithic/earlier Bronze Age scatters are being sample tested, but, thus far, to typically disappointing result. Yet to return to one of the main themes of the fieldwork – landscape movement and settling down – in future stages these ubiquitous scatters will clearly demand greater emphasis (teasing out from buried soil distributions). It has already been argued that the ring-ditch landscape 'parcelling' influenced field system 'blocking'. Therefore, the relationship of the ring-ditches to contemporary settlement will certainly become a major directive. As the project itself moves though the landscape, its research framework will clearly develop. Whilst some issues will remain constant given broader research agendas (eg early-Neolithic usage), if for no other reason than certain site 'types'/configurations will begin to repeat, and – in the spirit of long-term projects – prioritisation must change.

Sites 'seek' and/or create their own 'genealogies'. In the case of the Barleycroft excavations, in some ways more than Haddenham, its affinities are with Fengate, and the character of the archaeology poses similar questions of context and 'representality'. Perhaps relating to the junction of the river and fen,

does the intensity of Bronze Age usage at Barleycroft/Over indicate that it was a 'special' enclave (an argument that could be further supported by the frequency of round barrows) or is it typical of the middle/lower reaches of the river system? Necessary comparison will only be possible by the implementation of similarly comprehensive landscape sampling programmes elsewhere along its length.

Extending over more than 650ha and thirty years, ARC's lower Ouse quarries will together provide an unparalleled investigation of buried prehistoric landscapes. Allowing for the study of both formal sites and more general patterns of broader land-use, the fieldwork is 'groundbreaking' and will permit archaeology to address such central questions as the status of the river – a territorial social divide and/or communication corridor linking diverse environmental niches and distant communities? Other central concerns are the interrelationship between settlement and landscape movement; the changing role of monuments and the situation of the living/dead; and where 'wild' and domesticated or variously 'wet' and dry land were. Basic structures framing prehistoric life, all are key issues that can only be addressed by investigation at many levels.

Moving behind all these claims sits, of course, the river – in change and in flux. It is salutary to recognise from the outset that in its many guises the Ouse undoubtedly continues to escape us, no matter what our methodologies or how sophisticated our research frameworks.

Acknowledgements

A radical departure from much field practice, the project has been funded throughout by ARC Central (now Hanson Aggregates Ltd), where it has been promoted by B Chapman and, latterly, J Bown. Equally, the support of B Sydes, L Austin, and S Kaner of Cambridgeshire County Council has been instrumental to its instigation. Long-term specialist collaboration with Josh Pollard (ceramics and flint) and Charly French (environmental) has been fruitful and a key component to the fieldwork to date. Beyond this, we are indebted to P Walker and C de Rouffignac (English Heritage), and C A Shell (Dept of Archaeology, Cambridge); otherwise, the many site assistants and other collaborating specialist should be aware of the debt owed to them, particularly P Murphy and P Wiltshire.

Graphics within this contribution are the work of C Begg, A Dickens, and P White; the GIS imagery is by Colin Shell and Nick Burton, and we are grateful to M Cole and A David of the AMlab for permission to reproduce their Over barrow field geophysical plot.

Evans wishes to express his gratitude variously for discussion, debate with and information provided by R Boast, R Bradley, J Coles, M Edmonds, D Hall, I Hodder, I Kinnes, S Needham, and M L S

Sørensen. Finally, working on more northerly rivers, long-term discussion (and collaboration) with Francis Pryor is heartily acknowledged.

Postscript

Since writing this paper the first series of radiocarbon dates have been processed for the project. Two from the Mildenhall pit group 3780–3640 BC (2970 ± 40 bc; OxA-8110) and 3710–3510 BC (2870 ± 45 bc; OxA-8108) place the cluster between 3800–3500 BC. Oak charcoal from the grave fill of the crouched inhumation (F. 928) from the main Butcher's Hill ring-ditch (Monument 2) is dated to 2040–1770 BC (1630 ± 40 bc; OxA-8113) whereas charred seeds from the central *in situ* cremation pit-pyre produced a date of 1880–1620 BC (1474 ± 40 bc; OxA-8112). An outlying urned cremation from the same monument (F.680) is dated to 1300–1010 BC (1000 ± 35 bc; OxA-8111) giving the monument a time span of at least 800 years. Bone from the secondary fills of the C-shaped enclosure ditch associated with the Barleycroft Paddocks longhouse produced a date of 1260–970 BC (955 ± 35 bc; OxA-8109). A date providing a significant *terminus ante quem* for the Barleycroft field system which, in relationship to the ring-ditch series, can now be firmly located to the mid/later 2nd millennium BC.

Bibliography

CAU Barleycroft/Over Reports

Evans, C, 1992 *The Archaeology of Willingham/Over: A desktop study*. Cambridge: Cambridge Archaeological Unit

Evans, C, 1995 *Archaeological Investigations at Barleycroft Farm, Bluntisham, Cambridgeshire, 1994*. Cambridge: Cambridge Archaeological Unit (Barleycroft Farm/ARC Paper 1)

Evans, C, & Gibson, D, 1996 *Floodplain Investigations: Barleycroft Farm, Cambridgeshire, 1995*. Cambridge: Cambridge Archaeological Unit (Barleycroft Farm/ARC Paper 4)

Evans, C, & Knight, M, 1997 *The Barleycroft Paddocks Excavations, Cambridgeshire*. Cambridge: Cambridge Archaeological Unit (Barleycroft Farm/ARC Paper 5)

Evans, C, & Pollard, J, 1995 *The Excavation of a Ring-ditch and Prehistoric Field system at Barleycroft Farm, Bluntisham, Cambridgeshire, 1994*. Cambridge: Cambridge Archaeological Unit (Barleycroft Farm/ARC Paper 2)

Gdaniec, K, 1992. *Archaeological Observations at Barleycroft Farm, Bluntisham*. Cambridge: Cambridge Archaeological Unit

Gdaniec, K, 1995 *Archaeological Investigations at Barleycroft Farm: The Plant Extension Site*. Cambridge: Cambridge Archaeological Unit (Barleycroft Farm/ARC Paper 3)

Other sources

Barrett, J C, 1988 The Living, the Dead and the Ancestors: Neolithic and Early Bronze Age Mortuary Practice, in J C Barrett & I A Kinnes (eds) *The Archaeology of Context in the Neolithic and Bronze Age*. Sheffield: Department of Archaeology and Prehistory, University of Sheffield, 30–41

Barrett, J C, Bradley, R, & Green, M, 1991 *Landscape, monuments and society: The prehistory of Cranborne Chase*. Cambridge: Cambridge University Press

Bruck, J, 1995 A place for the dead: the role of human remains in Late Bronze Age Britain, *Proc Prehist Soc*, **61**, 245–77

Burton, N, 1995 GIS in Archaeology: Visualising the Palaeo-environment. Unpublished MPhil thesis, University of Cambridge

Clark, J G D, 1960 Excavations at the Neolithic site at Hurst Fen, Mildenhall, Suffolk, 1954, 1957 and 1958, *Proc Prehist Soc*, **26**, 202–45

Edmonds, M, Evans, C, & Gibson, D, 1999 Assembly and Collection – Lithic complexes in the Cambridgeshire Fenlands, *Proc Prehist Soc*, **65**,

Evans, C, 1987 Nomads in 'waterland'?: Prehistoric transhumance and Fenland Archaeology, *Proc Cambridge Antiq Soc*, **76**, 27–39

Evans, C, 1988 Excavations at Haddenham, Cambs: A 'planned' Causewayed Enclosure and its regional affinities, in C Burgess & P Topping (eds) *Enclosures and Defences in the Neolithic of Western Europe*, Brit Archaeol Rep Int Ser **403**. Oxford: British Archaeological Reports, 127–48

Evans, C, 1993 Lithic 'noise' – low density scatters – missing settlements? The Langwood Farm environs, *Fenland Res*, **8**, 14–16

Evans, C, nd The Fengate Depot Site, in F Pryor, *Archaeology and environment of the Flag Fen basin*. London: English Heritage Archaeological Report

Evans, C, 1997 Hydraulic Communities: Iron Age enclosure in the East Anglian Fenlands, in A Gwilt & C Haselgrove (eds) *Re-constructing the Iron Age*. Oxford: Oxbow Books, 216–27

Evans, C, forthcoming Testing the Ground – Sampling Strategies, in T Lane & A Crowson (eds) *The Fenland Management Project Summary Volume*

Evans, C, & Hodder, I, 1987 Between the Two Worlds: Archaeological Investigations in Haddenham Level, in J M Coles & A J Lawson (eds) *European Wetlands in Prehistory*. Oxford: Clarendon Press, 180–91

Evans, C, Pollard, J, & Knight, M, 1999 Life in Woods: Tree-throws, 'settlement' and forest cognition, *Oxford J Archaeol*, **18**, 241–54

Evans, C, & Serjeantson, D, 1988 The backwater economy of a fen-edge community in the Iron Age: the Upper Delphs, Haddenham, *Antiquity*, **62**, 360–70

Evans, C, & Pollard, J, nd Storey's Bar Road sub-site

– A re-appraisal, in F Pryor, *Archaeology and environment of the Flag Fen basin*. London: English Heritage Archaeological Report

Field, K, 1974 Ring-Ditches of the Upper and Middle Great Ouse Valley, *Archaeol J*, **131**, 58–74

French, C A I, Davis, M, & Heathcote, J, forthcoming Hydrological monitoring of an alluviated landscape in the lower Great Ouse valley, Cambridgeshire: Interim results of the first three years, *Environmental Archaeology*

French, C A I, & Wait, G A, 1988 *An archaeological survey of the Cambridgeshire river gravels*. Cambridge: Cambridgeshire County Council

Green, H S, 1974 Early Bronze Age burial, territory and population in Milton Keynes, Buckinghamshire, and the Great Ouse Valley, *Archaeol J*, **131**, 75–139

Hall, D, 1996 *The Fenland Project Number 10: Cambridgeshire Survey: Isle of Ely and Wisbech*, East Anglian Archaeology **79**. Cambridge: Cambridgeshire Archaeological Committee

Hall, D, & Coles, J, 1994 *Fenland Survey: an essay in landscape persistence*, NS report 1. London: English Heritage

Heawood, R, 1995 *An Archaeological Evaluation at Ashton Close, Needingworth*, Cambridgeshire County Council Archaeological Field Unit Report A57. Cambridge: Cambridgeshire County Council

Hodder, I, & Evans, C, forthcoming *The Emergence of a Fen-edge Landscape: The Haddenham Project 1981–87*. Cambridge: McDonald Institute Research Series

Hodder, I, & Shand, P, 1988 The Haddenham long barrow: An interim statement, *Antiquity*, **62**, 349–53

Lawson, A J, Martin, E A, & Priddy, D, 1981 *The Barrows of East Anglia*, East Anglian Archaeology **12**

Mortimer, R, & Evans, C, 1996 *Archaeological Excavations at Hinxton Quarry, Cambridgeshire - The North Field*. Cambridge: Cambridge Archaeological Unit

Needham, S, & Sørensen, M L S, 1988 Runnymede refuse tip: A consideration of midden deposits and their formation, in J C Barrett & I A Kinnes (eds) *The Archaeology of Context in the Neolithic and Bronze Age: Recent trends*. Sheffield: Dept of Archaeology and Prehistory, University of Sheffield, 113–26

Phillips, C W, 1970 *The Fenland in Roman Times*, Royal Geographical Res Ser **5**. London: Royal Geographical Society

Pollard, J, 1996 Iron Age Riverside Pit Alignments at St Ives, Cambridgeshire, *Proc Prehist Soc*, **62**, 93–115

Pollard, J, forthcoming 'These places have their moments': thoughts on occupation practices in the British Neolithic, in J Bruck & M Goodman (eds) *Making places in the prehistoric world: themes in settlement archaeology*. London: UCL

Pryor, F, 1980 *Excavation at Fengate Peterborough, England: The third report*. Northamptonshire Archaeol Soc Monogr **1**/Royal Ontario Museum Archaeol Monogr **6**

Pryor, F, 1982 Problems of survival: later prehistoric settlement in the southern East Anglian Fenlands, *Analecta Praehistorica Leidensia*, **15**, 125–44

Pryor, F, 1984 *Excavation at Fengate Peterborough, England: The fourth report*. Northamptonshire Archaeol Soc Monogr **2**/Royal Ontario Museum Archaeol Monogr **7**

Pryor, F, 1988 Earlier Neolithic Organised Landscape and Ceremonial in Lowland Britain, in J C Barrett & I A Kinnes (eds) *The Archaeology of Context in the Neolithic and Bronze Age: Recent Trends*. Sheffield: Department of Archaeology and Prehistory, University of Sheffield, 63–73

Pryor, F, 1996 Sheep, stockyards and field systems: Bronze Age livestock populations in the Fenlands of Eastern England, *Antiquity*, **70**, 313–24

Pryor, F, & French, C A I, 1985 *Archaeology and Environment in the Lower Welland Valley*, East Anglian Archaeology **27**. Cambridge: Cambridgeshire Archaeological Committee

Schlee, D E, 1995 *Excavation of a Romano-British Settlement on the Needingworth Bypass*, Cambridgeshire County Council Archaeological Field Unit Report 99. Cambridge: Cambridgeshire County Council

Taylor, M, & Pryor, F, 1990 Bronze Age building techniques at Flag Fen, Peterborough, England, *World Archaeology*, **21**, 425–34

Tilley, C, 1994 *A phenomenology of landscape: places, paths and monuments*. Oxford/Providence USA: Berg

Waller, M, 1994 *The Fenland Project No 9: Flandrian Environmental Change in Fenland*, East Anglian Archaeology **70**. Cambridge: University of Cambridge, Cambridgeshire Archaeological Committee

10 The Ouse Valley in the Iron Age and Roman periods: a landscape in transition *by Mike Dawson*

Introduction

The development of the Iron Age landscape and the impact of Roman imperialism have long been the focus of study in the Ouse Valley. In the last decade and a half something of a consensus has been reached in published work of how trends in the Iron Age related to and underpinned the development of the region in the Roman period. In a nutshell the orthodox vision sees increasing settlement density, settlement agglomeration, nascent urbanism, and developing centralisation as part of the diffusion of ideas in a Europe-wide core-periphery model. Within this general vision a subsidiary trend has been proposed with eastern England in the middle Iron Age seen as something of a backwater, peripheral to developments in central southern Britain (Cunliffe 1991). Later developments have been interpreted in terms of the wider core-periphery paradigm, focusing on the effects wrought by the advance of Rome (Champion 1989, 9–13). In this political model, during the contact period south-eastern Britain formed a core from which political centralisation and the development of coin-using economies spread outwards towards a periphery constituted by the south Midlands and south-western Britain (Cunliffe 1991). In landscape terms, large open sites with extensive bank and ditch configurations, such as Wheathamstead and Camoludunum, have been interpreted as proto-urban 'oppida' around which tribal territories developed.

In the Roman period, although there is presently no consensus regarding the extent of tribal territories (Millet 1990, 12–14), it is a common assumption that late-Iron Age tribal territories in the Ouse were organised around *civitas* centres at *Verulamium* (St Albans), *Venta Icenorum* (Caistor), and *Ratae Corieltauvorum* (Leicester) and their development, together with that of small towns and the establishment of 'villas', is seen to demonstrate the Romanisation of Britain, through the response of indigenous trajectories to the imposition of Roman rule (Millett 1990; Haselgrove 1989).

Despite these broad constructs, with the exception of the Fenland, where the creation of the Fenland Survey in 1932 initiated an extensive programme of landscape survey (Hall and Coles 1994, 6), little analysis of landscape development in the region has taken place. The earliest landscape survey within the Ouse drainage was Fox's influential 'Archaeology of the Cambridge Region' (Fox 1923), yet it was not until 1971 that the results of excavations in the Ouse basin were correlated with artefact distributions as part of a wider synthesis of the Iron Age

(dated introduction to Cunliffe 1974). Two early ceramic groups, Ivinghoe-Sandy and Chinnor-Wandlebury, were identified which extended across a large proportion of the upper and middle Ouse and drew this area into a ceramic province with the western Chilterns. This 'region' may have survived into the later Iron Age as the bowl continuum, *c* 100 BC, when Gallo-Belgic style ceramics had begun to appear. Highlighting the difficulties of linking settlement evidence to artefact distributions, Cunliffe's analysis also drew attention to the possibility of archaeological regions which transcended topographically determined areas.

In the 1970s and 1980s several landscape surveys followed Cunliffe's lead in attempting to link ceramic chronologies to settlement evidence. The landscape between the Nene and Ouse Valleys was surveyed in 1972 (Hall and Hutchins 1972), followed a year later by a more detailed study of the late Iron Age (Simco 1973). In the latter the distribution of 'Belgic' ceramics was generally found to be in locations which had no earlier Iron Age material and Simco proposed, not only that such locations represented settlement initiated by an immigrant or invading population, but that settlement density was probably increasing as a result. Little evidence, though, derived from formal excavation, and the ceramic chronology was based on a limited number of decorated metal artefacts and imports in the late Iron Age.

In Buckinghamshire the first survey of the Iron Age focused on the north of the county. Initiated by excavations at Bletchley, on the Ouzel, in 1964, the results were published in 1975 (Waugh *et al* 1975). Limiting their objectives to the provision of a gazetteer as the 'basis for future work' the authors concluded that, despite its proximity to the Chilterns, the late-Iron Age ceramic assemblage from the Saffron Gardens site was similar to more northerly sites close to the Ouse Valley (Waugh *et al* 1975, 378).

In 1984, a significant advance in the study of the Iron Age landscape was made with the completion of a doctoral thesis by Knight, based on the Iron Age of the Great Ouse and Nene valleys. For the first time, although relying heavily on Nene Valley excavations, a ceramic chronology was established which was not only based on decorated metalwork and import associations but on C14 dates and an extensive body of excavated evidence. Four broad periods were distinguished: (1) *Deverel-Rimbury variations*, dated by C14 and metalwork to the late Bronze Age; (2) *Iron Age 1*, the late-Bronze Age/Iron Age transition spanning the Ewart Park late-9th century BC to La Tene 1, based on metalwork associations; (3) *Iron Age 2*, later-5th century BC to earliest Belgic, later-1st century BC; (4) *Iron Age 3*, Belgic to earliest Romano-British (AD 43), based on the dating sequence at Irchester.

In the period 'late Bronze Age to Iron Age 2' Knight defined four settlement groups: hillforts; single enclosure settlements; multiple ditched enclosures; and open settlement. Animal bone and plant macrofossil remains indicated a mixed economy as the basis for settlement, in which animal husbandry and the cultivation of emmer wheat and hulled and naked barley were supplemented by later innovations, including the introduction of oats, rye, spelt, and club wheat. Knight also suggested arable farming intensified during the Iron Age concurrent with the beginnings of textile production and the seasonal use of floodplain locations. Settlement density, too, was assessed and was found to have increased across the region from Iron Age 2 to the late Iron Age by a factor of 2.5:1 (Knight 1984, figs 13 and 14). In contrast to earlier migration theories, however, Knight proposed that such changes may have resulted from the introduction of more labour intensive and productive crops, such as club wheat, as well as increased exploitation of iron ore. These developments may in turn have led to social tension, to the development of elite groups and the centralisation of settlement. Knight's study ended with the mid-1st century BC.

Analysis of the transitional period from late Iron Age to early Roman-Britain has focused on the increasing variety of imported artefacts. Distribution patterns of Mediterranean amphorae, European Celtic brooches, Gallo-Belgic ceramics, Gallo- Belgic coins, and decorated metalwork characterise the period. Some of the distributions may be an effect of Roman cultural imperialism, but wider cultural contacts between late-Iron Age polities must have been important in determining the range and final deposition of many imported artefacts. Concurrent with an increase in the variety of artefacts were changes in the settlement pattern, especially the growth of proto-urban centres. Within the Ouse catchment, oppida have now been identified at Baldock (Burleigh 1995) and Thetford (Gregory 1991). Oppida, early Gallo-Belgic coin distributions, Welwyn type burials, and Gallo-Belgic ceramics have become the defining characteristics of several tribal territories within which changes have generated several regional late-Iron Age political histories (Branigan 1985, Cunliffe 1991).

Surveys of the Roman period have tended to emphasise the role of specific historical events at the expense of processual explanations. In addition, concentration on the immediate impact of the Roman invasion on the landscape, particularly the construction of roads (Matthews 1989, 59) and the foundation of major towns, has tended to distract from the evidence of settlement trends in rural areas.

As with the Iron Age, the Fenland has been subject to the most intense landscape survey (Phillips 1970; Hall and Coles 1994). Settlement was influenced not only by natural changes in the water table but also by the creation of extensive drainage systems such as the Car Dyke. In the lower Ouse, early surveys focused on specific aspects of Roman archaeology such as burial (Liversage 1977) and artefactual studies (Taylor 1985). In 1977, Browne published a short history of the Roman period in Cambridgeshire. In 1984, the Royal Commission and Bedfordshire County Council collaborated in a survey of Roman Bedfordshire (Simco 1984) in the middle Ouse. Small towns, villas, and individual settlements were distinguished along with kiln sites and other task specific locations, but the extent and density of settlement estimates were based on SMR data, and the lack of excavated sites meant that no chronological analysis was possible (Simco 1984, figs 7 and 8). Areas of heavy or marginal soils which lacked evidence of settlement were assumed to have been empty in the past rather than a function of modern land-use. There has been little synthetic work in the upper Ouse where the most recent survey is that of Roman Milton Keynes, based on the work of the Milton Keynes Development Corporation (Mynard 1987).

The central weakness of the surveys outlined in this introduction have become clear. Evidence derived largely from aerial photographs, limited field survey and antiquarian sources, and the paucity of excavated evidence has conspired to generate a site specific view of landscape development which at best is based on a very broad dating framework. Inevitably patterns derived from these sources are skewed in favour of areas susceptible to aerial photography or areas of recent arable agriculture. The result is that the limited attempts which have been made to characterise the landscape, both in terms of settlement and land-use, have drawn extensively on analogies with other regions rather than focusing on the Ouse Valley. Lastly, as a result of the failure to characterise Ouse Valley settlement, there is no reliable indication of settlement density in either the Iron Age or Roman periods. Without these elements in place the orthodox vision of the Iron Age and Roman periods outlined at the beginning of this introduction is considerably undermined.

In the ten years since Knight's survey of the Iron Age in the Ouse and Nene valleys highlighted the complexity of Iron Age settlement, considerable changes have occurred both in the availability of evidence and in archaeological approaches to interpretation (Evans 1992a). Increased development and the issue of Planning Policy Guidance Note 16 (PPG 16), in 1990, have resulted in an exponential rise in both the number and scale of excavations in the catchment, which has gone some way to addressing the imbalance in evidence between regions and within the Ouse Valley. Equally significant is the change in archaeological approaches, and in the 1990s the analytical balance has moved towards the development of regional archaeologies, where inter-

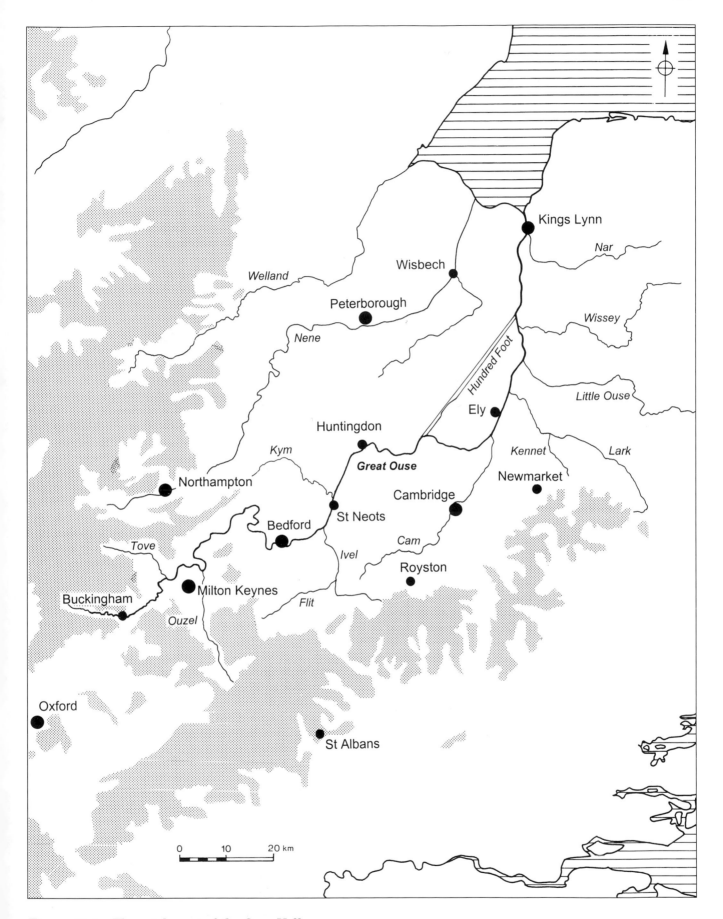

Figure 10.1   The catchment of the Ouse Valley

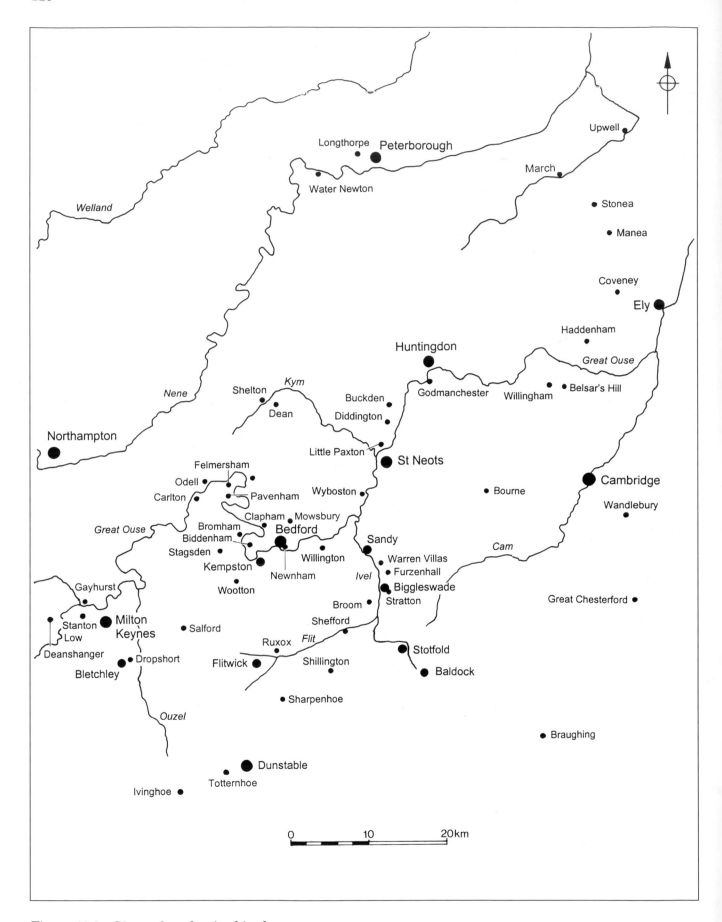

Figure 10.2   Sites referred to in this chapter

pretation of Roman, as much as Iron Age, landscapes is seen to be the product of discourse between groups in a society. The landscape is no longer a historical map over which invaders or cultural fashions advance or withdraw, rather the landscape has become a text through which the social system of a polity can be interpreted. The strength of this approach is that it recognises the force of embedded social value, ritual, and the ethnic identity of Iron Age people, opening up the possibility for interpretations of an archaeological landscape that was not predestined to be invaded by Rome. A third component of change comprises the advances made in the analysis of ecological factors and the impact they have had on landscape development (Robinson 1992). Focusing on the relationship between the physical environment and the impact of man (Scaife Chapter 3, this volume), the extent to which these underpin the human interpretation of the landscape, and the ways in which this may have affected what seemed otherwise rational choices, can be examined.

The survey which follows, therefore, is an attempt to bring together new evidence from the region (Fig 10.1), and to re-examine the balance between indigenous development and the impact of Rome. It is merely a preliminary study in which much of the recently excavated evidence quoted still remains to be analysed in full (Fig 10.2).

The topography of the Great Ouse Valley

Unlike many regions, few areas within the Ouse Valley provide an obstacle to settlement. The river Great Ouse drains from the Chilterns, the Cotswolds, and off the clay watershed between Ouse and Nene. Within this basin the river course is strongly controlled by the geology, although the topography of the catchment is low. In the north, undulating clay lands stretch as far as the Jurassic Ridge, whilst in the central region the Greensand Ridge, nowhere exceeding 50m OD, extends from Woburn Sands, Bedfordshire, to beyond the Gransdens in Cambridgeshire. To the south the topography is more diverse with hills of chalk and clay forming the Icknield Belt, part of the hinterland of the Chilterns, whilst beyond Huntingdon the flatlands of the Fens extend to the Wash, bordered on the south by the Gogmagog Hills and the east by the chalk downlands of Norfolk.

Originating in Buckinghamshire, the Great Ouse flows eastwards off the Cotswolds at Greatworth (165m OD), turning north in a loop through the clays towards Northampton, before flowing south to emerge at Clapham, north of Bedford town. Significant tributaries in the upper reaches include the Ouzel, which rises in the foothills of the Chilterns, and the Tove, which drains the Towcester area. From Clapham to Tempsford the Ouse meanders eastwards within a wide flat valley between the

Greensand Ridge to the south and the ridges of Gault Clay to the north. The drainage pattern here is predominantly from the south. Two important tributaries, the Flit and the Ivel, drain from the hinterland of the Chilterns to pass through a breach in the Greensand Ridge, near Sandy, and join the Ouse at Tempsford. From Tempsford the Great Ouse flows north until, joined by several west flowing tributaries including the Kim, it turns eastwards again. Past Huntingdon and Godmanchester it flows into the Fens where the drainage becomes predominantly eastern with tributaries Cam, Kennet, Lark, Little Ouse, Wissey, and Nar. At its northern extent the river drains into the Wash at Kings Lynn (Rogerson 1986, 22).

The Ouse Valley in the Iron Age and Roman periods (Figs 10.3 and 10.4)

Apart from the Fenland and Fen edge, the Ouse catchment appears uniformly appropriate to settlement, nevertheless both spatial and temporal variation frequently occurs. Some areas, such as Shillington, have localised drainage patterns which limit the extent of available land, whilst in other areas, like the Greensand Ridge, local topography placed practical limits on settlement location.

In the Fens, marine incursion early in the Iron Age resulted in an extension of the wetland around the wash and reduced islands such as Stonea, Coveney, and Ely. Consequently, in Lincolnshire, Cambridgeshire, and Norfolk, where peat growth took place, Iron Age settlement was restricted to Fen edge and island locations (Hall and Coles 1984, fig 59). In the Roman period water levels receded and settlement for the first time spread on to the Flandrian silts (Hall and Coles 1995, fig 68). Occupation was interrupted by probably extensive flooding again in the mid-3rd century, in the south Fen (Potter 1981 132). Short-lived reoccupation returned in the late-3rd century, but by the late-4th century settlement levels were gradually declining, although no sites have clear evidence that this was a result of marine transgression (Potter 1981, 132).

At Willington Mere, on the Fen edge, pollen analysis indicates that deforestation took place in this part of the Ouse Valley immediately before peat formation and the development of the Mere in c 825–790 cal BC (French and Wait 1988, 55). Further westwards, beyond the Fens, in the lower Ouse, evidence from Eynesbury suggests deforestation in these areas had been complete by the late Neolithic (French and Wait 1988) with settlement restricted to the first and second gravel terraces or to low gravel islands in the floodplain. In the middle Ouse at Warren Villas, Sandy, a probably Bronze Age pennanular ditch on the flood plain had, by the 2nd century BC, become filled by fine alluvial deposits, where ploughing was taking place in increasingly waterlogged conditions (Robinson 1992). By the late Iron Age, settlement in some parts had spread onto

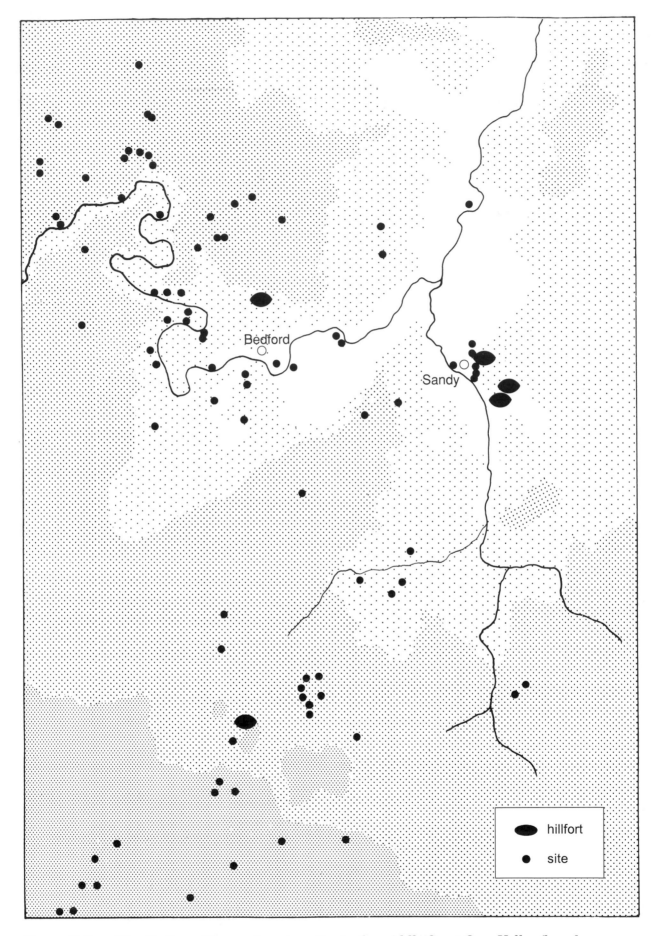

Figure 10.3   Distribution of known Iron Age sites in the middle Great Ouse Valley (based on Bedfordshire HER and Buckinghamshire SMR)

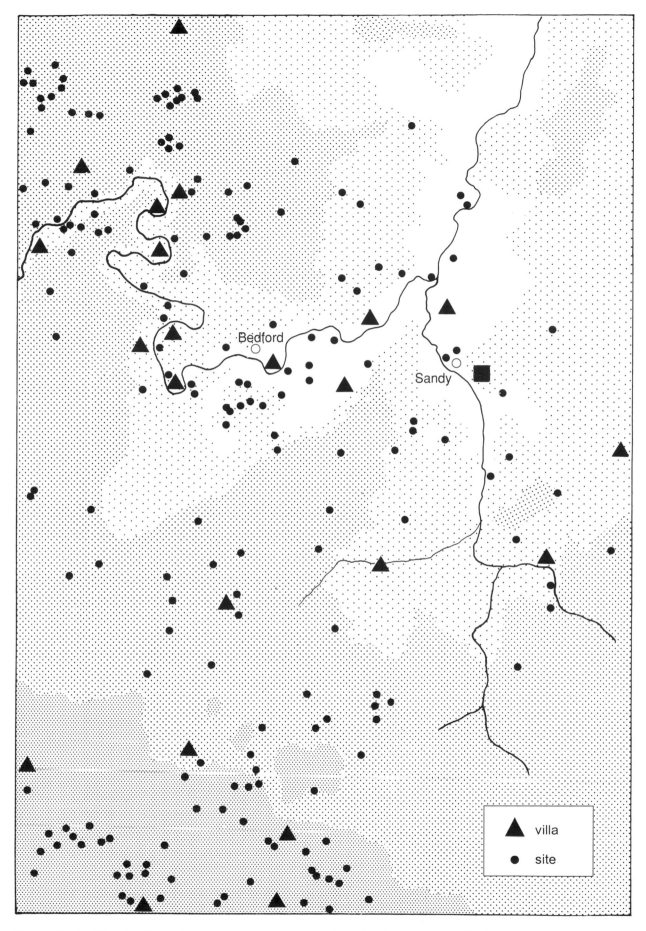

Figure 10.4 Distribution of known Roman sites in the middle Great Ouse Valley (based on Bedfordshire HER and Buckinghamshire SMR)

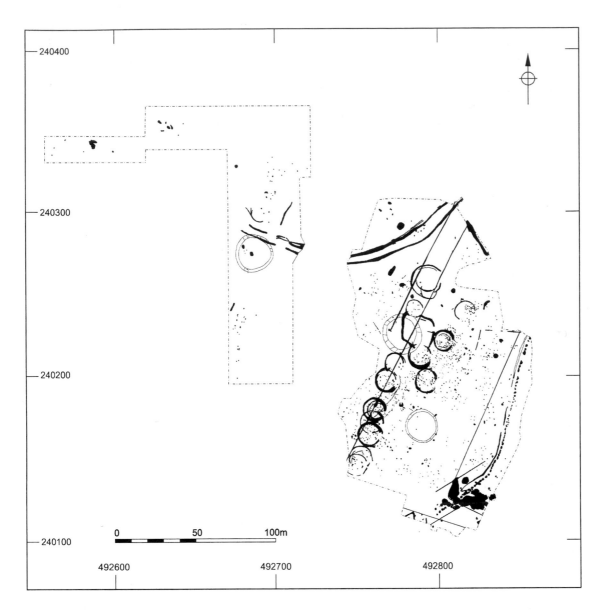

240400

240300

240200

240100

0   50   100m

492600   492700   492800

*Figure 10.5
The middle-
Iron Age settle-
ment at
Salford*

the floodplain, but the trend was soon reversed and sites as widely dispersed as Wyboston, Cambridgeshire (Tebbutt 1957), and Clapham, Bedfordshire (Tilson 1973, 1975), were abandoned when significant alluviation took place. At Haddenham Delphs, Cambridgeshire, an enclosed site was also abandoned during the 1st century AD and sealed beneath alluvium (Evans and Serjeantson 1988).

Conditions remained variable into the late-1st century AD, with evidence for alluviation at Buckden, Diddington, and Little Paxton (French and Wait 1988, 78), and for peat formation in the Flit Valley at Ruxox Farm. In the Ouse Valley, alluvial deposition appears to have largely ceased during the early-Roman period (Bell 1981), and at several sites, including Warren Villas (Dawson and Maull 1996) and Wyboston, Roman period ditches were dug through late-Iron Age alluvial deposits.

By the end of the Roman period, alluviation had returned to most areas and in the Ivel Valley the rising water table was probably responsible for the

loss of the Roman road between Stratton and Sandy in the 5th century (Dawson 1994).

The character of Iron Age settlement

Over sixteen years ago, four broad categories of Iron Age settlement were identified by Knight (1984) in the Nene and Ouse valleys. Hillforts, single enclosures, multiple enclosures, and open settlements (Knight 1984, 180–263) characterised the region. Many of the characteristics of individual settlement types have been confirmed in the intervening years, but recently increasingly large scale excavation and survey is suggesting that the balance and range of settlement in the Ouse Valley might be significantly different to that of the Nene.

Unenclosed settlement in the Ouse catchment existed from at least the beginning of the 1st millennium BC. At Salford, on the Greensand Ridge, Neolithic and Bronze Age activity suggests deforestation may have taken place in the 3rd millennium BC, and a single barley grain from a pit indicates early, possibly Neolithic, agriculture. Three Bronze Age barrows predate the growth of settlement in the late Bronze Age. Initial habitation restricted to five roundhouses had, by the middle Iron Age, increased to cover 2.8ha, with over 26 roundhouses identified (Dawson forthcoming c). The change in character was not an isolated occurrence and there is a similar early sequence at Bancroft, though here a single structure of three concentric post rings characterised the settlement rather than the smaller roundhouses at Salford (Fig 10.5).

In general the open settlements were characterised by roundhouses, defined by circular or sub-circular drip gullies or post rings, four and two post structures, and pits. These sites, known from Broom (French 1990), Biddenham (Luke forthcoming), Stagsden (Dawson forthcoming a), and Milton Keynes (Zeepvat 1989), were common throughout the Ouse Valley where they are usually found on higher slopes well above the flood plain. At several sites, pits and enclosures form distinct groups and, despite many instances of isolated pits and post-holes, such settlements were probably regularly divided into activity areas. Yet at many sites the configuration of roundhouses indicates few could have been contemporary. At Coveney (Evans 1992b) and Bancroft (Williams and Zeepvat 1994) pairing of roundhouses has been proposed as the basis of replicated settlement and a similar pattern is implicit in the layout of structures at Stagsden and possibly Salford (Dawson forthcoming c).

Open settlements were occupied for varying periods during the Iron Age with only a few, like Bancroft, occupied throughout the 1st millennium BC. Probably more typical is Salford, occupied in the late Bronze Age but deserted by the end of the late Iron Age, and Ursula Taylor and Stagsden which were occupied only in the late Iron Age.

As well as the varied pattern of occupation on open sites there is some evidence for change in their form during the 1st century BC. Sub-circular or sub-rectangular, often stone-filled gullies, rather than circular drip gullies, appear to enclose comparable areas to the roundhouses. Possibly indicating changes to the structure of dwellings, they originate in the 1st century BC at Eastcotts, Biddenham, and Warren Villas, where the new form may be part of a move to more marginal locations. A second innovation at these sites, absent from the earlier open settlements, is the proliferation of small enclosures. Probably gardens, their linear layout and repeated overlapping form suggests sequential occupation in a tradition similar to that proposed for paired roundhouses.

In addition to sites that have several roundhouses are an increasing number of locations with only a single roundhouse. Recently, at Biddenham, three isolated structures have been found within an area of over 10ha of excavation.

Coexisting with unenclosed settlement from the

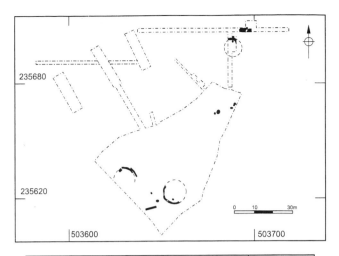

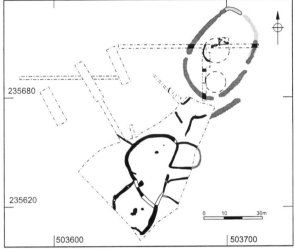

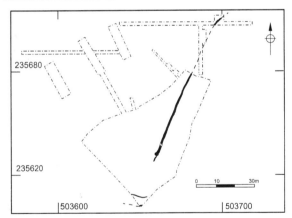

Figure 10.6 The Iron Age site at Hinksey Road, Flitwick, showing the progression from unenclosed to enclosed site and later field system

earliest Iron Age onwards were settlements within a single- or double-ditched enclosure. Such sites, often identified from aerial photographs, were not defensible; the ditches are shallow and lack evidence for palisades or revetments. In the Ouse Valley the variety of enclosed sites is probably wider than Knight's 1982 sample (Knight 1984, Group 2 and 3 enclosures, 200–31) suggested. At Willington

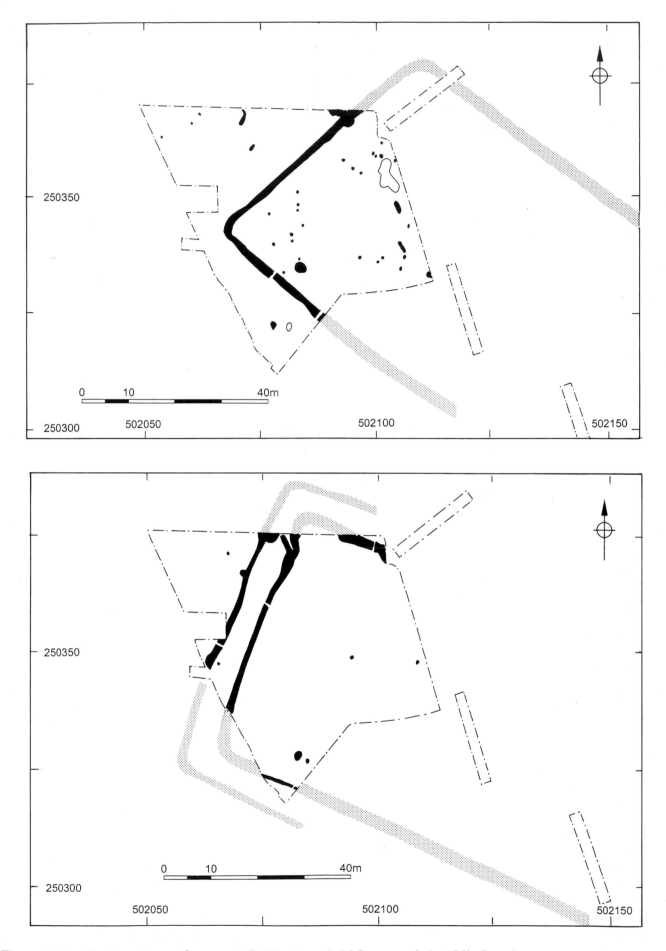

Figure 10.7   The Iron Age enclosures at Biddenham Gold Lane: early/middle Iron Age

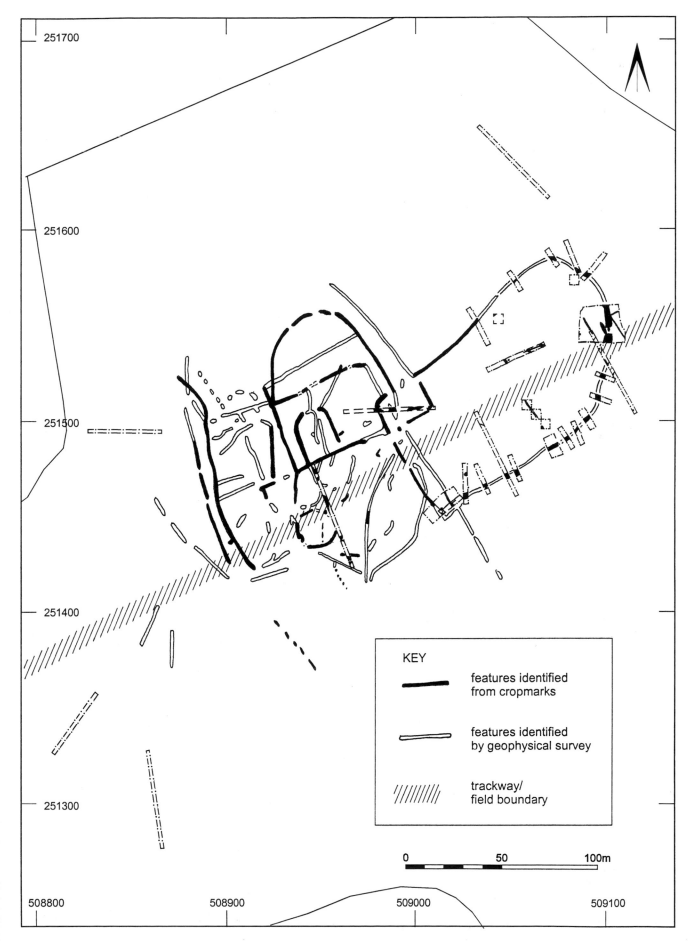

Figure 10.8   The Iron Age and Roman settlement at Norse Road, Bedford

(Pinder 1986) and Flitwick, Bedfordshire (Fig 10.6; Luke 1999), the main settlement was found to include a secondary enclosure and there is some evidence to suggest enclosed settlements in the Ouse Valley may be larger than in the Nene. In the latter, approximately 0.13ha was the maximum area enclosed (Knight 1984, table 19, 169) but at Gold Lane (Fig 10.7), Biddenham, and Norse Road, Bedford (Dawson and Gaffney 1995; Dawson 1997), two single-ditched enclosures extended to over c 0.36ha. Several recent excavations, including Shillington (Dawson forthcoming a) and Flitwick, indicate that contemporary activity areas often extended beyond the limits of the enclosures.

The third group of Iron Age settlements are those where habitation is surrounded by several, possibly focused enclosures. Familiar from the Upper Thames Valley, there are examples of such sites in the Ouse catchment at Norse Road, Bedford (late Iron Age) (Fig 10.8); Odell, Bedfordshire (Dix 1980); Pennylands (late Iron Age); Bradwell (Williams and Zeepvat 1994); and possibly Wavendon Gate, Buckinghamshire (Williams *et al* 1995). The characteristic focused enclosures of these sites suggest they could share a common agricultural tradition and at Norse Road geophysical survey certainly identified a 'habitation effect' central to the enclosures, at the highest point of the site (Dawson and Gaffney 1995). But at least two of the outer enclosures at Norse Road contained structural evidence suggesting that settlement like that at Odell (Dix 1981) had moved location within the area of the enclosures and it may be that the sites with focused enclosures are in fact no more than repeated occupation of a preferred location. Similar to the 'focused' sites are those where enclosure follows a common alignment. Washing line enclosures (MPP 1989) such as those in Dean and Shelton are known from aerial photographs, but few have been excavated. Recently, at Shillington, three enclosures aligned along a multiple-ditched boundary were sampled and found to have been occupied sequentially from the middle to late Iron Age. In common with other settlements the enclosures were characterised by zones of pitting, habitation, ironworking, and cereal production.

Hillforts in low places: the growth and decline of defensible space

The absence of hillforts in eastern England is a recognised regional characteristic and is used to support the contention that eastern England was peripheral to developments in central southern Britain for much of the Iron Age. Compared with earlier surveys (Dyer 1961) the number of hillforts has been reduced for lack of evidence at Limlow Hill and Burlow Hill (Hyde Hall Farm), whilst Arbury Banks may be the earthwork of an enclosed settlement (Bryant and Burleigh 1995, 94). Despite these reductions there are still several hillforts in the Ouse catchment, although the majority are located on the periphery of the region.

The most clearly defined series, Ravensburgh

(Dyer 1976a), Wilbury (Applebaum 1949), Arbury Banks, and Northfield, is on the north face of the Chilterns. Further west, Ivinghoe, still part of the Chiltern series, overlooks the Ouse–Thames watershed, and further west still is Rainsborough (Avery *et al* 1967), a hillfort located on the Ouse–Cherwell watershed. In the northern part of the catchment there are no hillforts, but at the northern limit of the region Hunsbury (Fell 1937, Jackson 1993–4) and Borough Hill (Audouy 1992) occupy locations on the edge of the Nene Valley. Within the catchment, Danesborough, Buckinghamshire (Croft and Mynard 1993), occupies a low hill above the Ouzel; Caesar's Camp, Bedfordshire (Dawson 1995), a contoured hilltop on the Greensand above the Ivel; and Mowsbury, Bedfordshire (Dring 1971a), a knoll on the clay ridge above Bedford town. On the chalk ridge of the Icknield belt is Sharpenhoe Clappers (Dix 1983). In the area of the lower Ouse, War Ditches, Belsars Hill, Arbury, Borough Fen, and Wandlebury are referred to as ringworks, to distinguish their near circular enclosures from the typical contoured hillfort (Evans 1992a, 14–26).

The character of hillforts and ringworks is varied: Danesborough may be the only regional example of a 'developed' hillfort; Ivinghoe (Cotton and Frere 1968), occupied a hilltop site; Sharpenhoe Clappers, on the chalk, and Sandy Lodge (Dyer 1971), above the Ivel, are promontory forts defined only by ramparts across the neck of a plateau. At Mowsbury, a hillfort with timber revetments has been identified but not fully characterised because of damage wrought by the imposition of a medieval moated site. As might be expected, details of the defensive sequence at several hillforts is well known: Ivinghoe and Wandlebury, like Mowsbury, have complex timber-reinforced revetments dating to the 5th century BC, whilst the revetments at Sharpenhoe and Sandy Lodge (and probably Caesar's Camp) were dump construction. Less is known of the internal arrangements of these sites. Ivinghoe and Ravensburgh yielded postholes, possibly of stockades and settlement, from limited areas of excavation. In contrast, at the ringwork site of Arbury the interior was rigorously sampled but produced no evidence of internal settlement; the foundations of a tower were, however, recovered near the entrance (Evans 1992b). At Arbury Banks, aerial photographs show extensive areas of pits, enclosures, roundhouses, and other evidence of habitation.

The variety of form, period of occupation, and location indicates the difficulty in assigning a single causal factor to the appearance of hillforts. Hill (1989) has coined the negative 'not-farmsteads' to express the one function not associated with the hillforts, and something of the variety of role he associates with these sites is found in the Ouse Valley. Arbury Banks and the Chiltern series may be the short lived remains of central places, a focus for small tribal groups along the Chiltern Ridge; in the Ouse the promontories at Sharpenhoe, Mowsbury, and Sandy may have been chosen for their exceptional positions which offer extensive views across the Ouse, Ivel, and Flit valleys, and Danesborough, together with the unfinished fort at Caesar's Camp, may be the remains of late, developed hillforts similar to those of central southern Britain. The ringworks, like the promontory 'forts' of the Ouse, were probably not settled, but provided a focus for unspecified activity (Hill 1989).

Territorial gains: land division and the growth of tribalism

The third component of the landscape where there is an increasing body of evidence is the division of land. Three major forms of physical division are known – dykes, ditched boundaries, and posthole alignments – whilst tribal or territorial subdivisions are derived from artefact, principally coin, distributions.

The dykes are distinguished from ditched field boundaries by their scale and, like the hillforts, are found predominantly on the periphery of the region. Initially regarded as tribal boundaries (Dyer 1961), there are two groups – those along the Chilterns extending into Cambridge as far as the Devils Ditch at Newmarket and those within the Ouse Valley (Knight 1984, map 20, 161). In several Chiltern examples a sequence in which pit alignments were replaced by bank and ditch boundaries, before becoming increasingly complex as double and triple ditches in their final phase, has been noted (Bryant and Burleigh 1995). The developed form of this model is rarely achieved in the Ouse Valley, where several posthole alignments are known from aerial photographs. One posthole alignment close to Bedford, at Plantation Quarry, Willington (Dawson 1996) has recently been excavated. Dating to the middle Iron Age, the Willington example extended over several hundred metres and connected penannular enclosures near the river flood plain with a single Bronze Age ring-ditch. The location in the river valley and its proximity to earlier burial monuments suggests that in some areas the alignments may be related to ceremony or are territorial markers, the alignments intended to focus attention on some aspect of the topography or construction in the environment. Short, unconnected stretches of pit alignment seem unlikely to relate to tribal divisions or function as territorial boundaries.

Ditched boundaries, in contrast, comprise the most extensive evidence for land division. They most commonly form localised field systems associated with settlement, but occasionally they may form part of more extensive boundary systems. There are clear regional differences in the field boundaries of the Ouse Valley. From the lower Ouse, Fen-edge settlements either comprise enclosures in linear alignments following water courses or roddons, or are part of apparently focused systems with settlement near the core. Further upstream, above Huntingdon, extensive networks of rectangular and sub-rectangular fields are known from a restricted number of locations, whilst at Biggleswade cropmarks in the Ivel Valley may be the remains of a limited coaxial system originating in the Iron Age, despite suggestions that they may be evidence of centuriation (Bigmore 1979). In the middle Ouse the present pattern of land division closely relates to settlement focus. In the valley bottoms linear arrangements of enclosures, often aligned along the edge of the first gravel terrace, have already been identified whilst the character of focused sites has been questioned. The origins of the latter date to the 1st century BC and settlement extended throughout the Roman period. In the upper Ouse, a biaxial system of field enclosures which stretches across Buckinghamshire into Bedfordshire has been found oriented on the Icknield Way, but the system is undated by excavation (Bull 1993).

Beyond the valleys, little is known of the Iron Age landscape. Cropmarks on the clay ridges of north Bedfordshire, and from the Greensand Ridge, are beginning to extend the areas of known settlement where linear patterns of enclosures are visible (Clark and Dawson 1995, fig 23). These still require investigation as many cropmarks could be the limited highlights of systems surviving on the ridge crests. Two projects, the Hemel to Humber pipeline (BCAS excavation) and the M1 widening scheme (Dawson and Edwards 1994), in particular, attest the absence of enclosures across extensive areas of the river valleys and their hinterland. Providing transects stretching across the Ouse catchment, which were intensively investigated during archaeological evaluation, they revealed that field boundary ditches were limited in focus with no hidden evidence for extensive field systems in areas which are not susceptible to aerial photography.

One ditched boundary type which does appear to subdivide larger areas of landscape is the triple ditch. One in particular has been excavated. Stretching north from the Elstow Brook in the south, across a neck of land to the River Ouse, it enclosed a large island of land which included several settlement sites and earlier ritual monuments (Shepherd forthcoming). Similar examples are known from the lower Ouse (Malim, Chapter 8 this volume).

The final component of landscape division is the tribal boundary. Caesar's reference to the Belgae has been especially influential in determining a Belgic tribal area in south-eastern England dating to the late-2nd century BC. From the later part of the 2nd century BC the distribution of Gallo-Belgic ceramics, coinage of Allen's type A and B (Allen 1961), and during the first half of the 1st century BC, the appearance of the Welwyn burial form have been used as the basis for assessing the extent of Belgic influence or territorial expansion. Current interpretations lay emphasis on the transmission of Gallo-Belgic styles rather than an extensive invading population. Little new evidence has been recovered to change the distributions: recent excavation at Biddenham, Marston Moretaine, Salford, and Stotfold (Steadman forthcoming) have increased the number of Welwyn style cremations, but these burials have not extended the distribution and, with recent finds of coins, have only contributed to the density of current patterns.

In the proto-historic period of the late Iron Age the regional subdivision of the landscape is given a political dimension with the evidence of tribal names. Three major tribal groups have been identified in the Ouse basin: the Trinovantes, the Iceni, and the Catuvellauni. Originally derived from Caesar (Cunliffe 1978, 68), tribal territories have been projected backwards into the late-2nd century BC on the basis of coin distributions (Allen 1961, Sellwood 1984, Van Arsdell 1989) and modified by detailed dynastic argument (Rodwell 1978). The latter was based on specific coin issues and indicated that the frontier between tribal groups was ill defined (Kimes et al 1982), although the idea of a linear boundary such as the Nene or Ouse is still common. Despite the tenacity of the formal boundary, the evidence of dynastic coin distributions suggests tribal territories remained unstable right up to the Roman invasion (Van Arsdell 1989).

The articulation of the landscape

The character of Iron Age settlement outlined so far contrasts markedly with the accepted vision of the region. There is no clear hierarchy of settlement and it is far from clear that any settlement agglomeration or nucleation took place in the 1st millennium BC. Occupation or activity at most of the hillforts either left little trace, or was related to such transient *activities* as seasonal assembly or religious dedication. Few of the hillforts were settled and none were occupied throughout the period; only one peripheral group on the Chilterns has sufficient evidence to even suggest a central place function. Two sites, Danesborough and Caesar's Camp, Sandy, respectively univallate and developed forms, are contenders for late proto-urban centres of the 1st century BC, but neither have been excavated and this must remain conjecture.

In addition, although a pattern of settlements divides into two principal forms, the overwhelming impression is of repeated reoccupation of preferred locations, concurrent with an increasing number of single roundhouse sites in areas that were once thought to be empty. Chronologically diagnostic artefacts, such as ceramics, provide only the broadest framework, but stratigraphic evidence clearly limits the scale of occupation at otherwise extensive sites like Salford and Bradwell.

The evidence of field boundaries is equally complex but attests a varied landscape dominated by small settlements in which agricultural enclosures were limited in extent. Less is known of the use to which these enclosures were put. Animal bone analysis has been undertaken on very few sites in the Ouse Valley and other areas are unhelpful in providing useful analogues. (In the Thames and Nene Valleys, sheep appear to replace cattle as the dominant domesticated species in the early Iron Age, whilst during the same period the trend in the south midlands is reversed, with cattle increasing in proportion to sheep (Maltby 1981). In general, horses are more abundant throughout the Iron Age than in the late Bronze Age (Robinson and Wilson 1983)).

In the Ouse Valley, only localised patterns have been identified. At Willington, Hartigans (Williams 1993), Pennylands, and Furzton (Williams 1988), where cattle predominated, their communities may have concentrated on herding. Horse, cattle, goat, and pig remain to be analysed in detail at Salford and evidence has yet to be analysed at other sites, though there is a possible structural link with stock rearing at Salford, Biddenham, and Hartigans, where some roundhouses had adjoining enclosures. At Bancroft, cattle predominated over sheep, but horses and pigs were present. Similarly, sheep, horse, and pigs were present at Pennylands. At Haddenham Delphs, exploitation of wildlife was clearly represented by the bones of beaver, swan, dalmatian pelican, common crane, heron, mallard, coot, and curlew; and this aspect of the food chain should not be forgotten on less well preserved sites. At many of these sites unenclosed areas between settlements indicate the potential for a landscape of mixed pasturage and woodland.

The predominance of cattle in the Milton Keynes area throughout the Iron Age, and the high proportion of pigs, was ascribed to the area's clay soils and the proximity of woodland for pannage (Holmes and Reilly 1994, 531). However, very little is known of the floral environment beyond a general trend towards deforestation throughout the Iron Age, and there is no automatic link between clay soils and either cattle or sheep as changing trends indicate.

The type of crop produced was possibly more susceptible to topography and soil type. Here the region seems to follow broadly the pattern established for the Thames Valley (Jones 1981). Spelt wheat was cultivated on a small scale at Salford and many other sites have evidence of cereal cropping as well as quern stones attesting processing on site. Asymmetrical plough marks have been found in a small enclosure on the flood plain at Warren Villas (Robinson 1992).

In other areas of rural activity the evidence is sparse but widespread. In the Ivel Valley, at Biggleswade and Warren Villas, hurdles attest woodland coppicing and the probability of wider woodland management, whilst the evidence of oak pollen from Warren Villas and oak charcoal from Salford indicates the proximity of oak woodland. Equally common may have been crafts such as thatching and basket making. In the Fenland, salt production is widely attested along the Fen edge (Hall and Coles 1994, 101–2). Loom weights at Willington, Bromham (Tilson 1975), and Chamberlains Barn (ex litt Slowokowski) suggest the importance of ovicaprids as providers of secondary products. Fine knife marks on animal bones, particularly on horses from Salford, may indicate leather production. Evidence of craft activity is similarly sparse but extensive. Iron production has been proposed in areas of the middle and upper Ouse (Hall and Hutchins 1972, 6–8) based on the collection of iron slags from fieldwalking, and slag, either from smelting or smithing, is regularly found on Iron Age sites in small quantities. The evidence of pottery manufacture is more circumstantial. Localised ceramic distribution patterns suggest production was widespread but localised, with much fired in bonfires leaving little or no evidence. Pottery kilns, such as those at Stagsden, only made their appearance late in the Iron Age.

Settlement density

In 1984 both Knight and Simco produced settlement patterns for the Ouse which were predominantly riverine (Knight 1984, figs 13 and 14; Simco 1984). Today it is clear these patterns are heavily biased towards areas of modern developments and land-use (cf Fulford and Nichols 1992). Increased ploughing on the clay uplands of Bedfordshire (Clark and Dawson 1995, fig 23) and, more recently, excavation on the Greensand Ridge, together with recent discoveries in the clay vale at Wootton (Pollard 1996) and at Marston Moretaine (BCAS 1996/18) have begun to fill the blanks in earlier distributions on the middle Ouse. Similarly on the lower Ouse, the publication of the Ouse gravels survey (French and Wait 1988) and the Fenland survey has considerably extended areas of known valley, Fenland, and fen-edge settlement.

Within the last decade several excavations, such as Gold Lane, at Biddenham (Dawson forthcoming a), and Stagsden, have taken place on sites which, although noted in sites and monuments records, could not have been identified as Iron Age from cropmarks alone. Further new sites have been recovered as a result of assessment and evaluation in otherwise blank areas. Thus the earlier bias in published survey data continues to be eroded by the wider integration of archaeology in the planning process.

Thirdly, the increased scale of excavation is affording new opportunities to examine, not just specific sites, but areas of landscape, and it is clear from recent work at Broom, Biddenham, Shillington, and Gold Lane that small scale settlement with, or adjacent to, limited enclosure systems may have been far more widespread from the Bronze Age onwards than hitherto realised.

Lastly there is increasing evidence of settlement patterns modified by regional environments. On the Fen edge and the marginal locations in the river valleys occupation may have been seasonal, yet although almost no areas remained without settlement (Hall and Coles 1994, 92–101), there is one notable exception – the Oxford clays of the southwestern Fen edge.

The breadth of evidence for agricultural diversity, the evidence for dispersed settlement, the broad dating framework, together with factors relating to the collection of data, has rendered estimates of settlement density elusive. Therefore, despite the advances made in site recognition and recovery, there is still insufficient data to make detailed observations regarding settlement density. It is clear though that the overall number of Iron Age sites is still increasing, and it is also clear that we cannot assume that Iron Age settlement increased consistently throughout the 1st millennium BC. Even evidence from this brief survey suggests significant changes were occurring which could have dramatically affected settlement densities.

Towards a model of the Iron Age landscape

Contemporary approaches to landscape studies, whilst acknowledging the interrelationship of human activity and the physical environment, stress the importance of embedded social relationships on landscape development. In phenomenology and post-processual analysis, reading of the landscape and its meaning for a specific population may be more important to the way the landscape was developed than central place theory or site catchment analysis.

Current published interpretations of the Iron Age in the Ouse Valley vary from the quasi-historical, but otherwise static, vision of hillforts as central places in a network of tribal territories which ultimately provided the location, at Ravensburgh, for the final conflict in Caesar's campaign (Dyer 1976b), to a more benign Ouse Valley as a backwater to developments in central southern Britain (Cunliffe 1991). The use of terms like 'backwater' invoke a core-periphery model of regional development, which implicitly marginalises the dynamic of in situ change in favour of external causation, and there is no doubt that such a view becomes more compelling as the Roman invasion approaches. In the earlier Iron Age, the evidence for the increasing establishment of sedentary settlement, together with the evident rise in cereal cultivation, suggests the shift from pastoralism to sedentary agriculture at this time may have led to conflict or tension between competing groups. In this situation 'hillforts' and changes in ceramic styles may have been statements in the discourse between communities, where a heightened sense of identity was played out in terms of land-use, land tenure, and ownership. The resolution of this situation was expressed through the abandonment of hillforts by the end of the 5th century BC and in the increasing subdivision of the land. Without detailed survey this can be carried too far: posthole alignments and limited field systems were evident throughout the period, but clearly any tentative move towards centralisation based around the hilltop enclosures was discarded in the middle Iron Age. Until the very end of the Iron Age evidence of nucleation or agglomeration is elusive, environmental evidence suggesting that subsistence, non-specialist agricultural practice, and settlement of the Ouse Valley remained small scale, dispersed, and characterised by cyclical occupation of preferred sites. Status in this model was rarely expressed in settlement form, only at Coveney where the layout of roundhouses and enclosing ditches was significantly complex has high status for the occupants been claimed (Evans 1992b). Alternatively status may have been expressed through ceremony, which only in the late Iron Age was visible in the new burial practice of cremation.

Comment on the nature of such a society has generally been left to Caesar or Tacitus, yet such a dispersed settlement pattern might be attributed to partible male inheritance, and archaeological evidence is certainly beginning to develop an image of deeply conservative communities. The latter has been invoked to account for the lack of continental imports on late-Iron Age sites in the Ouse Valley and Chilterns (Farley 1995) and for the longevity of middle-Iron Age ceramics (Evans and Sarjeantson 1988) on the Fen edge. It may also account for the presence of 1st-century BC cremations placed in wheel-turned urns at Salford, adjacent to a site where the majority of ceramics were handmade.

During the late Iron Age, the proximity of Rome was made increasingly explicit through the importation of Italian artefacts, which were initially deposited as grave goods. Samian, decorated metalwork, and amphora may indicate the higher status of some Iron Age settlements but were only found on settlements in the immediate pre-conquest period. Their importance lies in the date of their appearance. Recently excavations have extended the known range of later Iron Age cremations at Stotfold, Biddenham, and Salford, but nowhere, except Shefford (Kennett 1970) and possibly Harlington (Dawson forthcoming b), has the combination of Roman imports and indigenous artefacts been found in possibly pre-conquest contexts in the region. Yet on the eve of the Roman conquest Sandy seems to have developed in accordance with the orthodox model. Several die-linked coins suggest a mint and political centre; over 30 Iron Age coins in a stream bed indicate a religious/ritual aspect; and the presence of a large univallate hillfort hints at nascent urban development. But the hillfort is unexcavated, the coins are those of Tasciovanus, the religious deposit part of a wider Iron Age phenomenon, and the extent of Iron Age Sandy is unknown, with only a single roundhouse which can be confidently dated to the pre-conquest period (Dawson 1995).

The shock of the new: continuity, colonisation, and enclosure in the Roman period

Innovative approaches to burial tradition, the expression of status through imported artefacts, the adoption of coinage, and the growth of oppida characterise the radical changes in the Ouse Valley dur-ing the contact period, and continuing adaptability must have been a significant factor after the conquest. Nevertheless, developments in the landscape must not be over-simplified merely as the negotiation between two interacting cultures. From the Roman standpoint, negotiation meant successfully moving through the transition from military hegemony to civil authority, but for the indigenous population the advent of Rome meant the entire renegotiation of established value systems. In the early stages of this transition the emphasis was clearly on military disposition and in the years following the Roman invasion significant additions were made to the landscape of the Ouse Valley. The military campaigns, which lasted until the final conquest of the Iceni, established forts at Longthorpe (Dannell and Wild 1987), Godmanchester (Wait 1991), and *Magiovinium* (Woodfield 1977). Major roads, including subsidiary routes, passed close to several local centres: Baldock (Stead and Rigby 1989; Burleigh 1995), Braughing (Burnham and Wacher 1990), and Sandy, in the west; Maiden Bower (Matthews 1976) and Danesborough in the east. Although there is no evidence of temporary campaign camps in the region, the roads, constructed in the 1st century AD, link forts to river crossings and may reflect the early campaign routes (Frere 1967).

Concurrent with the physical development of the landscape, the power structure of Britain was being transformed by the creation of a hierarchy of administrative and legal relationships. Based on the *civitas*, the region was placed under the jurisdiction of centres at Leicester (*Ratae Corieltauvorum*), St Albans (*Verulamium*), and Caistor (*Venta Icenorum*) (Rivet 1958), with the hierarchy of territories extending down to the *vicii* attested at Water Newton (Wild 1974, 147), Sawtry (Collingwood and Wright 1965), and Thrapston (Browne 1977).

The early restructuring is assumed to have drawn on the political framework of the late Iron Age, reflecting earlier tribal areas in which the '*civitas*' centres legitimised Roman authority by drawing on earlier tribal organisation. The civitas, therefore, did not necessarily constitute a significant re-orientation of the landscape. However, the major towns were also the focus of a road network, which in the 1st century AD was provided with a series of posting stations (Black 1995), and it was this which radically redirected earlier patterns of communication.

In the landscape the processes of renegotiation can be measured in continuities and discontinuities of late-Iron Age patterns. Continuities in rural habitation have already been noted on some open sites, as well as sites of aligned and focused enclosures, but earlier settlement mobility disappeared in the Roman period. Sequential occupation of the same sites continued but no new sites of these types were founded after the conquest. One reason for this may be in the extension of field systems. New ditched boundaries such as those at Old Covert, Salford

Figure 10.9   The Iron Age and Roman enclosures at Warren Villas

(Petchey 1978), and an area of rectangular fields oriented on the Fenland Causeway in Cambridgeshire (Hall and Coles 1995, 119) suggest enclosure was taking place on a large scale in the Roman period.

With dating evidence improved, it is clear that by the 2nd century AD a settlement hierarchy had emerged in which individual farms, hamlets, villas, and small towns played a part. Individual farms are known in three forms. The units which made up the linear sites, like Upwell (Hall 1982), Warren Villas (Fig 10.9), Ruxox (Dawson forthcoming a), and East-

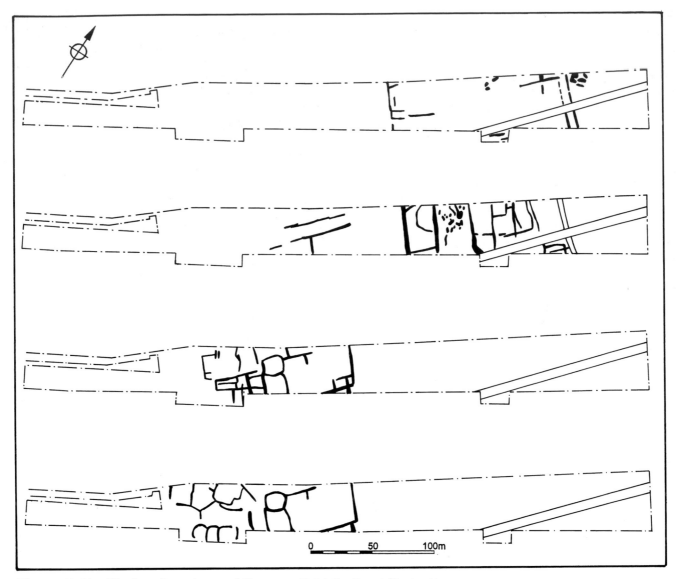

Figure 10.10   The late-Iron Age and Romano-British site at Eastcotts

cotts (Fig 10.10); the farms, such as Odell, Peartree Farm (Shepherd forthcoming), and Bunyans Farm (Shepherd forthcoming) characterised by limited field systems and short stretches of double-ditched drove way, often zig-zagging past one side of the site; and lastly, enclosed sites. These sites all have origins in the late Iron Age and many exhibit functional continuities, such as pit groups and metal-working; but enclosed sites like the single round-houses do not seem to have survived the 1st century AD. In the Fenland, the number of single farm sites was found to have fallen from over 70% of known settlement in the 1st century AD to 35–40% in the late-2nd and early-3rd centuries (Hingley 1989, 75).

In contrast to the general decline of farm sites, the rise of the villa, a synonym for the country estate of approximately 300 acres, seems particularly significant. In the upper Ouse, over 40 villas sites are known, many clustering around the small town of Towcester. In the middle Ouse they favour lighter

soils, which overlay the gravels in the river valleys, or the mixed deposits on the Greensand Ridge or the chalk marls of the Icknield belt (Simco 1984, fig 8). Away from the towns and roads a significant number of villas are found along the Ouse as it winds its way through the claylands of Buckinghamshire, Northamptonshire, and Bedfordshire. Around the Ouzel and Ouse confluence, Wymbush and Bradwell may owe their success to the proximity of Watling Street, but Carlton, Odell, Bletsoe, Felmersham, Pavenham, Biddenham, and Newnham Marina indicate that the mixed topography of the river valley was at least as valuable. There are still no known examples from the claylands of northern Bedfordshire. Similarly on the lower Ouse, whilst recent discoveries indicate the wider dispersal of villas than hitherto recognised (cf Hingley 1989, 137) the distribution still tends to focus on the towns of Godmanchester and Water Newton.

In the Fens there are no villas, but on the eastern Fen edge 'there is a continuous band of Romano-

British settlement ... comprising a small number of substantial masonry buildings' (Gurney 1986). Stonea may be the centre of an imperial estate (Potter 1989).

At Bradwell and Newnham Marina (Simco 1984), evidence of late-'Belgic' Iron Age settlement underlies the villa complex in a pattern which has become increasingly familiar in south-eastern England. A similar process may be at work at Aston Well (Dawson forthcoming a) and Bletsoe (Dawson 1994) where villas were founded close to Iron Age settlement, but the temporal pattern of villa development in the region remains anecdotal. Bancroft, Stanton Low (Woodfield and Johnstone 1989), and Deanshanger (Branigan 1985) developed in the 2nd century AD from Iron Age predecessors whilst Gayhurst and Stantonbury were only founded in the 3rd century, but nevertheless developed on sites with roundhouses. Further south Wymbush and Bletchley were founded in the 3rd century. Thenford, initially a timber structure, was converted to stone in the 3rd century (Branigan 1985). In the Icknield belt, a courtyard villa at Totternhoe, close to Dunstable, which may have been founded in the 1st century AD, has been ascribed to the manager of a *mansio* (Matthews *et al* 1992, 65) and there is a similar courtyarded villa near Sandy at Furzenhall (Johnstone 1959).

As they developed throughout the 2nd–5th centuries, the differential growth of villas and their affinity for specific topographical locations separates them increasingly from the pre-Roman pattern and illustrates the reorientation of the settlement hierarchy. Villas are often found on south-facing slopes, close to a water source, but not on marginal ground or in exposed locations, suggesting their distribution probably results from an economic system in which only a specific agricultural regime could generate sufficient profit to develop a pre-existing farm site or maintain a new foundation.

Concurrent with the development of the villa and the individual farm is the growth of nucleated settlement. These are not numerous in the Ouse Valley. They occupy the middle ground within the settlement hierarchy and are commonly referred to as 'hamlets and small villages' (Hingley 1989, 76–8). The settlement form has proved difficult to identify. Recently referred to as 'extended sites', investigation of two locations, Ruxox and Willington, indicates the need for a clear definition of settlement type. At Ruxox, rather than a village, the landscape components divide into a linear site of aligned enclosures similar to Eastcotts, and, approximately 500m away, a villa. At Willington the settlement comprises a site of focused enclosures at the western end of a cropmark, with a series of aligned enclosures at the eastern extremity (*contra* Simco 1984, 31–2). Both sites, rather than constituting nucleated settlement, conform to the pattern of continuity suggested by other pre-Roman sites.

On the other hand, Kempston (Dawson forthcoming a), a recently excavated site in Bedfordshire, may exemplify the Roman village (Fig 10.11). It extends over 10ha on a low island in the Ouse Valley, has a gridded network of gravel-metalled tracks and comprises several stone-built farms set within the street grid. Although not entirely excavated, the farms were probably occupied concurrently and it is this which distinguishes nucleated from repetitively occupied sites. Further examples of nucleated settlement with this characteristic are known from the Fenland at Grandford (Potter and Potter 1982), Flaggrass, and Coldham (Potter 1981), but few are known from the upper Ouse.

The origins of nucleated settlement are far from clear. Grandford may have originated with a post-Boudiccan fort but others, like Kempston, may have grown up around earlier Iron Age sites.

The paucity of village sites in the region is significant in comparison with the small towns, despite the potential overlap. Bourne (Potter 1981), a village which may have grown large enough to have become a small town, is, for instance, an exception. There are several small towns in the Ouse Valley. *Durocobrivis* (Dunstable) (Matthews 1989) and Sandy developed around *mansiones* or *mutationes* of the *cursus publicus* (Black 1995), whilst *Magiovinium* (Dropshort Farm) and Towcester (Burnham and Wacher 1990) on the Watling Street; Godmanchester; and *Durolipons* (Cambridge) (Browne 1974) originated as forts.

Agglomeration, centralisation and urbanisation

Reorientation of settlement patterns, enclosure, the nucleation of settlement, and the development of urbanisation characterise the 1st and 2nd centuries AD, but throughout the period all three were subject to changes both in scale and intensity. Some of these changes have been directly attributed to imperial policy. In the Fenland, west of Akeman Street, extensive settlement in the early-2nd century AD has been attributed to deliberate colonisation under Hadrian (Potter 1989), on the eastern Fen edge in Norfolk, Gurney (1986) has attributed a series of villas to assistants of the provincial procurator, and on the upper Ouse the regular dispersal of villa estates has been attributed to colonisation around Towcester (Branigan 1985). The origin of small towns is attributed to the location of forts or the *cursus publicus* (Black 1995).

The initiation of small town development with an official foundation suggests market forces were part of the indigenous response to the Roman occupation (Burnham 1986; Hingley 1989). But it is also possible that the move towards settlement nucleation and the growth of small towns is part of a survival strategy linked to the rise of the villa estate. In Bedfordshire, at Biddenham, across the river from the village site at Kempston, where 17ha has been explored, several small-scale Iron Age settlements, comprising single roundhouses, were abandoned be-

126

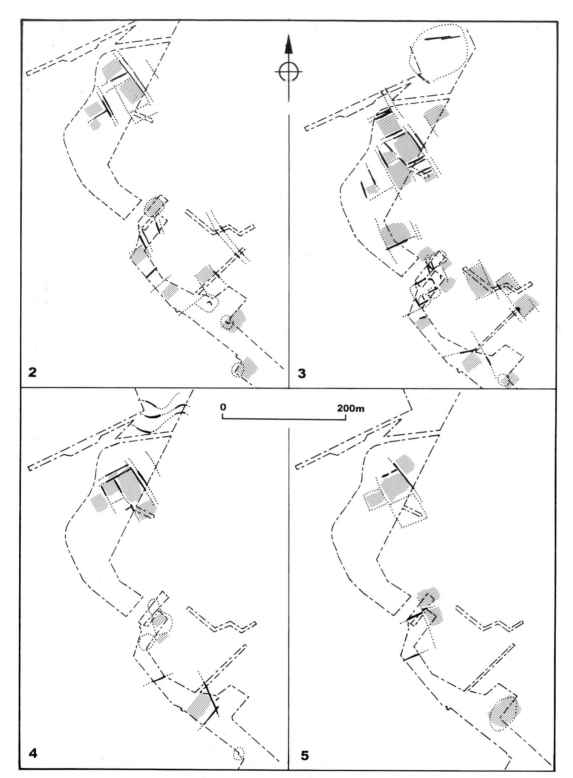

Figure 10.11 The Roman-British site at Kempston, Bedfordshire. This may exemplify the Roman planned village, with a gridded network of streets and several farm structures. The plan shows the development of the site from phase 2 (late-1st to mid-3rd century AD) to phase 5 (mid- to late-4th century). The locations of the buildings are shown as toned rectangles, solid lines represent drainage ditches alongside gravelled tracks. The limits of the excavation are shown as broken lines. the full report is Dawson forthcoming a.

fore Roman period ceramics found their way to the sites. Nearby, at Stagsden, occupation of a larger farm may have been abandoned in the early-2nd century AD. At Shillington a late-Iron Age site was similarly abandoned. All these sites have in com-

mon the proximity of a villa foundation. In the Biddenham area the villa is located close to the river Ouse and the house may have been built by the early 2nd century, at Shillington the Aston Well villa is less than 1km away. In such a situation a rural population displaced by the growth of a villa estate may have sought alternative employment in the service of Rome or the economies of scale offered by nucleated agricultural settlement.

However, colonisation, the foundation of forts, and the construction of *mansiones* do not automatically lead to the sort of landscape patterns noted in the Ouse Valley. Hingley (1989) has suggested that the driving force behind the development of towns and local centres was a market economy based on coinage. Small towns and nucleated settlement therefore grew up as the population was drawn away from the countryside by economic opportunity. The spread of the villa, whether its origins lay with veteran settlement or indigenous response, has also been attributed to these same market forces. However, the paucity of early coinage, continuity of settlement at many sites other than villas, and the lack of many nucleated sites suggest that only a small proportion of the population were able to take advantage of the new situation. It is at least as likely that some of these developments were required by the provincial administration, rather than a voluntary response to economic temptation.

In this scenario, the early foundation of the villa estate dispossessed a proportion of the rural population, whilst at the same time the new infrastructure required labour. Subsequently, in the late-1st to early-2nd century, as the villa estates developed, the nucleated settlements were growing. Colonists were available from the rural population and in the countryside strategies such as kiln-based pottery production were implemented. These trends were to continue throughout the Roman period but, increasingly, new developments became part of the social renegotiation that took place in the Roman province.

Despite this assertion, changes are difficult to identify in the region. Province wide there is a shift in the relationship between large and small towns, and in the development and decline of villas. In the Fenland, Stonea was abandoned, whilst elsewhere there is a shift in burial practice with inhumations becoming the dominant practice. In the late-4th century a significant factor appears on the margins of the region with the fortification of the Saxon shore, and it is possible that the fortification of Great Chesterford had a role in this system (Draper 1986; Going *ex litt*). Changes in the landscape occur more clearly in the 5th century when sites such as Kempston fell into decay and became largely derelict. At Biggleswade, one of the products of decay may have been a rise in the water table. As drainage systems fell out of use in this area, not only was the Warren Villas site abandoned but the line of the Roman road between Sandy and Biggleswade was lost (Dawson 1994).

Bibliography

Allen, D F, 1961 The origins of coinage in Britain: a re-appraisal, in S S Frere (ed) *Problems of the Iron Age in Southern Britain*. Univ London Inst of Archaeol, Occasional Paper No **11**, 97–308

Applebaum, E S, 1949 Excavations at Wilbury Hill, an Iron Age Hillfort near Letchworth, Hertfordshire, *Archaeol J*, **106**, 12–45

Audouy, M, 1992 *Archaeological Fieldwork at Borough Hill, Daventry, Northants*. Northampton: Northants Archaeology Unit

Avery, M, Sutton, J E G, & Banks, J W, 1967 Rainsborough, Northants, England: Excavations 1961–5, *Proc Prehist Soc*, **33**, 207–306

BCAS 1996/18 *Land off Beancroft Road, Marston Moretaine*. Bedford: Bedfordshire County Council

Bell, M, 1981 Valley sediments and environmental change, in M Jones & G Dimbleby (eds) *The Environment of man: the Iron Age, Roman and Anglo-Saxon Periods*, BAR Brit Ser **87**. Oxford: British Archaeological Reports, 75–91

Bigmore, P, 1979 *The Bedfordshire and Huntingdonshire Landscape*. London: Hodder & Staughton

Black, E W, 1995 *Cursus Publicus. The infrastructure of government in Roman Britain*, BAR Brit Series **241**. Oxford: British Archaeological Reports

Branigan, K, 1985 *The Catuvelaunii*. Stroud: Alan Sutton

Browne, D M, 1974 An archaeological gazetteer of the city of Cambridge, *Proc Cambridge Antiq Soc*, **LXV** (I), 1–38

Browne, D, 1977 *Roman Cambridgeshire*. Cambridge: Oleander Press

Bryant, S, & Burleigh, G, 1995 Later prehistoric dykes of the eastern Chilterns, in R Holgate (ed) *Chiltern archaeology. Recent work. A handbook for the next decade*. Dunstable: The Book Castle, 92–5

Bull, E J, 1993 The bi-axial landscape of prehistoric Buckinghamshire, *Rec Buckinghamshire*, **35**, 11–18

Burleigh, G, 1995 A late Iron Age oppidum at Baldock, Hertfordshire, in R Holgate (ed) *Chiltern archaeology. Recent work. A handbook for the next decade*. Dunstable: The Book Castle, 103–12

Burnham, B, 1986 The origins of Romano-British small towns. *Oxford J Archaeol*, **5** (2), 185–203

Burnham, B, & Wacher, J, 1990 *The 'small towns' of Roman Britain*. London: Batsford

Champion, T, (ed) 1989 *Centre and Periphery*. Southampton: One World Archaeology

Clark, R, & Dawson, M, 1995 Later pre-historic and Romano-British landscape in mid-Bedfordshire, in R Holgate (ed) *Chiltern archaeology. Recent work. A handbook for the next decade*. Dunstable: The Book Castle, 56–68

Collingwood, R G, & Wright, R P, 1965 *The Roman Inscriptions of Britain*. Volume I. Oxford: Clarendon Press, RIB I, 230

Cotton, M A, & Frere, S S, 1968 Ivinghoe Beacon, 1963–5, *Rec Buckinghamshire*, **18**, 187–260

Croft, R A, & Mynard, D C, 1993 *The changing land-*

scape of Milton Keynes, Buckinghamshire Archaeol Soc Monogr Ser **5**

Cunliffe, B W, 1974 *The Iron Age Communities of Britain*. London: Routledge & Kegan Paul

Cunliffe, B W, 1991 *The Iron Age Communities of Britain*. 3rd edition (1st ed 1974, 2nd ed 1978) London: Routledge & Kegan Paul

Dannell, G B, & Wild, J P, 1987 *Longthorpe II, the military works depot: an episode in landscape history*, Britannia Monogr Ser **8**. London: Society for the Promotion of Roman Studies

Dawson, M, 1994 *A Late Roman Cemetery at Bletsoe, Bedfordshire*, Bedfordshire Archaeol Monogr **1**

Dawson, M, 1994 Biggleswade West, *Bedfordshire Archaeol*, **21**, 119–37

Dawson, M, 1996 Plantation Quarry, Willington. Excavations 1988–91, *Bedfordshire Archaeol J*, **22**, 2–49

Dawson, M, 1995 Sandy, in A E Brown *Roman Small towns in Eastern England and Beyond*, Oxbow Monogr **52**. Oxford: Oxbow, 167–77

Dawson, M, 1997 Post fieldwork assessment of potential for analysis Norse Road BCAS Rep 97/41. Unpublished report

Dawson, M, forthcoming a (2000) *Archaeology in the Bedford Region*, BAR Brit Ser Monogr. Oxford: British Archaeological Reports

Dawson, M, forthcoming b (2000) Harlington Roman cemetery, Bedfordshire, *Bedfordshire Archaeol*, **24**

Dawson, M, forthcoming c *An Iron Age settlement at Salford, Bedfordshire*, Bedfordshire Archaeol Monogr **5**

Dawson, M, & Edwards, B, 1994 Environmental Impact Assessment M1 Widening Junctions 10–15, ACER Consultants. Unpublished report

Dawson, M, & Gaffney, C, 1995 The application of geophysical techniques within a planning application at Norse Road, Bedfordshire (England), *Archaeological Prospection*, **2**(4), 103–15

Dawson, M, & Maull, A, 1996 Warren Villas Quarry, Upper Caldecote: interim report on excavations 1989–1994, *Bedfordshire Archaeol*, **22**, 58–66

Dix, B, 1980 Excavations at Harrold Pit, Odell 1974–1978 A preliminary report, *Bedfordshire Archaeol J*, **14**, 15–18

Dix, B, 1981 The Romano-British farmstead at Odell and its setting: some reflections on the Roman landscape of the south-east Midlands' Landscape History, **3**, 17–26

Dix, B, 1983 An excavation at Sharpenhoe Clappers, Beds, *Bedfordshire Archaeol*, **16**, 65–74

Draper, J, 1986 Excavations at Great Chesterford, Essex 1953–5, *Proc Cambridge Antiq Soc*, **LXXV**, 3–41

Dring, G J, 1971a Iron Age pottery from Mowsbury Camp, Ravensden, near Bedford, *Bedfordshire Archaeol J*, **6**, 68–9

Dyer, J F, 1961 Dray's ditches, Bedfordshire, and early Iron Age territorial boundaries in the eastern Chilterns, *Antiq J*, **41**, 32–43

Dyer, J F, 1971 Excavations at Sandy Lodge, Bedfordshire, *Bedfordshire Archaeol J*, **6**, 9–17

Dyer, J F, 1976a Ravensburgh castle, Hertfordshire, in D W Harding (ed) *Hillforts: later prehistoric earthworks in Britain and Ireland*. London: Academic Press, 153–9, 421–3

Dyer, J F, 1976b The Bedfordshire region in the first millennium BC, *Bedfordshire Archaeol J*, **11**, 7–18

Evans, C, 1992a Wetland Central? Iron Age centres in the Cambridgeshire Fenlands, *Fenland Res*, **7**, 14–15

Evans, C, 1992b Commanding gestures in lowlands: the investigation of two Iron Age ringworks, *Fenland Res*, **7**, 16–26

Evans, C, & Serjeantson, D, 1988 The backwater economy of a fen-edge community in the Iron Age: the Upper Delphs, Haddenham, *Antiquity*, **62**, 360–70

Farley, M, 1995 The Buckinghamshire Chilterns in late Prehistory, in R Holgate (ed) *Chiltern archaeology. Recent work. A handbook for the next decade*. Dunstable: The Book Castle, 28–30

Fell, C I, 1937 The Hunsbury hillfort, Northants: a new survey of the material, *Archaeol J*, **93**, 57–100

Fox, C, 1923 *The archaeology of the Cambridge region*. Cambridge: Cambridge University Press

French, C A I, 1990 Broom, Southill, Bedfordshire: Environmental Assessment – Archaeological Statement. Fenland Archaeological Trust unpublished report

French, C A I, & Wait, G A, 1988 *An archaeological survey of the Cambridgeshire river gravels*. Cambridge: Cambridgeshire County Council

Frere, S S, 1967 *Britannia: a history of Roman Britain* Routledge & Kegan Paul

Fulford, M, & Nichols, E, (eds) 1992 *Developing Landscapes of Lowland Britain. The Archaeology of the British Gravels: A Review*, Oxbow Monogr **27**. Oxford: Oxbow

Gregory, T, 1991 *Excavations in Thetford, 1980–82, Fisons Way*, E Anglian Archaeol Rep **53**(i–ii)

Gurney, D, (ed) 1986 *Settlement, religion and industry on the fen edge; three Romano-British sites in Norfolk*, E Anglian Archaeol Rep **31**

Hall, D, 1982 The countryside of the South East Midlands and Cambridgeshire, in D Miles (ed) *The Roman-British countryside*, BAR Brit Ser **103**(i–ii). Oxford: British Archaeological Reports, 337–50

Hall, D, & Hutchins, J B, 1972 The distribution of archaeological sites between the Nene and the Ouse Valleys, *Bedfordshire Archaeol J*, **7**, 1–16

Hall, D, & Coles, J, 1994 *Fenland Survey: an essay in landscape persistence*, NS report 1. London: English Heritage

Haselgrove, C, 1989 The later Iron Age in southern Britain and beyond, in M Todd (ed) *Research on Roman Britain 1960–89*, Britannia Monogr Ser **11**. London: Society for the Promotion of Roman Studies

Hingley, R, 1989 *Rural settlement in Roman Britain*. London: Seaby

Hill, J D, 1989 Re-thinking the Iron Age, *Scott Archaeol Rev*, **6**, 16–24

Jackson, D A, 1993-4 Iron age and Anglo Saxon settlement and activity around the Hunsbury hillfort, Northampton, *Northamptonshire Archaeol*, 26, 3–32

Johnstone, D, 1959 Furzenhall Farm excavations, provisional report. Unpublished Bedford Museum Coll Acc No 1992/110

Jones, M, 1981 The development of crop husbandry, in M Jones & G Dimbleby (eds) *The Environment of man: the Iron Age, Roman and Anglo-Saxon Periods*. BAR Brit Ser **87**, Oxford: British Archaeological Reports, 95–127

Kennett, D H, 1970 The Shefford burial, *Bedfordshire Mag*, **12**(93), 201–3

Kimes, T, Haselgrove, C, & Hodder, I, 1982 A method for the identification of the location of regional cultural boundaries, *J Anthropological Archaeol*, **1**, 113–31

Knight, D, 1984 *Late Bronze Age and Iron Age settlement in the Nene and Great Ouse Valleys*, BAR Brit Ser **130** (i–ii). Oxford: British Archaeological Reports

Liversage, J, 1977 Roman burials in the Cambridge area, *Proc Cambridge Antiq Soc*, **67**, 11–38

Luke, M, 1999 An enclosed, pre-'Belgic' Iron Age farmstead with later occupation at Hinksley Road, Flitwick, *Bedfordshire Archaeol*, **23**, 43–88

Luke M (forthcoming) Archaeology in the Biddenham Loop, Bedford

Maltby, M, 1981 Iron Age , Romano-British and Anglo-Saxon animal husbandry – a review of the faunal evidence, in M Jones & G Dimbleby (eds) *The Environment of man: the Iron Age, Roman and Anglo-Saxon Periods*, BAR Brit Ser **87**. Oxford: British Archaeological Reports, 155–203

Matthews, C L, 1976 *Occupation sites on a Chiltern Ridge. Excavations at Puddlehill and sites near Dunstable, Bedfordshire. Part 1: Neolithic, Bronze Age and early Iron Age*, BAR Brit Series **29**. Oxford: British Archaeological Reports

Matthews, C L, 1989 *Ancient Dunstable: a prehistory of the district*, 2nd ed revised and enlarged by J.P. Schneider. Dunstable: Manshead Archaeology Society, Dunstable

Matthews, C L, Schneider, J, & Horne, B, 1992 A Roman villa at Totternhoe, *Bedfordshire Archaeol*, **20**, 41–96

Millett, M, 1990 *The Romanisation of Britain*. Cambridge: Cambridge University Press

MPP, 1989 *Monuments Protection Programme Single monument Class description: clothes line enclosures*. London: English Heritage

Mynard, D, (ed) 1987 *Roman Milton Keynes*, Buckinghamshire Archaeol Soc Monogr Ser **1**

Petchey, M R, 1978 A Roman field system at Broughton, Buckinghamshire, *Rec Buckinghamshire*, **20**(4), 637–45

Phillips, C W, (ed) 1970 *The Fenland in Roman times*, Royal Geogr Soc Res Ser **5**. London: Royal Geographical Society

Pinder, A, 1986 Excavations at Willington 1984: II Iron Age and Roman periods, *Bedfordshire Archaeol*, **17**, 22–40

Pollard, J, 1996 Roman settlement at Keely Lane, Wooton: an interim statement. Unpublished report in Historic Environment Record, Bedfordshire

Potter, T W, 1981 The Roman occupation of the central Fenland, *Britannia*, **12**, 79–133

Potter, T W, 1989 Recent work on the Roman Fens of eastern England and the question of imperial estates, *J Roman Archaeol*, **2**, 267–74

Potter, T W, & Potter, C F, 1982 *A Romano-British village at Grandford, March, Cambridgeshire*, Brit Mus Occas Pap **35**. London: British Museum

Rivet, A L F, 1958 *Town and country in Roman Britain*. London: Hutchinson

Robinson, M R, 1992 Environment archaeology and alluvium on the river gravels of the south Midlands, in S Needham & M G Macklin (eds) *Alluvial Archaeology in Britain*, Oxbow Mono **27**. Oxford: Oxbow

Robinson, M R, & Wilson, R, 1983 A survey of environmental evidence from the South East Midlands. Unpublished report for English Heritage 1983

Rodwell, W R, 1978 Relict landscapes in Essex, in H C Bowen & P J Fowler, *Early land allotment in the British Isles: a survey of recent work*, BAR Brit Ser **48**. Oxford: British Archaeological Reports, 89–98

Rogerson, R J A, 1986 The terraces of the River Great Ouse. Unpublished PhD thesis, University of London

Sellwood, L, 1984 Tribal boundaries viewed from the perspective of numismatic evidence, in B W Cunliffe & D Miles (eds) *Aspects of the Iron Age in central southern Britain*, Univ Oxford Comm Archaeol Monogr **2**. Oxford: OUCA, Institute of Archaeology, 191–204

Shepherd, N J, (forthcoming) Excavations on the A428 Bedford Southern Bypass

Simco, A, 1973 The Iron Age in the Bedford Region, *Bedfordshire Archaeol J*, **8**, 5–20

Simco, A, 1984 *Survey of Bedfordshire. The Roman Period*. Bedford: Bedfordshire County Council/RCHME

Stead, I, & Rigby, V, 1989 *Baldock: the excavation of a Roman and pre-Roman settlement 1968–1972*, Britannia Monogr **7**. London: Society for the Promotion of Roman Studies

Steadman, S, (forthcoming) Excavations at Norton road on the Stotfold Bypass, Bedford

Taylor, A, 1985 Prehistoric, Roman, Saxon and Medieval artefacts from the southern Fen edge, Cambridgeshire, *Proc Cambridge Antiq Soc*, **74**, 1–52

Tebbutt, C F, 1957 A Belgic and Roman Farm at Wyboston, Bedfordshire, *Proc Cambridge Antiq Soc*, **50**, 75–84

Tilson, P, 1973 A Belgic and Romano-British site at Bromham, *Bedfordshire Archaeol J*, **8**, 23–66

Tilson, P, 1975 The excavation of an Iron Age hut circle at Bromham in 1971 with a note on two post medieval finds from Clapham, *Bedfordshire Archaeol J*, **10**, 19–23

Van Arsdell, R D, 1989 *Celtic Coinage of Britain.* London: Spink

Wait, G A, 1991 Archaeological excavations at Godmanchester (A14/A604 Junction), *Proc Cambridge Antiq Soc*, **80**, 79–95

Waugh, H, Mynard, D C, & Cain, R, 1975 Some Iron Age pottery from mid and north Bucks with a gazetteer of associated sites and finds, *Rec Buckinghamshire*, **19**(4), 373–421

Wild, J P, 1974 Roman settlement in the lower Nene Valley, *Archaeol J*, **131**, 140–70

Williams, R J, 1988 North Furzton, Iron Age settlement, *South Midlands Archaeol*, **18**, 41–5

Williams, R J, 1993 *Pennylands and Hartigans: two Iron age and Saxon sites in Milton Keynes,* Buckinghamshire Archaeol Soc Monogr Ser **4**. Aylesbury: Buckinghamshire Archaeological Society

Williams, R J, Hart, P J, & Williams, A T L, 1995 *Wavendon Gate: a late Iron Age and Roman settlement in Milton Keynes,* Buckinghamshire Archaeol Soc Monogr Ser **10**. Aylesbury: Buckinghamshire Archaeological Society

Williams, R J, & Zeepvat, R J, 1994 *Bancroft the late Bronze Age and Iron Age settlements and Roman temple-mausoleum and the Roman villa,* Buckinghamshire Archaeol Soc Monogr **7**(i–ii). Aylesbury: Buckinghamshire Archaeological Society

Woodfield, C, 1977 A Roman military site at Magiovinium, *Rec Buckinghamshire*, **XX**(3), 384–409

Woodfield, C, & Johnstone, C, 1989 A Roman site at Stanton Low on the Great Ouse, Buckinghamshire, *Archaeol J*, **146**, 135–279

Zeepvat, R J, 1989 The Milton Keynes project: landscape archaeology in the new city. Unpublished report, Milton Keynes Archaeology Unit/Buckinghamshire County Museums

11 A river valley landscape: Excavations at Little Paxton Quarry, Cambridgeshire 1992–6 – an interim summary

by Alex Jones with illustrations by Nigel Dodds

Introduction

This paper provides an interim summary of results of an ongoing programme of archaeological excavation at Little Paxton Quarry, Diddington, Cambridgeshire (hereinafter called the 'study area'), located on the west bank of the River Great Ouse, 3.5km to the north of St Neots (Figs 11.1A and B). The fieldwork was undertaken by Birmingham University Field Archaeology Unit on behalf of Bardon Aggregates Limited (formerly CAMAS Aggregates). The programme of fieldwork at the site is incomplete, and the provisional models presented here will doubtless be amended following completion of the fieldwork, and the detailed analysis and reporting of the results.

Extensive cropmarked features recorded within the study area (French and Wait 1988, fig 26: Air Photo Services 1992 and 1998), included possible ring-ditches of Bronze Age date, and ditched enclosures and associated field systems of probable Iron Age or Romano-British date, although it was suspected that the visibility of the cropmarked features may have been restricted by localised alluvial deposits.

The work forms part of an integrated programme of excavation and research within the quarry concession which is intended to determine the changing function and economy of the area, in particular focusing upon the potential for comparison of structural and economic data from the two Iron Age settlements, an Iron Age square barrow, and two Romano-British foci. Integrated analysis of settlement forms and patterning is also intended to contribute towards a broader, multi-period, landscape-based study of changes in settlement in the River Great Ouse Valley, and in other river valley environments.

Initial site evaluation involved air photo analysis (Air Photo Services 1992 and 1998), geophysical survey (Geophysical Surveys of Bradford 1992), and trial-trenching (Leach 1992, Jones 1992), which targeted the cropmark concentrations, and also investigated areas for which no archaeological information was available. Following evaluation, Fields 1 and 2 have been further tested by fieldwalking and test-pitting (Bevan 1996 a and b; Bevan 1997a and b). Three open area excavations have been completed to date, and the results have been summarised in interim reports. The first (Area A, Field 1) examined a 'ladder' enclosure of Romano-British date (Jones and Ferris 1994). The second (Area B, Field 4), investigated features of Neolithic/Bronze Age date

and an Iron Age settlement complex (Jones 1995). The third excavation (Areas C and D, Field 1) examined a possible Iron Age square barrow and other cropmarked features (Jones 1998). Data from these excavations is supplemented by the results of salvage recording and watching briefs maintained during soil-stripping outside the areas of the main feature concentrations. The results of these three excavations are conflated in the following interim summary and discussion. Further analysis and reporting of the results will be undertaken upon completion of the full fieldwork programme.

Results

Mesolithic to Bronze Age

The recovery of a few stray flint tools of Mesolithic date from Fields 1 and 4 (Fig 11.1C; Bevan 1996a) could suggest an early date for sporadic activity in the vicinity, but the finds of this date are few in number. It is hoped that future fieldwork will elucidate the extent and nature of this early exploitation of the river terrace gravels.

The earliest features, of late-Neolithic to early-Bronze Age date, were found in Area B (Fig 11.1C, Field 4). These features comprised three clusters of postholes or small pits, measuring between 0.2–0.7m in diameter and an average of 0.3m in depth (Figs 11.2 and 11.3). Although difficult to interpret in the absence of clearly identifiable structures, or a well-defined context, the form of the northern cluster could perhaps indicate that it formed part of a pit circle (eg Maxey: Simpson 1985). Alternatively, these features may not have been associated with coherent structures. This feature group contained small fragments of burnt bone, fragments of Peterborough Ware, Beaker fragments, and flint artefacts, including a knife. Isolated pits and pit 'groups' formed of two or three examples (not illustrated), and have also been identified in Fields 2 and 5 during further excavation, in 1998.

More widespread late-Neolithic to early-Bronze Age activity within the study area is suggested by the recovery of Neolithic flint artefacts from fieldwalking in Fields 1 and 2 . Fieldwalking over part of Field 1 (Fig 11.1C) recovered an assemblage of 76 flint artefacts, diagnostically Neolithic in date, including cores, arrowheads, scrapers, knives, and retouched blades. The presence of unfinished arrow-

132

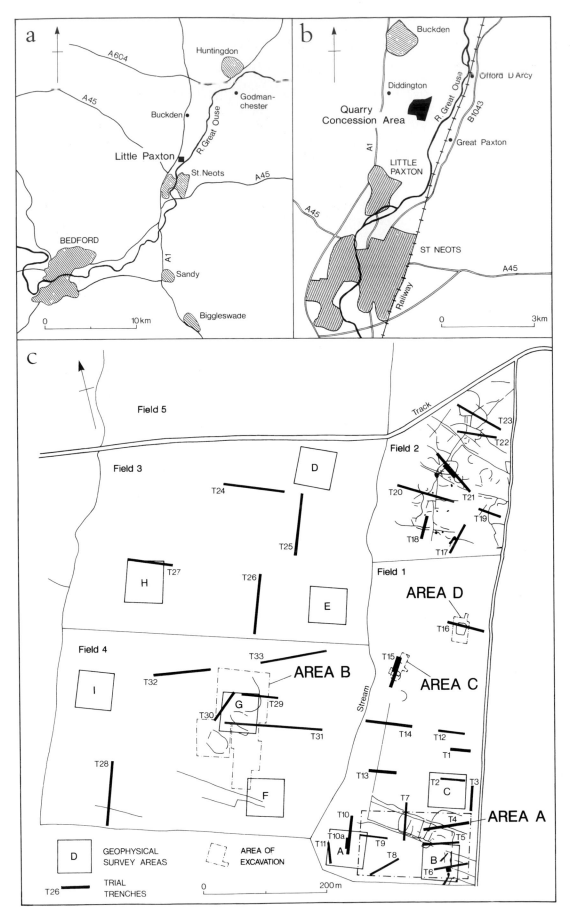

Figure 11.1   A, The Little Paxton Quarry site and the River Great Ouse Valley; B, St Neots and the Little Paxton Quarry site; C, Little Paxton Quarry: areas of archaeological investigation, Fields 1-4 and simplified plan of cropmarked features (Air Photo Services)

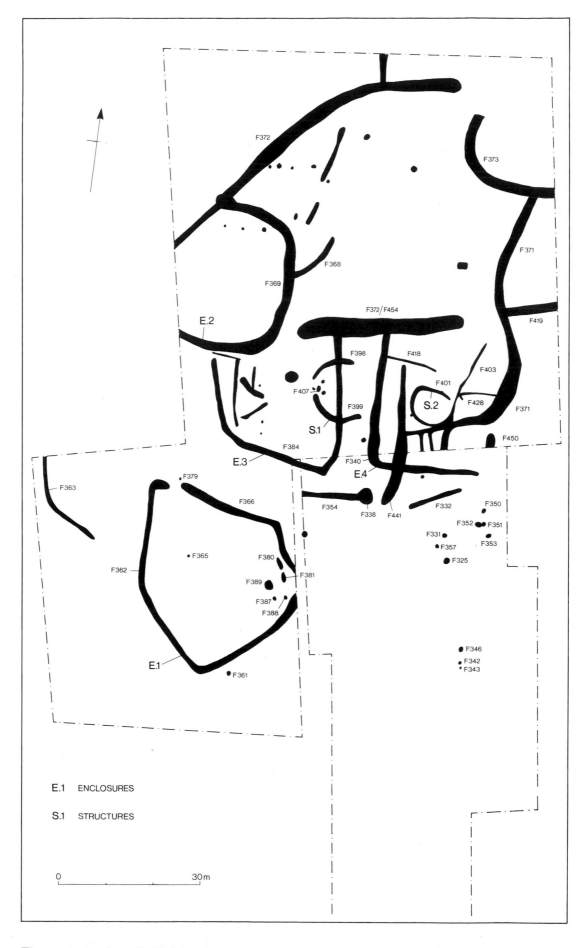

Figure 11.2   Area B, Field 2, Simplified plan of features of all phases

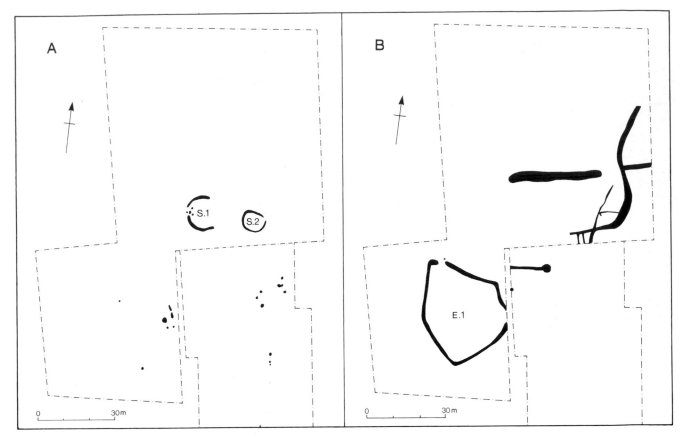

Figure 11.3   Area B, main features, Neolithic-Bronze Age (A); early middle-Iron Age (B)

heads and scrapers suggests contemporary settlement in the vicinity.

Two roughly circular structures (S1 and S2: Figs 11.2 and 11.3), were represented by gullies cut into the subsoil, adjoining the late-Neolithic focus in Area B. Structure 1 was represented by two curvilinear gullies (F398–9), probably associated, which together defined two-thirds of the circumference of a circle measuring approximately 15m in diameter. Both gullies appear to have been dug in sections, with slight changes in angle. These gullies could have formed eaves-drips around a circular hut with an entrance to the west, also defined by a cluster of postholes (Figs 11.2 and 11.3). Structure 2 (Fig 11.4) was sub-oval in plan, measuring a maximum of 8m in diameter. It was defined by an eaves-drip gully which measured an average of 0.6m in width and 0.3m in depth. An entry-gap, measuring 2m in width and located on the eastern side of the structure, was further defined by an arrangement of postholes, cut just inside the line of the two eastern gully terminals. The pottery from Structures 1 and 2 comprised soft, black laminated fabrics of early-Bronze Age date.

More widespread Bronze Age activity within the study area was suggested by the identification of a number of possible cropmarked ring-ditches (Air Photo Services 1992, fig 1), located in Fields 1 and 2.

Iron Age

Three apparently discrete foci of Iron Age activity have been located, in Fields 1, 2, and 4 (Fig 11.1C). The Field 2 complex, under excavation in 1998, will be reported upon separately (Jones forthcoming), while further foci of Iron Age activity, located elsewhere within the quarry (not illustrated), remain to be investigated later in the fieldwork programme.

The earliest Iron Age settlement in Area B (Field 4) was represented by an irregularly-shaped, pentagonal, ditched enclosure (Figs 11.2 and 11.3, Enclosure 1). It was defined by a ditch (F362, F366) which measured a maximum of 1.6m in width and an average of 1m in depth, and was probably complemented by an internal bank. Entry-gaps were recorded along its northern and eastern sides. Although no contemporary structures were noted within its interior, a number of features located to the east of its perimeter, including a well (F338), a group of deeply-cut ditches (eg F372, Fig 11.5) and shallower field boundary ditches, may have been associated. The early middle-Iron Age pottery from this enclosure was dominated by sandy wares, although some shelly wares were also present.

Following the abandonment of Enclosure 1, two adjoining ditched enclosures (Figs 11.1 and 11.6, Enclosures 3–4) were dug to the north. Three sides of Enclosure 3 were defined by vertically-sided ditches; part of its northern side was formed by a

*Figure 11.4 Area B,
Structure 2, view north
(Photograph C Cavanagh)*

*Figure 11.5 Area B, Ditch
F372, view east
(Photograph C Cavanagh)*

recut (F454) of early middle-Iron Age ditch F372. A number of internal features, including gullies, a pit, and two hearths, were identified within the interior of this enclosure. Part of the northern side of the adjoining, and possibly contemporary, Enclosure 4, was also formed by a recut (F454) of ditch F372. The western and southern bounds of this enclosure were defined by a single ditch, which was L-shaped in plan. These two enclosures were distinguished by the presence of contemporary internal features in Enclosure 3 and their absence from the interior of Enclosure 4, and also by the evidence for their abandonment. The fill sequence in the enclosure ditches suggests that the Enclosure 3 ditches were rapidly

backfilled after they went out of use, while the Enclosure 4 ditches had more weathered profiles, and appeared to have been infilled more gradually after going out of use. The later middle-Iron Age pottery from Enclosures 3 and 4 was dominated by sandy wares, with only a small quantity of Scored Ware recovered.

The final phase of Iron Age activity in this settlement focus was represented by the excavation of a further ditched enclosure (Figs 11.2, 11.3, and 11.6, Enclosure 2), located to the north of Enclosures 3-4. The southern, eastern, and northern sides of Enclosure 2 were curvilinear, the northern side ending in an enlarged, round-ended terminal. The sequence of ditch fills suggests that it was complemented by an inner bank which gradually weathered into the ditch. The ditch fills contained pottery of late-Iron Age date, including ribbed and corrugated fine-ware bowls, with a large proportion in sandy fabrics.

The plant remains recovered from the Iron Age settlement in Field 4 suggest that crop processing was one of the activities undertaken here, although such remains were absent from the early middle-Iron Age enclosure. The bone assemblage suggests that cattle, sheep, and goats predominated among the domesticated animals, although dog, pig, and horse bones were also identified.

The main cropmarked feature investigated in Area D was a square barrow or enclosure, occupying a slightly raised plateau in the east of Field 1 (Figs 11.1C and 11.7). It was defined by an enclosing ditch (F550–F551, Fig 11.8). The ditches defined an area measuring 9m north-east to south-west, and 7m south-west to north-east (measured from the innermost edges of the ditches). Two entry-gaps, measuring 0.1m and 2m in width were recorded along the northern and eastern sides of the enclosure respectively. The regular rectilinear form and comparatively small size of the Area D ditched feature does not appear to be paralleled at Little Paxton. The small size and form of this feature is perhaps most closely paralleled by ditched square enclosures of Iron Age date, such as those excavated at Maxey (Pryor 1985, fig 44). These are interpreted as ditched barrows of Arras type, principally found in East Yorkshire (Stead 1991). Although no trace of a

burial was found, it is possible that it may have been removed by plough truncation. Equally, the presence of one (possibly two) entrance causeways is not necessarily contrary to the interpretation of the features as belonging to a square barrow. Stead interprets a number of 'causewayed' enclosures at Garton Station and Kirkburn as ditched enclosures (Stead 1991, figs 20 and 23), although the interpretation of these Yorkshire sites is complicated by their association with other square barrows without such entrances, and by their later reuse. An alternative interpretation of the Area D ditched feature is a small enclosure associated with farming, its small size, and form determined by functional factors.

A group of features including a pit (F570), gullies, and postholes were recorded both inside and outside the Area D barrow or enclosure, but were not associated. The pit, gullies, and postholes contained pottery of middle-Iron Age date.

The settlement remains in Field 2 (see Fig 11.1C for simplified plot of cropmarked features), under excavation at the time of writing (not illustrated in detail), comprise two discrete zones. The earliest features in the northernmost zone (to the north of Evaluation Trench 22) include shallow gullies, and repeatedly recut eves-drip gullies, belonging to a phase of unenclosed settlement. This feature group was succeeded by a cluster of seven ditched enclosures. Both phases of activity in this northern zone have been dated by preliminary spot-dating of the pottery to the middle Iron Age. The settlement re-

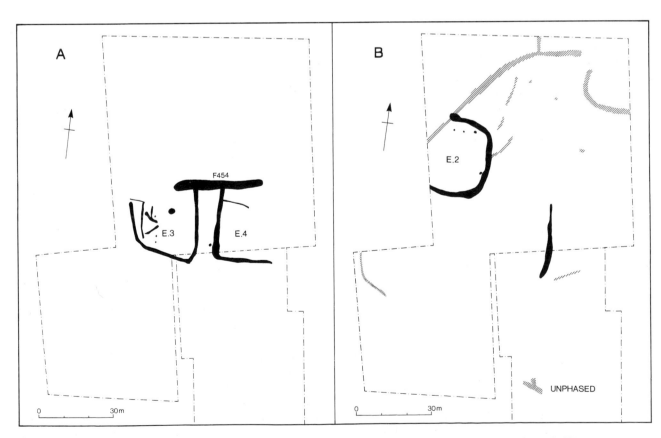

Figure 11.6   Area B, main features, later middle-Iron Age (A); late-Iron Age and unphased (B)

Figure 11.7   Area D, Overhead view of square barrow or enclosure, view north (Photograph E Newton)

mains in the south of the field (to the south of Trench 21) are differently aligned, and run east–west or north–south. The earliest main feature group in this zone comprise shallow-ditched enclosures interpreted as stock enclosures. Later activity was focused in an irregularly-shaped ditched enclosure (in the area of Trench 21), which yielded a quantity of Belgic Ware.

Romano-British

Romano-British settlement appears to have been mainly concentrated in the extreme south of Field 1 (Fig 11.1C), occupying a slight north-west–south-east aligned gravel ridge (Figs 11.9 and 11.10, Area A). Three phases of Romano-British activity were defined here by preliminary spot-dating.

The earliest phase of activity (Phase 1) was represented by a number of linear and curvilinear field boundary ditches, probably representing more than one period of activity. These features may have defined small fields or market-garden plots, although subsequent plough truncation makes their identification difficult. No clear dating evidence was recovered, although the morphology of the curvilinear fields could even suggest an Iron Age origin.

Following abandonment of the linear field system, in Phase 2, a ditched 'ladder' enclosure was laid out (Enclosure A, Figs 11.9–11.11). It measured an average of 27m in width, and was recorded for a length of over 180m, although it was suspected, from examination of the cropmark evidence, that it had continued to the east of the excavated area. The northern side of this 'ladder' was defined by two roughly parallel ditches (F305, F306), cut approximately 4.5m apart (measured centre to centre). The fill sequence in these ditches indicates gradual in-filling, rather than deliberate backfilling, followed

by re-excavation. The southern side of the ladder was defined by a parallel double- or triple-ditched arrangement (F307–F309), cut parallel to the northern pair of ditches. The fills of the enclosure ditches contained pottery of late-3rd and 4th-century date; a barbarous radiate coin dating to AD 270–90, and a coin of Crispus (AD 320) were also recovered.

The main focus of activity within the enclosure was within its north-western corner, which contained traces of timber-framed buildings, possibly barns, as well as rubbish pits and hearths. Of particular interest was a flat-based cut (F209), rectangular in plan, which may be interpreted as a water tank or trough. This feature was cut below the contemporary water-table, and may have been positioned to receive water channelled along the southern enclosure ditches. Feature F209 was filled with waterlogged black organic silts. This feature is paralleled by a 'pond-like depression', recorded by Tebbutt (1969, 55) at Little Paxton, filled with peaty soil containing Roman pottery. Two further foci of activity were recorded within the interior of the enclosure. One comprised a group of postholes, which probably defined a barn. To the east lay a further occupation area which contained a well (F304), and the possible traces of a further timber-framed building.

Other enclosures (Figs 11.9 and 11.10, Enclosures B, D, and E), only partly exposed, may have been contemporary with the 'ladder'.

The final phase of Romano-British activity is marked by the abandonment of the 'ladder' and the other contemporary enclosures, and the laying-out in the east of the excavated area of a new grid field system and ditched enclosure (Enclosure C, Figs 11.9 and 11.10), following a common north–south alignment. The exposed north-western corner of the

138

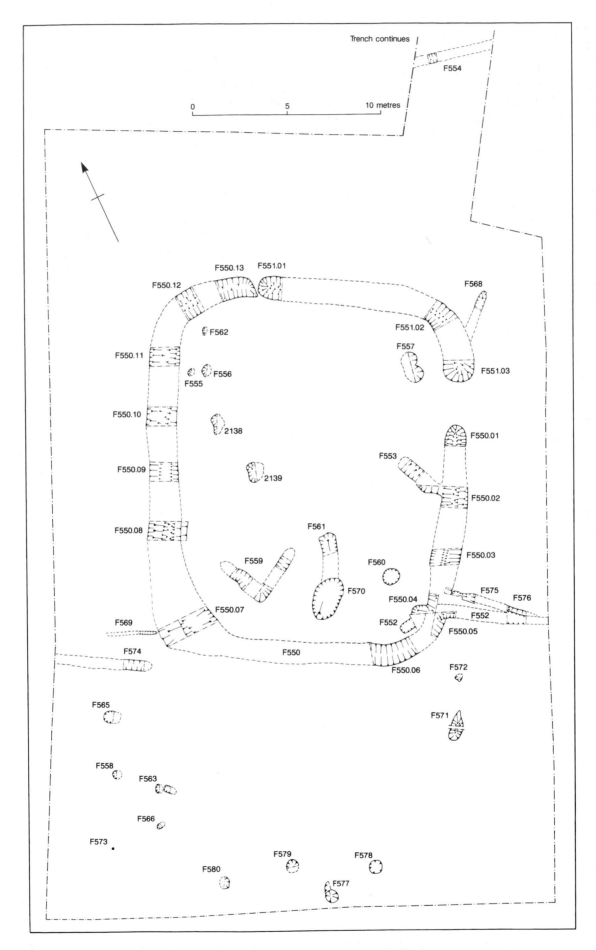

Figure 11.8   Area D, Field 1, simplified plan of features of all phases

enclosure was cut into the infilled ditches of Phases 1 and 2, and a Phase 3 well (F281) was cut into the infilled ditches of the 'ladder' enclosure. The pattern of Phase 3 field boundaries suggests that these may have defined individual small fields or market-garden plots. Once again, the sequence of ditch fills suggested gradual silting-up of the field boundary and enclosure ditches. The dating evidence for this enclosure comprises pottery with a mid-4th-century date, while a coin of Valens (AD 364–378) suggests some later activity.

The pottery assemblage includes mostly locally produced grey wares, and Nene Valley grey and colour coated wares; the main non-local pottery was Horningsea ware, and Oxford wares were notable by their absence. The insect remains recovered from waterlogged deposits suggest an open pastoral environment, where grazing animals were present. The deposition in a ditch of a single human infant bone, or of a burial of which only a single bone remained, might represent a symbolic 'marker' associated with the control of the agricultural domain by women through manipulation of symbols and actualities of reproduction and fertility (Scott 1991), although finds of infant burials are relatively common on Romano-British settlement sites. Cattle and sheep were the dominant livestock animals, while horse and pig were scarcer.

A second focus of Romano-British activity was located in the south-west of Field 2, in the area under excavation at the time of writing. Preliminary spot-dating of the pottery from this possible farmstead and livestock enclosure complex suggests it had been abandoned by the early-2nd century AD.

Post-Romano-British

The zone surrounding the Area A Romano-British settlement was farmed in the medieval period as one of the open fields of the village of Boughton, located immediately to the south of the study area. Traces of 'lazy bed' ditches of probable medieval date have been located in Field 2. The surviving earthworks of this village include the manor house, and traces of a number of individual tofts laid out along the main village street. The village was documented in 1279. Since ridge and furrow earthworks overlie part of the upstanding village remains, it has been suggested that the village could have had an earlier medieval date (French and Wait 1988, 79).

Discussion

Mesolithic to Bronze Age

The earliest artefacts found by the present fieldwork at Little Paxton are Mesolithic in date, which suggest some form of early, sporadic hunter-gatherer activity. No features of Mesolithic or early-Neolithic date have been found.

The three late-Neolithic feature clusters in Area A (Figs 11.2 and 11.3) may have been located to take advantage of a slightly raised plateau here. The interpretation of these features is difficult in the absence of clearly defined structures. The apparently deliberate placing of flint artefacts, principally knives, at the base of these features could suggest a ritual, rather than a structural, function. This interpretation is supported by the absence of evidence for post-pipes within the features. Richards and Thomas (1984, 219) have noted that 'the performance of ritual involves formalised repetitive actions which may be detected archaeologically through a highly structured mode of deposition'. The composition, and clustering of the flint assemblages recovered from the ploughsoil in Fields 1 and 2 indicates settlement. Few features of this date have, however, survived plough truncation of up to 0.5m (C French pers comm). An irregularly-shaped ring-monument measuring approximately 42–3m in diameter, dated in the range 1840–1780 cal BC (Evans 1997, 19) was excavated to the east of Field 2.

The identification of two possible early-Bronze Age roundhouses (Figs 11.1C and 11.2–11.4, Area B) is of particular importance, since the evidence in the Ouse valley for Bronze Age activity is presently largely confined to possible ring-ditches (eg Field 1974, Green 1974), identified by aerial photography. The Area B discoveries could also suggest that some of the cropmarked features presently identified as ring-ditches may possibly be reinterpreted as hut eaves-drip gullies, as also demonstrated by the results of evaluation trenching at Margett's Farm immediately to the north of the study area (Tempus Reparatum 1992, 10), and by Evans (1997, 24). This possible, partial reinterpretation of the air photograph evidence would have important implications for our understanding of the nature and relative distribution of Bronze Age settlement and funerary foci. Further testing of the other possible cropmarked ring-ditches elsewhere in the study area will hopefully clarify the nature and distribution of Bronze Age activity here. Possible cropmarked ring-ditches are presently recorded within Field 2 (Fig 11.1C).

Field (1974) published an early survey of the distribution of cropmarked ring-ditches in the Ouse valley. He suggested ring-ditches were predominantly sited on river terrace deposits, although a possible bias in their identification by aerial photography was acknowledged. The greatest concentrations of these features were mapped at the junction between the Ouse and the Ivel. Ring-ditches did not appear to cluster close to the riverbank, although 60% of the identified sites lie within 0.6 km of the River, and 71% within a distance of 0.8km (Field 1974, 128). He noted (op cit, fig 3) that linear groups of three or four ditches, or double parallel lines of three and two sites, are common. Such a cluster, comprising two or possibly three sites has been identified by aerial photography in Field 1 (Fig

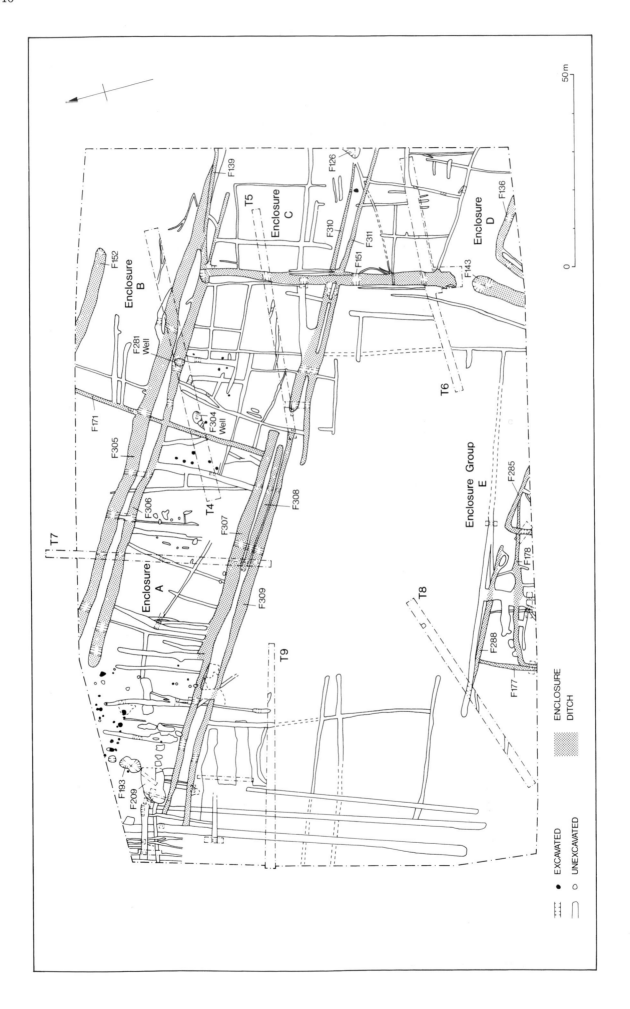

Figure 11.9   Area A, Field 1, simplified plan of features of all phases

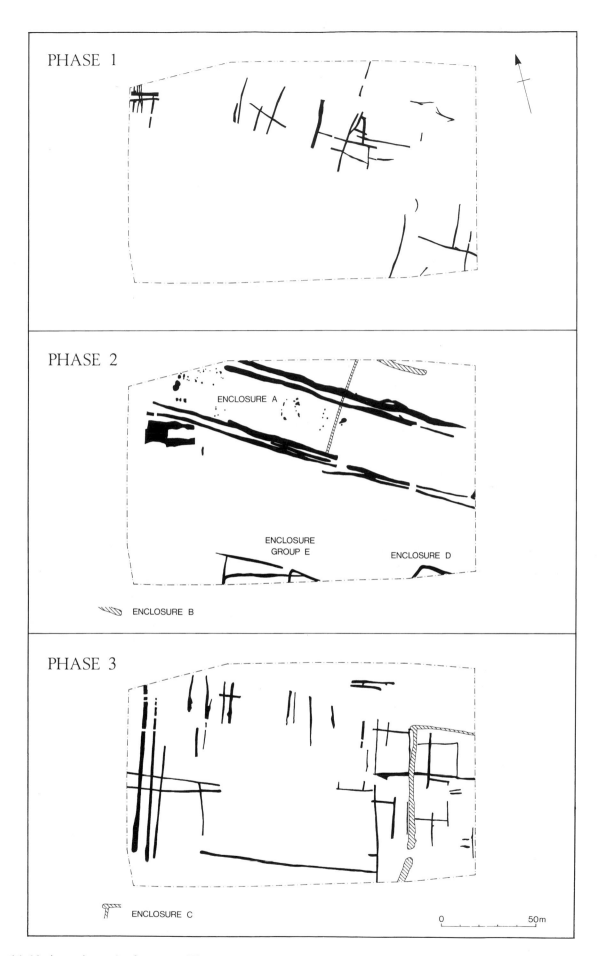

Figure 11.10 Area A, main features, Phases 1-3

11.1C: Trench 15 area), although excavation (Area C) failed to identify any surviving traces. The distribution of ring-ditches is generally dispersed in the Diddington area, although four of the cropmarked examples (out of a total of 17) appear to form a cluster (Field 1974, 61).

Iron Age

No settlement or artefactual evidence for activity in the early Iron Age has been identified to date in the study area.

Settlement in the middle Iron Age was concentrated in Field 4 (Area B), and also in Field 1 (Area D) and 2 (excavation ongoing). The earliest Iron Age activity in Field 4, of early-middle Iron Age date, was focused on Enclosure 1, and an area to the east of this enclosure, which contained field and other, more deeply-cut, boundaries and a well. Although later phases of Iron Age activity here are characterised by marked changes in structural arrangements, an element of continuity is provided by their location within a well-defined, and slightly raised, plateau. Although the recutting of ditch F372 (Figs 11.2 and 11.5), in the later middle Iron Age provides a degree of continuity with the arrangements of the preceding phase, the later activity is otherwise characterised by the excavation of two new, and adjoining enclosures (Enclosures 3 and 4). The former contained traces of internal structures, while the other could have functioned as a cattle enclosure.

The identification of a possible square barrow (Field 1, Area D) adds an element of diversity to the Iron Age landscape. Although clustering is a typical attribute of square barrows, a quarter of the examples identified by Whimster (1981, 112) were solitary, as was the excavated example.

Romano-British

The earliest Romano-British activity in Field 1, albeit undated, was represented by arable cultivation within small fields or market garden plots (Figs 11.9 and 11.10). The layout of the Phase 2 enclosure reflects a change in site function. The Phase 2 ladder enclosure contained some evidence of internal features, comprising timber-framed buildings, possibly including stores or stables, rubbish-pits, and hearths. However, the relative dearth of internal buildings and the identification of a possible animal drinking trough (Fig 11.9 and 11.10) could indicate that the enclosure functioned at least partly as a compound for livestock. Alternatively, it is possible that evidence of structures, such as timber-framed buildings, could have been removed by ploughing. It is notable that the area in the north-west of the ladder was relatively low lying, and it is possible to speculate that it was abandoned after flooding from the nearby stream to the west (Fig 11.1C).

Later Roman settlement appears to have been concentrated within Enclosure C, located over 150m to the east of the contemporary stream channel. This enclosure may have continued in use until the late-4th century AD.

The farmstead enclosure appears to be the dominant form of settlement in the vicinity. A small enclosure, initially established in the Iron Age, was excavated by Greenfield (1969, 48) to the south of Little Paxton church, 200m north of the river. It was interpreted as a small farmstead of predominantly 3rd- to 4th-century date, surrounded by rectilinear field systems. Further Romano-British settlement is recorded to the west of Wray House, including pits and possible ovens or kilns (Addyman 1969). Of particular interest is the identification of a possible boat quay near Wray House (Tebbutt 1969, 57),

Figure 11.11 Area A, Overhead view of the northern side of 'ladder' enclosure, view northwest (Photograph E Newton)

which could have provided an important link with the east bank of the river, connecting the area with Ermine Street and the town of Godmanchester to the north.

The evidence of Roman rural settlement at Little Paxton is not confined to farmstead enclosures. A rectangular ditched enclosure located to the northeast of the study area was interpreted as a *temenos* or ritual area (Alexander nd). The ditch enclosed a pit which contained bronze letters, paralleled at other Roman religious sites. The Little Paxton complex was dated by coins dated AD 270–5, and AD 337–46. The relationship of this *temenos* with the excavated farmstead in Field 1, and with a suggested Roman settlement to the east, is undefined.

Spot dating of the pottery from the ongoing excavations in Field 2, suggest the area was abandoned by the early-2nd century AD, with a possible settlement shift to the higher ground in the south of Field 1 (Area A), perhaps caused by rising water levels. This interpretation is necessarily tentative.

Post-Romano-British

Although no evidence of settlement in the immediate post-Roman period has been found within the study area or its environs, a number of important nearby late-Saxon settlement foci have been partially excavated, notably at Little Paxton (Addyman 1969) and St Neots (Addyman 1973). A Saxon settlement dated to the late-9th to 11th centuries, located to the south-east of Little Paxton church and to the north of the Ouse, was excavated by Addyman. Its location may have been determined by the proximity of a nearby river crossing, near Wray House, which will have provided an important link with Great Paxton, on the opposite, eastern bank of the River Great Ouse, as in the Roman period. Addyman did not interpret this settlement as a precursor of medieval Little Paxton, but rather as a fragmented estate within a parish, an interpretation also supported by the subdivided nature of the manor and its many free tenants (Addyman 1969, 76).

Conclusion

The scale of archaeological investigations at Little Paxton, when the planned fieldwork programme is complete, will provide a good quality data set, including environmental evidence, whose study should make a significant contribution to local, regional, and national research. Excavation will provide an understanding of the Neolithic ritual landscape, and help to elucidate the nature of the relationship – chronological and spatial – between late–Bronze Age settlement and burial ritual.

Detailed investigation of the two main Iron Age settlements in Fields 1 and 2, and the Romano-British settlement in Field 1, will permit the development and testing of models of social and economic change. The scale of these investigations will also

hopefully elucidate the interrelationship between the various settlements, and changes in the river valley environment, which will be of relevance at a regional, and also a national level.

(This text was prepared in 1995 and was slightly revised in 1998.)

Acknowledgements

The fieldwork was sponsored by Bardon Aggregates Limited (formerly CAMAS Aggregates). The fieldwork was managed and directed by Alex Jones. I thank the field staff and specialists for their assistance. The fieldwork was monitored for Cambridgeshire County Council by Bob Sydes, and by Iain Ferris for BUFAU, who also edited this report.

Bibliography

Addyman, P V, 1969 Late Saxon Settlements in the St Neots Area. II The Little Paxton Settlement and Enclosures, *Proc Cambridge Antiq Soc,* **62**, 59–93

Addyman, P V, 1973 Late Saxon Settlements in the St Neots Area. III The Village or Township at St Neots, *Proc Cambridge Antiq Soc,* **64**, 45–99

Alexander, M, nd A Romano-British Shrine Site Near Diddington. Unpublished manuscript

Air Photo Services 1992 Little Paxton, Cambridgeshire, Aerial Photographic Assessment 1992. Unpublished report

Air Photo Services 1998 Little Paxton, Cambridgeshire, Aerial Photographic Assessment, updated for Phase 3 Area. Unpublished report

Bevan, L, 1996a Little Paxton Quarry, Diddington, Cambridgeshire. Field 1 Fieldwalking, February 1996. Summary Report. BUFAU Report No 219.04. Birmingham University Field Archaeology Unit unpublished report

Bevan, L, 1996b Little Paxton Quarry, Diddington, Cambridgeshire. Field 1 Test- Pitting, March 1996. Summary Report. BUFAU Report No 219.05. Birmingham University Field Archaeology Unit unpublished report

Bevan, L, 1997a Little Paxton, Diddington. Field 2 Fieldwalking and Test-Pitting 1997. BUFAU Report No 211.07. Birmingham University Field Archaeology Unit unpublished report

Bevan, L, 1997b Little Paxton, Diddington. Field 2 Further Test-Pitting 1997. BUFAU Report No 211.08. Birmingham University Field Archaeology Unit unpublished report

Evans, C, 1997 The Excavation of a Major Ring-Ditch Complex at Diddington, near Huntingdon, with a Discussion of Second Millennium BC Pyre Burial and Regional Cremation Practices, *Proc Cambridge Antiq Soc*, **85**, 11–26

Field, K, 1974 Ring-Ditches of the Upper and Middle Great Ouse Valley, *Archaeol J,* **131**, 58–73

French, C A I, and Wait, G A, 1988 An Archaeological Survey of the Cambridgeshire River Gravels. Cambridgeshire County Council, unpublished

Geophysical Surveys of Bradford 1992 Little Paxton Quarry, Stage 2. Report No 92/89. Unpublished report

Green, H S, 1974 Early Bronze Age burial, territory and population in Milton Keynes, Buckinghamshire, and the Great Ouse Valley, *Archaeol J*, **131**, 75–139

Greenfield, E, 1969 The Romano-British Settlement at Little Paxton, Huntingdonshire, *Proc Cambridge Antiq Soc*, **62**, 35–57

Jones, A E, 1992 Little Paxton Quarry, Diddington, Cambridgeshire, Phase 2 Archaeological Assessment. BUFAU Report No 223. Birmingham University Field Archaeology Unit unpublished report

Jones, A E, 1995 Little Paxton Quarry, Diddington, Cambridgeshire: Archaeological Excavations 1992–3. Second Interim Report: The Southwest Area. Settlement and Activity from the Neolithic to the Iron Age, *Proc Cambridge Antiq Soc*, **83**, 7–22

Jones, A E, 1998 An Iron Age Square Barrow at Diddington, Cambridgeshire. Third Interim Report of Excavations at Little Paxton Quarry, 1996, *Proc Cambridge Antiq Soc*, **86**, 5–12

Jones, A E, forthcoming Little Paxton Quarry, Fourth Interim Report. Iron Age and Romano-British Settlement in Field 2, *Proc Cambridge Antiq Soc*

Jones, A E, & Ferris, I M, 1994 Archaeological Investigations at Little Paxton, Diddington, Cambridgeshire, 1992–3: First Interim Report: The Romano-British Period, *Proc Cambridge Antiq Soc*, **82**, 55–66

Leach, P J, 1992 Little Paxton Quarry, Diddington, Cambridgeshire, Archaeological Assessment, Phase 1. BUFAU Report No 219. Birmingham University Field Archaeology Unit unpublished report

Pryor, F, French, C, Crowther, D, Gurney, D, Simpson, G, & Taylor, M, 1985 *The Fenland Project, No 1: Archaeology and Environment in the Lower Welland Valley, Vol 1*, E Anglian Archaeol Rep **27**(i). Cambridge: Cambridgeshire Archaeological Committee

Richards, C, & Thomas, J, 1984 Ritual Activity and Structured Deposition in Later Neolithic Wessex, in R Bradley & J Gardner (eds) *Neolithic Studies: A Review of Some Current Research*, BAR Brit Ser **133**. Oxford: British Archaeological Reports, 177–8

Scott, E, 1991 Animal and infant Burials in Romano-British Villas: A Revitalisation Movement, in P Garwood, D Jennings, *et al* (eds) *Sacred and Profane: Proceedings of a Conference on Archaeology*. Oxford: Oxford Committee for Archaeology, University of Oxford, 115–21

Simpson, W G, 1985 The Excavations at Maxey, Bardyke Field, 1962–3, in Pryor, F, French, C, Crowther, D, Gurney, D, Simpson, G, & Taylor, M, *The Fenland Project, No 1: Archaeology and Environment in the Lower Welland Valley, Vol 2*, E Anglian Archaeol Rep **27**(ii). Cambridge: Cambridgeshire Archaeological Committee

Stead, I M, 1991 *Iron Age Cemeteries in East Yorkshire*. English Heritage Archaeol Rep **22**. London: English Heritage

Tebbutt, C F, 1969 Appendix A. Gravel Pit Finds in the Neighbourhood of St. Neots, Huntingdonshire, in E Greenfield 1969, 55–7

Tempus Reparatum 1992 An Archaeological Evaluation at Margett's Farm, Buckden, Cambridgeshire. Unpublished report

Whimster, R, 1981 *Burial Practices in Iron Age Britain. A Discussion and Gazetteer of the Evidence c 700 BC– AD 43*, BAR Brit Ser **90**(1). Oxford: British Archaeological Reports

12 Estate, Village, Town? Roman, Saxon, and medieval settlement in the St Neots area *by Paul Spoerry*

Introduction

In the 25 years since the publication of the third of Peter Addyman's papers on Saxo-Norman sites around St Neots (Addyman 1973), there has been only limited discussion and no additional major pieces of work concerning the post-Roman archaeology of this part of the Ouse Valley. Over the last few years the impact of PPG16-led evaluations and recording work has resulted in a need to look again at this area, to collate and reassess the old evidence with the intention of understanding more fully the new.

This paper has two main themes; i) observations of settlement dynamics in the St Neots area from the Roman period through to the medieval, and ii) a reappraisal of the late-Saxon to medieval topography of the settlement of St Neots itself.

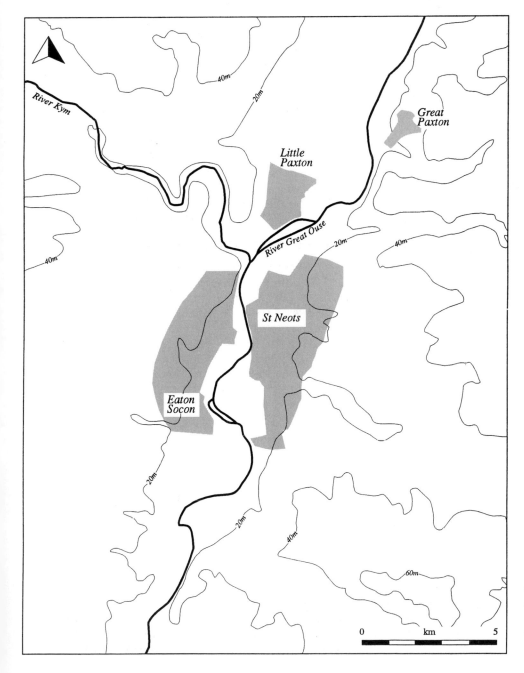

Figure 12.1 The topography and modern settlement of the Huntingdonshire stretch of the River Great Ouse

145

Background and Roman settlement

The St Neots area is geographically dominated by the River Great Ouse, flowing south-south-west to north-north-east (Fig 12.1). The geology is essentially river gravels surrounded by boulder clay, both masking the solid geological background of Oxford Clay.

The normally held view on the Romano-British period in the St Neots area is that there is no known settlement of a size large enough to be called a town between Sandy, to the south, and Godmanchester, to the north. A sizeable Roman road that joins these two towns runs approximately north–south a few kilometres east of the river Ouse (Margary 1967). This established Roman road (Margary No 22), known as 'Brown Street' further south (Viatores 1964), does not deviate from its straight path in the Eynesbury/St Neots area. St Neots does, however, lie close to a possible Roman river crossing, where a supposed east–west minor route (Margary No 231) cuts a corner to a link road between Ermine Street and Watling Street further to the west (Margary 173d). The presence of this east–west road was first suggested by 'the Viatores' in a publication in 1964, and has since also been represented in Bigmore's *The Making of the English Landscape* volume for Bedfordshire and Huntingdonshire (Bigmore 1979). The evidence for the existence of this road is rather scanty and, in fact, the line of the exact route close to St Neots has never been adequately shown. The work of the Viatores suggests that it may have been preserved in the old line of the A45 to the east of St Neots, and that on the west side of the Great Ouse it joined the probable south-west to north-east 'Ermine Street to Watling Street link road' at a point just west of modern Staughton Moor. The Roman Ouse crossing would therefore have been a few hundred metres north of the later medieval bridge at St Neots, in the area on the east bank known historically as Island Common. The place name Eaton Ford on the western side opposite St Neots bridge, although indicative of an early crossing point here, presumably relates to a crossing of the post-Roman period, rather than being a folk memory of an earlier route.

A single tantalising piece of information in support of the presence of this east–west Roman road is visible on the 1757 Map of Sir Stephen Anderson's (formally The Priory) Estate (Huntingdonshire Records Office Acc 223A). This map shows a large part of the area of St Neots parish to the north-east of the town. It shows the line of the Cambridge road east of Wintringham, and also at the east end of Market Street in St Neots. Three to four hundred metres to the north of this road can be seen another east–west linear feature, represented by a cart track ('to the Goare Piece') in the east of the parish and as 'the Rowley Hedge' as it approaches the northern edge of St Neots town. This latter is particularly interesting as no other 'hedge' is worthy of an individual name on the whole map. This very straight line was still present as field boundaries and a track in the early part of this century and it follows exactly the line that the Roman road should take if extrapolated from the old A45 Cambridge Road. This is by no means conclusive information for the existence of a Roman road, but it does add considerable weight to the argument for its existence.

Roman roads are, of course, only part of the known Roman landscape in the area. If this more varied evidence is studied as a whole, a better explanation of the individual elements is usually possible.

Chance finds over many decades have indicated that even if no Roman 'town' existed near St Neots, some form of significant occupation did indeed take place in this period. Many Roman coins and pottery are listed on the Cambridgeshire Sites and Monuments Record (SMR) around St Neots (Fig 12.2), but this may be indicative of dense rural activity/settlement rather than a suggestion of anything else. Certainly a similar number of relevant SMR points can be identified at various points along the river valley, for instance around the Paxtons (Fig 12.2), where excavation and aerial photographic data have identified an intensively-farmed landscape with a dense scatter of farmsteads (eg Greenfield 1969) which is the background of activity from which those chance finds derive. It ought to be noted here that the SMR data used to complete Figures 12.2 and 12.4 derives only from those parishes that are shown as unshaded in Figure 12.3.

The area around Eynesbury, however, undoubtedly had some form of concentrated occupation in the Roman period. In earlier times it was thought that there was a Roman fort, or forts, at 'the Conygeare' between Eynesbury village and the river (Gorham 1820). The origins of this interpretation are difficult to untangle, especially as, according to Gorham, the larger part of this area was already quarried away for gravel by the early-19th century. Many reports of Roman period finds during this extraction phase have ended up in the County SMR, but it was Tebbutt's excavations earlier this century (Tebbutt 1935) that confirmed the earthworks surviving at that time were indeed Roman in date. Whether they were actually the remains of fortifications is impossible to judge from the information now available. Tebbutt's report is very scanty by modern standards and no early maps show the feature in detail. By the time of the Ordinance Survey 25 inch update in 1926, the only portion left is shown as a riverside embankment with a narrow east–west rectangular platform on top of it. This could easily be a product of the quarrying, and it does not appear to have any of the main characteristics of Roman forts. Thus all that can currently be said about the Conygeare earthworks is that they were certainly of Roman date and they were associated with Roman buildings, but that the presence of a fort is not proven.

These remains would be of only casual interest on their own. They represent, however, only the north-

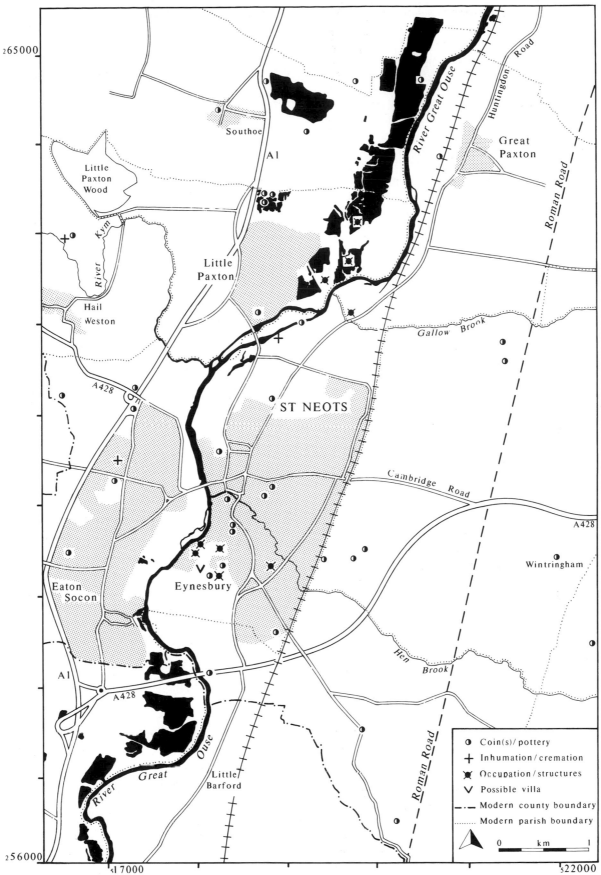

Figure 12.2   Roman period (SMR entries) and other known sites in the St Neots area (data only from parishes shown unshaded on Figure 12.3). Recent quarrying, built-up areas, and the road system are shown as their presence influences the discovery of archaeological material, thus biasing apparent ancient distributions. Despite this the focus of Roman material around Eynesbury is clear, as is a general increase of activity along the river valley

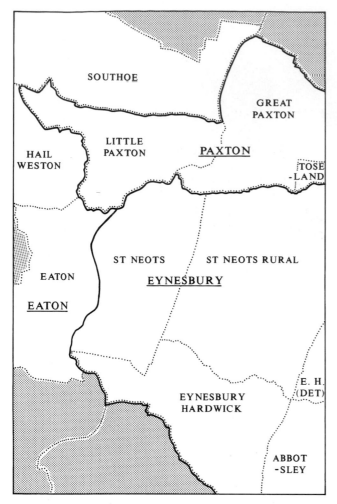

Figure 12.3   Modern parishes in the study area. The shaded areas have not been studied. The heavy lines are the suggested boundaries of the late-Saxon minster parishes of Eynesbury and Paxton, based on information in the Domesday Book and from other early sources

ern edge of a group of SMR records, and more recently identified remains, that must be seen as a sizeable zone of Roman occupation. This stretches for 500m south-eastwards from the riverside at the Conygeare to the recently identified occupation features at Ernulf School (Alexander 1993). A possible villa site, where tesserae and building materials have been recovered in the ploughsoil, is present on the southern edge of this zone, and a number of other records report pottery and building materials being recovered.

The 1993 work by Cambridgeshire County Council at Ernulf School produced very good quality evidence for Roman settlement, bearing in mind that, due to the need to continue using the sports fields, the evaluation was confined to geophysical surveying and test pitting. Magnetometer and resistivity survey, followed by test pits, mostly located to test geophysical anomalies, identified a group of enclosures and associated pitting lying west of, and adjacent to, a north–south metalled trackway (Fig 12.4). This trackway almost certainly represents the eastern boundary of the whole zone of occupation that

runs from here to the river at the Conygeare. The artefact density in the features studied was very high and the dating of both the pottery and coins suggests very little activity before the late 3rd century, with a sizeable 4th-century component, and probably some 5th-century material.

It is not known whether the Eynesbury Roman settlement is all mostly late in date, or whether it is just this eastern area that survives until the end of the Roman period. It is worth noting, however, that almost all of the dated finds from the western part of Eynesbury have been from the 3rd century or later.

What this evidence represents is perhaps the most important question to resolve. Bigmore (1979) suggests that the concentration of Roman-period evidence around Eynesbury might represent a Celtic-type Multiple Estate Centre, perhaps conforming in its boundaries with the very large Domesday parish of Eynesbury. He argues for a similar estate being centred on the villa at Eaton Socon across the river. The status of this land unit as a 'Soke', operating outside of the usual hundredal control in the late-Saxon to medieval periods, is perhaps a strong argument for it being a separate estate, already in existence when the hundredal system was set up in the 9th century and perhaps having Romano-Celtic origins. The argument for Eynesbury also having its origins as a Romano-Celtic estate is much less persuasive on only purely documentary grounds, however, the material evidence for a substantial Roman settlement cannot be ignored and it is difficult to see what this settlement could be if it is not a major estate centre. If the area of Roman settlement remains is truly about 500m across, then it is large enough to represent a Roman small-town. I do not suggest that this is indeed the correct and only interpretation of Roman Eynesbury, but I cannot see that it was much smaller than this even if it was all part of one estate.

With this is mind, the presence of the east–west Roman road and river crossing a short distance away seems more plausible. Why the settlement was not closer to the road line, which appears to be about 1500m to the north, cannot, however, be explained.

According to Hart (1968), the historic county boundaries of Bedfordshire and Huntingdonshire owe their existence to the wholesale adoption by Edward the Elder of the territorial units corresponding to the Danish 'armies' that occupied the Eastern Danelaw in the 40 years prior to their defeat in 917–18. Hart suggests that the imposition of these Danish organisational units may have 'wiped the slate clean' with regard to earlier territorial arrangements. I, for one, do not think that Bigmore's arguments for estate survival are necessarily negated if one accepts Hart's thesis; provided that the latter is only applied to the Shire and Hundredal boundaries, with parochial and estate arrangements being subject to rather more varied histories.

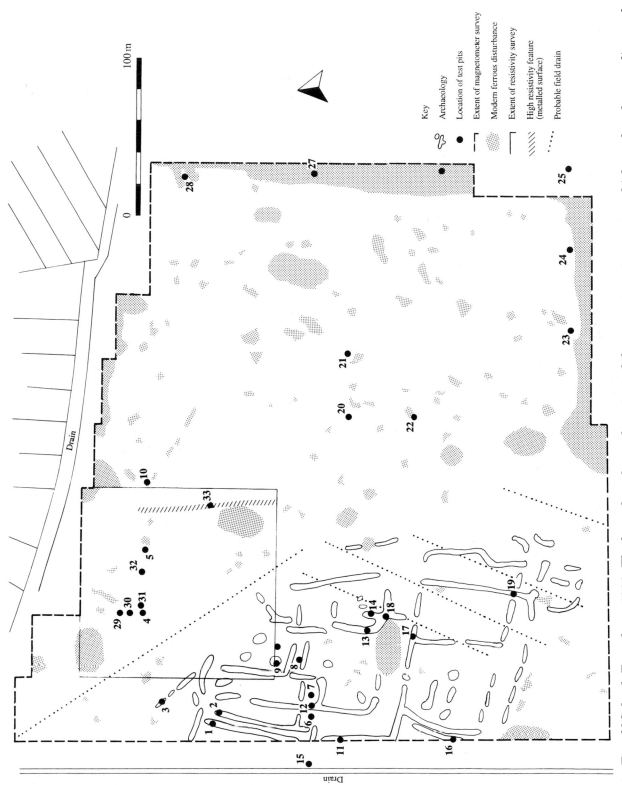

Figure 12.4   Ernulf School, Eynesbury 1993. The large box shows the extent of the magnetometer survey, which produced anomalies as shown. Test pits confirmed their origin as late-Roman features, their morphology suggesting small enclosures and refuse pits close to settlement. The small box represents the resistivity survey from which one linear, a roughly metalled track, was identified. The cluster of test pits in the north-west corner of the site investigated stone wall foundations, which proved to be discrete and remain undated

Saxon occupation

Good evidence of pagan Saxon remains in this part of the river valley is surprisingly thin on the ground. The four locations of pagan Saxon burials around St Neots and Eynesbury, as shown on Figure 12.5, are all a result of evidence for only occasional burials, rather than being representative of the cemetery of a sizeable community. It could be assumed that this picture is erroneous and that, for example, the small number of individuals represented in each case is a result of only partial investigation of each area. However, as all of these finds are in areas of modern development, the absence of further discoveries during this century is puzzling and one of the possible explanations is, therefore, that all four are, in reality, only small groups of burials. No locations for settlements of this period are known, although the Romano-Saxon wares from Ernulf School might point to a continuation of use of this area as settlement into the 5th century. If Bigmore's suggestions of estate continuity are right, then we might find that pagan Saxon period occupation was close to the pre-existing Roman estate centres, although this assumption has no grounding in fact.

With a neighbouring, possible, Roman river-crossing point, and its descriptive place-name, Eaton Ford may have been a focus for activity over many centuries. Middle-Saxon settlement centres of note in the St Neots area are not, however, known with any certainty. Speculation that Eaton and Eynesbury both had sizeable populations in this early period seems reasonable, but this is only based on their apparent importance 200 or 300 years later. The only find shown on Figure 12.5 that can be attributed to the middle-Saxon period is a small group of organic-tempered sherds that were recovered from features below the priory remains in St Neots during Tebbutt's excavations (Tebbutt 1966). This find is, however, at odds with the location of the presumed late-Saxon centres discussed below, and thus cannot be taken too seriously without corroboration. A find of an undated group of 'Saxon' loom weights near the Conygeare is also too vague to be of much use. The second element of the place name Eynesbury (Einulbesberie) may possibly indicate a substantial centre from an early time, but it may also relate to the presence of a pre-existing earthwork (the Coneygeare). It is only for the late-Saxon period onwards that solid evidence for occupation here is, however, available (see below).

The parochial and manorial arrangements from the medieval period onwards often hold clues as to the shape of the minster parishes of the late-Saxon period, and possibly also indicate estate relationships from earlier centuries. Figure 12.3 shows the current understanding of the Domesday minster territories, alongside the early modern parish boundaries for Eynesbury and the Paxtons. In addition, it must be remembered that adjacent and to the west lay the 'Soke' of Eaton which was almost certainly a land unit that operated as both a major independent estate and also as a minster parish in the pre-(Norman) Conquest period. The presence of a late-Saxon burial ground, and possibly also a church, were identified under the northern bailey of the Norman castle at Eaton during excavations in the 1940s (Tebbutt 1952). This, alongside further evidence for late-Saxon buildings predating the Norman fortifications (Addyman 1965), can be interpreted as indicative of a well-established estate centre and settlement being located here in the centuries leading up to the Norman Conquest, probably alongside a minster church. This would have been the focal point for the Soke of Eaton, but again the early history of this settlement is unknown, and the possibility of continuity from Peter Bigmore's suggested Roman origins is nothing more than an interesting hypothesis that has yet to be tested.

From the entries in the Domesday Book, Eynesbury is known to have been a sizeable community in the 11th century. It also possessed a church and priest and, in addition, separate entries are given for the holdings in the attached settlements of Cotton (Caldecote) and St Neots. Thus, Eynesbury should perhaps be seen as the centre of another substantial estate and as the site of another minster church from the late-Saxon period. Figure 12.3 indicates the possible shape of the minster parish.

The rather well preserved Minster church at Great Paxton suggests a third population centre in this part of the Great Ouse Valley, completing the picture that this area was well-settled, with the river valley continuing to act as a focus for economic and social activity of all kinds.

The late-Saxon landscape would therefore have been one of a thin distribution of larger villages, often representing the site of minster churches and each acting as the focal point for a sizeable territory. In addition, each of these settlements would have possessed satellite hamlets or 'berewicks' – many of which developed into individual parishes in later centuries. Within this distribution, variation would most often derive from geographic/topographic factors. Thus the major transportation routeways would often act as enhancing factors, either increasing the number of settlements or, more, often encouraging the growth and economic diversification of some centres into the precursors of the medieval 'market village'. Settlement growth often has a snowballing effect, with increasing size, status, and diversification attracting more of the same. At Eaton and Eynesbury a doubling-up of major estate centres and minster churches seems to have taken place, with one in each Shire either side of the river. This phenomenon is known from border areas in all sorts of locations the world over, where two communities attempt to benefit from common economic factors, particularly from trade funnelled through rare 'crossing points'.

In the case of Eynesbury, it would seem that a successful estate centre and minster parish focus grew up not far from the river, possibly inheriting

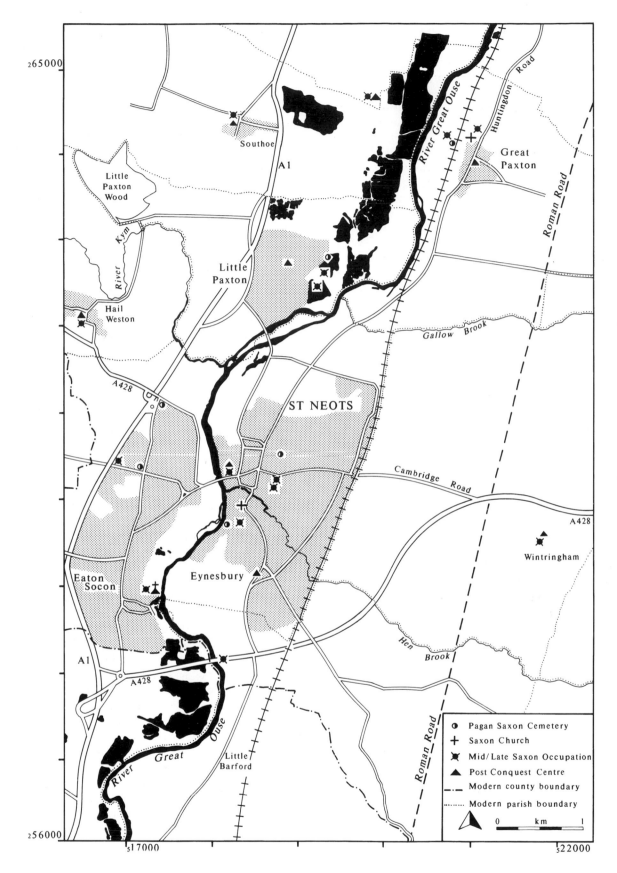

Figure 12.5   Saxon to medieval (SMR entries) and other known sites in the St Neots area (data only from parishes shown unshaded on Figure 12.3). Pagan Saxon cemeteries appear to have a consistent spatial relationship with the known later settlement foci, being close to, but outside of, the later villages. Possibly suggesting continuity from earlier centres. Even at this small scale some shift in the position of each main settlement focus is evident between the late-Saxon and medieval periods. Early settlements that may have disappeared by the Norman conquest may have existed at Duloe Bridge and close to the river on the present line of the St Neots southern bypass

an occupation site from a sizeable late-Roman community. At sometime in the late-Saxon period, and according to the medieval sources (*Liber Eliensis*) by c 980 AD, a monastic foundation was set up, but instead of it being at Eynesbury itself, it appears to have been located a few hundred metres to the north, across the Hen Brook. Perhaps the fact that the river crossing was located here might have been the impetus for the new location. Alternatively it might have been purely that as the new foundation was in the form of a manor separate to the main manor of Eynesbury, the buildings themselves were sited within these lands, but fairly close to the river and to the old settlement at Eynesbury. Whatever the reasons, the new settlement appears to have flourished and eventually it became fully independent as the parish of St Neots.

Addyman's work at Eaton Socon (1965) brought together data previously gathered by Lethbridge and Tebbutt, plus the Ministry of Works excavations from 1962. His suggestion that the late-Saxon settlement is liable to have been the head manor of Wulfmar under Edward the Confessor (later the centre of the so-called Barony of Eaton) seems perfectly acceptable today. The archaeological data available to Addyman concerning Eaton has not been added to appreciably in the last 30 years, and his suggestion of a late-Saxon settlement stretching across 200m or more east to west, starting west of the one building excavated in 1962 and finishing at the large graveyard (and thus church) under the later castle bailey, also seems entirely plausible. Much of this settlement was levelled during the construction of the castle in the 12th century and this precipitated a shift of the village to a site around a green south-west of the new castle, resulting in the relocation of the church to its current position north of the green, commanding access to the castle and river.

Eaton Socon was certainly successful as the main centre of the Barony of Eaton, enjoying good road and river contacts from its favourable position. Across the Great Ouse in Huntingdonshire, however, an even greater success story was unfolding.

Figure 12.5 shows the location of Saxon remains in the study area, as recovered from the Cambridgeshire SMR and other documents, particularly the Victoria County History of Huntingdonshire (Jamison 1932 a and b). On the west side it is apparent that there are late-Saxon origins for the villages of Southoe, Hail Weston, and Little Paxton, with the latter perhaps showing a settlement shift away from the river after the 11th century. The settlement at Eaton Socon is evident to the south, and in between are symbols representing pagan Saxon activity and possibly late-Saxon settlement on the line of the road from Eaton Ford to Duloe, west of St Neots bridge. What this latter represents is not entirely clear; the SMR entry referring to one post-built building, pottery, and a loom weight (Cambridgeshire SMR 495). It may well be that it represents nothing more than an isolated structure,

located close to a crossing point of east–west and north–south routes, rather than being indicative of a true settlement in its own right.

On the eastern bank of the river the archaeological evidence for Saxon occupation is mostly concentrated at Great Paxton and at three points in Eynesbury/St Neots. The exceptions to this are the hamlet of Wintringham (Cambridgeshire SMR 1117), which had a late-Saxon manorial phase (Beresford 1977), and which is believed to have been a satellite of Eynesbury, and a site on the St Neots southern bypass, close to the river. This latter site relates to unpublished excavations from the early 1980s on the site of a Bronze Age ring-ditch which experienced secondary use, perhaps in the Saxon period (Herne 1984). Rubbish pits were cut into the ring-ditch fill and these were associated with at least one post-built building and a possible well. Of particular interest were five graves, aligned east–west and located around the mound edge. Grave goods were restricted to personal items such as knives. The excavator believes these graves to be contemporary with the settlement remains, although in his interim report he describes the ceramics from the rubbish pits as of 8th–10th-century date, whilst the burials, and their location, have the character of the pagan to Christian transition period at latest. I would, thus, suggest that the two are not contemporary, and that the burials are 7th-century at latest, with the occupation being middle- to late-Saxon in date. The burials probably relate to earlier settlement somewhere in the vicinity and, as yet, unlocated. I do not believe that the occupation remains that were found represent anything more than a 'farmstead' and it is unlikely to have been very long-lived.

Eynesbury was originally the mother parish of St Neots. The status of the latter as a separate, named settlement seems, from the historical data, to date to sometime well before 1086 AD as the Domesday Book records the settlement and its inhabitants, although it was still within Eynesbury parish at this stage. Tradition has it that the monastery was founded in the late-10th century by Ethelwold, on petition by the estate owner Leofric and his wife Leoflaed. In her detailed discussion of the historic background to the priory, Marjorie Chibnall (in Tebbutt 1966) stated her belief that the essence of this story was likely to be true, even if the detail were not. Thus, we should expect there to have been a religious foundation and an ancillary 'village' settlement present in the late-Saxon period somewhere within Eynesbury parish and, as discussed above, presumably located north of the Hen Brook, within the area of the medieval and later town and parish of St Neots. The SMR data, as illustrated in Figure 12.5, shows two possible locations – north-east of the bridge, under the later medieval priory, and in the triangle of land between the later Church Street, Cambridge Road, and the Hen Brook.

The nature and location of the various elements in the late-Saxon settlement pattern at St Neots and Eynesbury were discussed in detail by Addyman (1973), with reference to his own work and that of Tebbutt over the previous decades. I must record my debt to these two scholars here, as many of the points I will make from now on were first proposed in their work.

Tebbutt first identified a late-Saxon settlement on the east side of St Neots in the 1920s. His work there, followed by the Ministry of Works rescue excavations published by Addyman in 1973, appears to have identified a settlement that spanned the period from, perhaps, the 10th century to late-12th or early-13th centuries. This is shown as two symbols lying close together in the centre of the modern town on Figure 12.5. It is likely that during the last century of this bracket the main period of occupation in this area was over, however, this does not mean that 12th-century activity in the St Neots area as a whole had diminished in comparison to the late-Saxon situation. Addyman's and Tebbutt's work resulted in the indication that this late-Saxon settlement reached eight hectares or more in size, an order of size almost comparable to that of the medieval town, which reached, perhaps, fifteen hectares at its peak.

As discussed above, pagan and middle-Saxon evidence for occupation around Eynesbury and St Neots is rather sparse. The only definite find spot of the latter period is the discovery of some early pottery and a 7th-century *sceatta* by Tebbutt during his excavations of the medieval priory.

Addyman points out (1973) that we do not know where, within the large pre-Conquest parish of Eynesbury, the middle- to late-Saxon settlement of Eynesbury actually was. He suggests that the late-Saxon settlement discovered by Tebbutt and himself might in fact be Eynesbury, or alternatively that this might conceivably have been the Saxon monastic foundation. Both of these points deserve consideration.

Both Eynesbury and St Neots have parish churches dedicated to St Mary. Eynesbury St Mary's has some late-12th-century fabric, whilst St Neots St Mary's has some of 13th-century date. A late-12th-century reference to the Rectory of St Neots suggests a church was in existence by then, whilst the Domesday Book records one church in the parish of Eynesbury, listed with the entry for this settlement rather than that of the emergent St Neots. Addyman proposes that the reason that the parish church of St Neots is located on the edge of the medieval town is that it predates the market foundation (early-12th century) and the formal laying-out of the market place. It lies next to the known late-Saxon settlement, separated by a large late-Saxon north–south ditch and, thus, it might be concluded that these elements together represent a major pre-conquest settlement, perhaps possessing a Saxon church on the site of the later one, lying immediately outside of the main settlement enclosure. This would then be a very strong candidate for the original late-Saxon Eynesbury.

Addyman did not claim that this suggestion was undoubtedly correct. I believe that it is incorrect. I cannot understand why a separate, second 'Eynesbury' would then spring up, complete with late-12th-century church, only 300m away to the south. This would certainly be too early to represent a suburban development around the main settlement (now called St Neots), and I would thus conclude that the village of Eynesbury always has been Eynesbury. If that is the case why does St Neots appear only 300m to the north? The answer to this has already been partially addressed insofar as the settlement was tied to a separate estate within the parish of Eynesbury and, would have been 'created' on land within that estate. Also St Neots is a 'special' foundation. Its two prime factors are access to trade and travel at a river crossing and possession of a monastery. The decision on the siting of the new settlement would have been affected by all these factors, plus normal considerations such as the availability of clean water and dry land.

The second question posed was whether the late-Saxon settlement found by Tebbutt and Addyman was itself the late-Saxon monastery? The buildings here, that were excavated to any great extent, were a large boat-shaped building (granary?) and sunken-featured buildings. These could easily represent ancillary structures in any type of settlement. If the argument from the previous discussion is used, however, then this settlement must indeed be at least related to, or part of, the late-Saxon monastery. The desire and opportunity to build a monastery was the primary prompt for the creation of a separate settlement. The growth of this latter was probably a secondary outcome of the monastery initiative. This still does not tell us, with any absolute certainty, where the main focus of the Saxon monastery was. It might have been under the later Priory foundation, as suggested by Tebbutt, or it might have related to the eastern Saxon settlement and the parish church. I support Addyman's suggestion that the off-centre location of St Mary's in St Neots does indeed need explaining, and it could certainly be that this site was chosen for the medieval church because of an historic association with a Saxon monastic church on the same site. Whatever the answer, I do not think that too much effort should be expended in looking for the site of the Saxon monastery, not because its presence and location are unimportant, but because I doubt it would be very easy to identify it as such, especially as it supposedly survived for less than forty years before being destroyed by the Danes in 1010. If the monastery did indeed last for only a few decades, then its remains are likely to be dwarfed by those deriving from all later settlement, especially if it be of a late-Saxon/Saxo-Norman domestic nature, and thus very similar in character.

After the Norman Conquest, why then was the medieval priory established further west and adjacent to the river? This could easily be a result of nothing more than a 'new broom' effect, with the

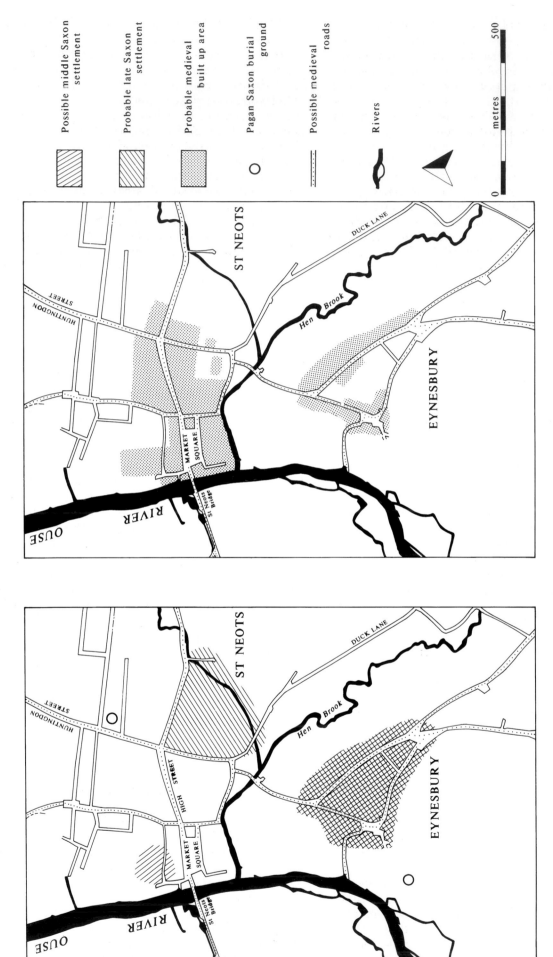

Key:

Possible middle Saxon settlement

Probable late Saxon settlement

Probable medieval built up area

○ Pagan Saxon burial ground

Possible medieval roads

Rivers

metres 0 500

Figure 12.6 An attempt to suggest the settlement-pattern shift at Eynesbury and St Neots. The main 19th-century roads are shown for orientation, with those that are likely to have had an early origin marked with a dotted line. The road layout of the Saxon settlement at Eynesbury is not known, although it may have been located around the later green, as shown. The only evidence for the middle-Saxon focus north of the market square is a small amount of organic-tempered pottery and one sceatta. The late-Saxon settlement of St Neots is comparatively well known, as is the formalised town around the market square. The low lying areas along the Hen Brook were only settled after the ground surface here was substantially raised in the 17th century (after Addyman and Tebbutt)

founders not wanting to fit a brand new foundation around the pre-existing village. This act, in line with many medieval monastic initiatives, was undoubtedly entrepreneurial as well as pious, and the opportunity to site a new priory close to a ford across the Ouse must have been recognised. The degree to which various individuals were involved in the foundation of the post-Conquest priory is, however, not fully known. The original impetus seems to have derived from Robert Fitz Wimarc, the post-Conquest owner of Eynesbury, and Bishop Anselm of Bec who was so taken with his 'discovery' of an indigenous saint here, that he brought part of the remains of St Neot back with him to Bec where they were venerated for several hundred years (Chibnall in Tebbutt 1966 and Haigh 1988). Almost three decades later it was Robert's daughter-in-law, Rohais, who finally gave the manor of Eynesbury to the monks of St Neots at the formal refoundation in 1113.

Figure 12.6 is an attempt to identify the areas of occupation in the middle-Saxon to medieval periods. The road plan shown is that of the major late-19th-century routes, which provide orientation, with those routes of probable medieval date identified as on the key. The first map shows the location of the late-Saxon settlement at St Neots, plus also the presumed continuity of settlement at Eynesbury throughout the period in question. The 'green' at Eynesbury is covered by tone representing occupation, as there is no guarantee that the early settlement plan here was based on the same roads as were in existence later on. I feel that the curvilinear nature of the boundaries and roads in the area around the church and towards the river does indeed suggest great antiquity of settlement, especially as this is close to the Roman settlement site. The size and shape of the Saxon settlement here is, however, very much a guess. The representation of middle-Saxon settlement north of the market square, on the site of the later medieval priory, represents the pottery, *sceatta*, and some archaeological features that Tebbutt found. This is thus only a possible settlement site, and therefore should be treated with some scepticism. The late-Saxon settlement at the eastern edge of historic St Neots is well-attested by excavation and the only question mark here is whether it continued further west through the later medieval churchyard, and whether it represents the site of the Saxon monastery as well as a lay settlement?

The shape of the medieval town of St Neots

Tebbutt's excavations on the site of the medieval priory in the late 1950s and early 1960s (Tebbutt 1966) revealed a substantial part of the ground plan of the medieval foundation. The detail of this must, however, be taken with some caution. As pointed out by Haigh (1988), if the conjectured portions of Tebbutt's plan of the priory are removed, then it is apparent how little has actually been excavated and many options for differing interpretative reconstructions are then available. Whilst not wishing to belittle Tebbutt's enormous contribution to the study of archaeology in and around St Neots, the above facts, coupled with the lack of detailed information in his report on the priory excavations, must lead one to exhibit caution when using his findings as the basis for wider interpretation. His report makes several vague statements about earlier features, but none of that described can be taken to indicate significant occupation of pre-12th-century date on this site. Thus it is probably reasonable to assume that the new Priory was founded on land that was not occupied by earlier buildings. It is not my intention to discuss the detail of Tebbutt's findings here. It is sufficient for my purposes to note that the buildings were both timber-framed and stone, and were in use from the 12th century until the Dissolution. Of more significance here is the way in which the priory plan related to the development of the town as a whole.

Tebbutt's suggestion that the priory church was on the south side of the monastic precinct is certainly correct. Initially the east–west road to the river crossing ran almost immediately south of the precinct boundary. The bridge will have formalised the crossing point when first built around 1180 and, from that point at least, the road ran east from the bridge to 'the Cross' at the east end of the High Street. The area along this road and the space south of it would have provided a formal market place south of the precinct and between the river and the Cross. The location of this latter, being positioned close to the pre-existing late-Saxon settlement, might be indicative of the earliest market area that existed, before the formal market place was laid out. The large regular market place and elements of the street plan and property boundaries all suggest some formal organisation in the laying out of the town between the pre-existing settlement at the eastern end, the river to the west and the new priory precinct to the north. Addyman (1973) and Tebbutt (1956 and 1978) have both discussed in detail aspects of the development of the medieval town of St Neots. The source of the data for most of this interpretation is Tebbutt's observations of sewer renewal sections through most of the town's streets (1956). He detailed a number of very significant discoveries here, including the late-medieval open sewers that ran through the market place and main streets, and the replacement of this system, probably in the 17th century, by brick and stone constructions. This probably coincided with a general raising of the level of the market place, to a point above that necessary to avoid flooding, which appears to have been a periodic problem in earlier centuries. It was also around this time that the land surface of the Hen Brook 'valley' was raised on both the St Neots and Eynesbury sides, a feat that involved considerable quantities of hard core and rub-

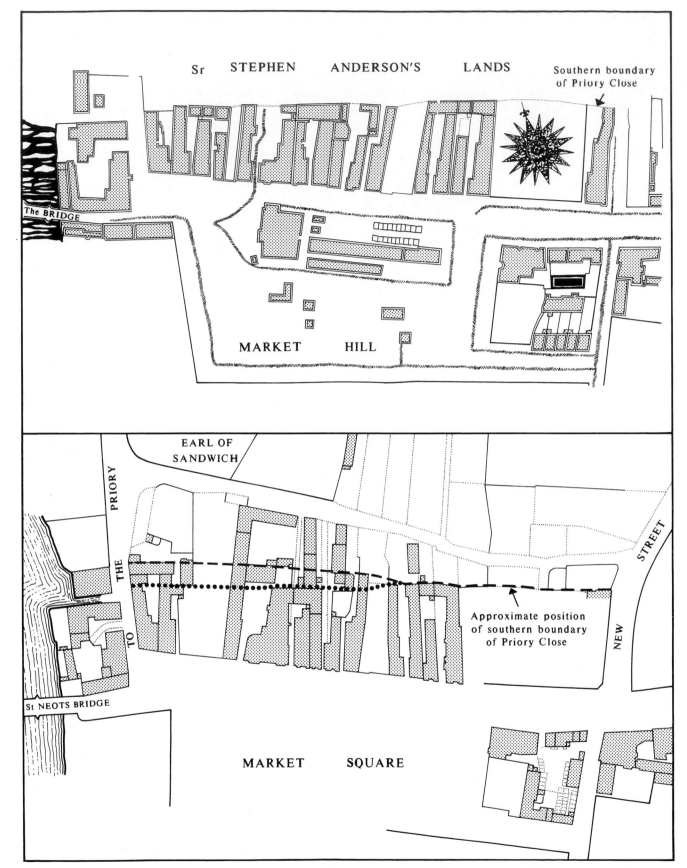

Figure 12.7   Two early maps showing the process of incorporation of former parts of the priory precinct into the commercial town. The upper is a 1756 map of Sir Stephen Anderson's Lands only (HRO). Tebbutt suggested the whole row of shops on the north side of the square were taken out of the precinct in the 15th century. The lower map, of 1848 (Cambridgeshire County Council Archaeology), shows piecemeal expansion of these units up to the new back lane after the former priory estate began to be broken up. As discussed in the text two possible lines of the late-medieval precinct boundary are shown

Figure 12.8 Excavations at the rear of 25-27 Market Square in 1993. The absence of any precinct boundary suggests its line was very slightly to the south of this site. The large sub-round pit, predating the burials, is shaded

bish. Almost all of the properties between the churches of the two settlements have been constructed on top of this make-up, and it is no surprise that several 17th-century buildings survive here, with no earlier construction being evident. The impetus for all these works was certainly commercial and, as identified by Tebbutt (1956), was probably linked to the introduction of locks on the Great Ouse in this same period. This enabled much larger vessels to navigate up river to St Neots and it is worth noting that the town quay was located at the mouth of the Hen Brook.

Bearing in mind that Tebbutt noted the preservation of the line of the southern boundary wall of the priory precinct north of the market square as shown on two 18th-century maps (the 1756 map of The Priory Estate which were by then 'Sir Stephen Anderson's Lands' HRO Acc 223B and a 1757 map of the Market Place HRO 223/13, the latter here Figure 12.7 upper), it is surprising that he did not also refer to the sewers shown on this map. They are undoubtedly the late-medieval system that he discovered, as discussed above, and presumably therefore date their replacement and the raising of the market square surface to some time after the map was drawn.

Chibnall in Tebbutt (1966) explained how the waning fortunes of the priory in the later Middle Ages eventually resulted in drastic action being taken. The poverty of the house by 1432 is well-documented and known to be mostly a result of taxation and restrictions placed upon 'alien' houses during the 100 Years War. Surprisingly, however, by the time of its dissolution, just over a century later, the priory was again comparatively wealthy and well-maintained. Tebbutt recognised the source of this as being revenues from the thriving town of St Neots. The construction of a large new parish church in the early-15th century is a good indicator of the success of the town as a whole. The priory appears to have been able to cash in on this by contracting the south side of its precinct and leasing the land made available as commercial properties along the north side of the Market Square. It is necessary to study in greater detail the morphology of this part of the town to understand the process fully.

Tebbutt's 1956 paper included descriptions of a number of observations he carried out during construction work in properties on the north side of the Market Square. He had identified the line of the old priory precinct wall in advance of this work and observed a robber trench in the correct location, along with evidence for an outer ditch that was filled in during the medieval period. In addition he found evidence suggesting that an insubstantial building had been built up against the southern face of the wall after the ditch was filled in. He found the rough stone foundations of a large building with a glazed tile floor 10m north of the priory wall, this he later suggested might be the Priory Church (Tebbutt 1966, 37–8). Of particular interest was the fact that he discovered Christian burials on both sides of the

precinct wall and also beneath it. Tebbutt suggested that this resulted from the construction of the wall after long use of the whole area between the church and the market place as a graveyard. Although virtually no dating evidence was available he suggested that the wall might have been constructed in the 15th century. This tied in with the priory's resurgence and increased rents from commercial properties. The insubstantial building outside of the wall was interpreted as one of the early shops. Tebbutt's plan and early cartographic information suggest that the wall he discovered is likely to have been aligned as shown by the dashed line on Figure 12.7 (lower).

In 1993, the Archaeological Field Unit of Cambridgeshire County Council carried out a small excavation just to the north of the presumed line of the precinct wall at the rear of 25–27 Market Square (Alexander 1994). The expectation was that significant numbers of burials would be recovered, but also it was hoped that this work would shed some light on Tebbutt's suggestions which, although perfectly reasonable, were essentially untested with regard to date and their applicability along the whole boundary. Over two phases the full or partial remains of 45 individuals were recovered (Fig 12.8), however, no evidence for the line of the precinct wall was discovered. This would seem to suggest that Tebbutt's suggested wall-line is not entirely correct and this data, coupled with a reappraisal of the early maps (Fig 12.7), has led the author to conclude that the actual line of the wall was probably the alternative dotted line as shown on the lower part of that Figure 12.7. This appears to be in accordance with the maps shown, which show excellently the absorption of the southern edge of the former priory lands into the commercial properties on the north side of the market place; the upper map being from 1756 (HRO Acc 223/13) and the lower a sale map of 1848 (from a photocopy held by Cambridgeshire County Council Archaeology, location of original unknown). If Tebbutt is right in his suggestion that the very earliest precinct boundary was at the very front of these properties, as suggested by the burials he found in the 1950s, then the whole sequence of the changing boundaries can be traced in Figure 12.7.

Unfortunately, the 1993 excavations failed to provide a better dated framework for this sequence. Of particular interest, however, was a very large pit that is shown on Figure 12.8. The pit was subround, 5–6m across, and c 1.5m deep where bottomed. It was backfilled with clay, within which were small amounts of chalk rubble, burnt daub, and charcoal. The lowest fills of the pit were a creamy-white mortar deposit, overlying a burnt deposit which included carbonised branches and fragments of burnt red sandstone. Around the edges of this pit the natural sands had been singed, implying that either hot material was dumped into the pit, or that it was used for burning itself. Only one late-Saxon/Saxo-Norman sherd was recovered from all of these fills, thus dating is very uncertain. The upper fills of this pit were cut by five burials. The sequence here can, therefore, be interpreted as a phase of late-Saxon/Saxo-Norman activity, involving the digging and use of the pit, followed by its backfilling with clay and the remains of demolished of wattle and daub buildings. The area was then, at a later date, incorporated into the medieval priory graveyard. This is by no means detailed evidence for a substantial pre-Priory phase in this part of the town, however, it does suggest that activity, possibly industrial, was taking place here, at least as late as the early-12th century and certainly before the priory graveyard was consecrated and in use.

Figure 12.6 (right hand) shows the probable area of buildings across St Neots and Eynesbury by the late-medieval period. In addition the roads that were likely to have been in existence at that point have been indicated. The earliest map of St Neots studied by the author is a small-scale semi-pictorial map of 1730, known as Gordon's map and reproduced by Tebbutt in his book on the town's history (1978). This shows all the roads marked here (Fig 12.6), except for Brook Street, which may have been in existence as a short-cut or track, if nothing more. It seems reasonable to assume that the 1730 plan of the town was little different to that of 300 or 400 years earlier and thus Figure 12.6 is not likely to be very inaccurate. The main points of change in the medieval plan, when compared with the pre-Conquest settlement, are that the town had moved west towards the river and adjacent to the priory, and that all the land between the priory and the Hen Brook is likely to have been in commercial, as well as domestic, use. The river, east–west roads, the bridge, and the priory all exerted influence on the shape of the settlement. There may also have been wharves on the Hen Brook, representing a third commercial focus after the Market Place and the Cross/High Street area. The eccentric location of the church, with respect to the town plan, is very evident on the figure and this illustrates well Addyman's suggestion that this anomaly may have been due to the early church being located to service the late-Saxon community to the east. Eynesbury was not necessarily reduced in size, but the streets, and thus the locations of frontage structures, were now formalised, and thus the shading on this figure is more accurate than that shown for the Saxon periods.

Conclusions

A great range of data has been tackled in this paper, drawing on the work of earlier scholars from Gorham through to Addyman, but most of all, of course, Tebbutt. By drawing together so many disparate strands, alongside more recent information, we have hopefully contributed to the understanding of the history of a very ordinary English town and its hinterland. This description is not meant to be in

any way demeaning to the inhabitants of Eynesbury and St Neots, be they of the 4th or 20th centuries, or from any point in between. It is, perhaps, this very 'ordinariness' that makes the study of a centre such as this so important. The lives of most of the individuals that shaped the town and village do not figure in the recognised histories of England, but they all contributed to a story that stands as a testament to continuing endeavour and human aspirations across the centuries. In dealing with the gross morphology of the region and the settlements I have not concentrated on particular properties or locations to any great degree. This synthesis will hopefully, however, clarify which parts of the landscape are likely to have been important at which time, and this will certainly aid in the protection and management of the archaeological resource, and will help archaeologists tackle the detail of specific excavations when and where the need arises.

If research priorities were to be proposed for archaeology in this part of the Ouse valley, I would argue strongly that the following points were considered.

1 The nature and size of the Eynesbury Roman settlement need to be adequately understood, as does the development from the 4th–5th-century evidence to the middle- and late-Saxon settlements.

2 The small, but significant, body of evidence for pre-priory occupation north of the Market Square needs to be supported by some well-dated information. The character of this activity needs identifying and the suggested sequence of changes to the precinct boundary line still needs support through excavation. It would be very satisfying if the supposed late-Saxon priory could be located for certain. It is likely, however, to be indistinguishable from other settlement of this period.

3 Opportunities to look at remains of earlier buildings around the parish church should be taken where possible, particularly with a view to determining the antiquity of activity in this area.

4 Good quality modern data concerning the economic life of the late-Saxon to medieval town is not available. Opportunities to investigate the complete depth of properties from the frontage back to, in particular, the Hen Brook should be seen as of prime importance.

Acknowledgements

I have already acknowledged my debt to earlier scholars, in particular Dr Peter Addyman and the late C F Tebbutt, without whose earlier synthetic and specific work, my task would have been vastly

160

more difficult. I am indebted to colleagues, past and present, at the Archaeological Field Unit, Cambridgeshire County Council and in particular my former colleague Mary Alexander, whose recent work at Ernulf School and Market Square provided the new data that prompted this piece. I must thank Jon Cane for drawing Figure 12.1, Caroline Gait and Mary Alexander for drawing Figures 12.4 and 12.8, and my wife Pam Spoerry for drawing Figures 12.2, 12.3, 12.5, 12.6, and 12.7. Finally I would like to thank the organisers of the Ouse Valley Conference and Publication for the invitation to contribute.

Bibliography

Addyman, P V, 1965 Late Saxon Settlements in the St Neots Area. I: The Saxon Settlement and Norman Castle at Eaton Socon, Bedfordshire, *Proc Cambridge Antiq Soc*, **58**, 38–73

Addyman, P V, 1973 Late Saxon Settlements in the St Neots Area. III: The Village or Township of St Neots, *Proc Cambridge Antiq Soc*, **64**, 45–99

Alexander, M, 1993 *Roman Settlement Evidence at Ernulf School, St Neots,* Cambridgeshire County Council Archaeology Report Series **91**. Cambridge: Cambridgeshire County Council

Alexander, M, 1994, *Medieval Burials at 25–27 Market Square, St Neots,* Cambridgeshire County Council Archaeology Report Series **89**. Cambridge: Cambridgeshire County Council

Beresford, G, 1977 Excavations of a moated site at Wintringham in Huntingdonshire, *Archaeol J,* **134**, 194–286

Bigmore, P, 1979 *The Bedfordshire and Huntingdonshire landscape.* London: Hodder & Staughton

Chibnall, M, 1966, History of the Priory of St Neots, in C F Tebbutt, 1966, appendix

Gorham, G C, 1820, *The History and Antiquities of Eynesbury and St Neots in Huntingdonshire and of St Neots in the County of Cornwall*, London: privately published

Greenfield, E, 1969 The Romano-British Settlement at Little Paxton, Huntingdonshire, *Proc Cambridge Antiq Soc*, **62**, 35–57

Haigh, D, 1988 *The Religious Houses of Cambridgeshire*. Cambridge: Cambridgeshire County Council

Hart, C, 1968 The Hidation of Huntingdonshire, *Proc Cambridge Antiq Soc*, **61**, 55–66

Herne, A, 1984 Eynesbury Excavation June 1984. Unpublished manuscript held at Cambridgeshire County Council SMR

Jamison, C M, 1932a Eynesbury, in W Page (ed) *The Victoria History of the Counties of England, Huntingdonshire, Vol 2*. London: University of London, 272–80

Jamison, C M, 1932b St Neots, in W Page (ed) *The Victoria History of the Counties of England, Huntingdonshire, Vol 2*. London: University of London, 337–46

Margary, I D, 1967 *Roman Roads in Britain.* London: John Baker

Tebbutt, C F, 1935 Excavations at Eynesbury Conygear, *Trans Cambridgeshire Huntingdonshire Archaeol Soc*, **15**, 266–8

Tebbutt, C F, 1952 Excavations on 'The Hillings' at Eaton Socon, Beds, *Proc Cambridge Antiq Soc*, **45**, 48–60

Tebbutt, C F, 1956 Excavations at St Neots, Huntingdonshire, *Proc Cambridge Antiq Soc*, **49**, 79–87

Tebbutt, C F, 1966 St Neots Priory, *Proc Cambridge Antiq Soc*, **59**, 33–74

Tebbutt, C F, 1978 *St Neots: the History of a Huntingdonshire Town*. London: Phillimore & Co Ltd

The Viatores, 1964 *Roman Roads in the South-east Midlands*. London: Victor Gollancz Ltd

Index *by Susan Vaughan*

Illustrations are indicated by page numbers in *italics* or by *illus* where figures are scattered throughout the text.